Changing Cuba-U.S. Relations

"This book provides an insightful analysis of the evolving relations between Cuba and the United States. Its uniqueness lies in the contributors' presentations from a Caribbean international relations perspective and the book is a valuable contribution to the IR literature."
—Mark Kirton, *Honorary Research Fellow, Institute of International Relations, The University of the West Indies, St. Augustine, Trinidad and Tobago*

"This should be an intriguing study on U.S.-Caribbean relations. Since the end of the Cold War, the geopolitical importance of the Caribbean has changed from an arena of East-West confrontation to a "third frontier" that presents a dual security problem: migration and drug traffic.
  Twenty-first-century geopolitics present new challenges and this book is an attempt to tackle them."
—Emilio Pantojas García, *Senior Researcher and Professor, Center for Social Research, University of Puerto Rico*

"A well-researched geopolitical must for understanding recent US-Cuba relations, its impact on the Caribbean and international relations of SIDS."
—Andrés Serbin, *President, Coordinadora Regional de Investigaciones Económicas y Sociales (CRIES); and former Chair, Caribbean Studies Association (CSA)*

Jacqueline Laguardia Martinez
Georgina Chami • Annita Montoute
Debbie A. Mohammed

Changing Cuba-U.S. Relations

Implications for CARICOM States

palgrave
macmillan

Jacqueline Laguardia Martinez
Institute of International Relations
University of the West Indies
St. Augustine, Trinidad and Tobago

Annita Montoute
Institute of International Relations
University of the West Indies
St. Augustine, Trinidad and Tobago

Georgina Chami
Institute of International Relations
University of the West Indies
St. Augustine, Trinidad and Tobago

Debbie A. Mohammed
Institute of International Relations
University of the West Indies
St. Augustine, Trinidad and Tobago

ISBN 978-3-030-20368-9   ISBN 978-3-030-20366-5 (eBook)
https://doi.org/10.1007/978-3-030-20366-5

© The Editor(s) (if applicable) and The Author(s), under exclusive licence to Springer Nature Switzerland AG 2020
This work is subject to copyright. All rights are solely and exclusively licensed by the Publisher, whether the whole or part of the material is concerned, specifically the rights of translation, reprinting, reuse of illustrations, recitation, broadcasting, reproduction on microfilms or in any other physical way, and transmission or information storage and retrieval, electronic adaptation, computer software, or by similar or dissimilar methodology now known or hereafter developed.
The use of general descriptive names, registered names, trademarks, service marks, etc. in this publication does not imply, even in the absence of a specific statement, that such names are exempt from the relevant protective laws and regulations and therefore free for general use.
The publisher, the authors and the editors are safe to assume that the advice and information in this book are believed to be true and accurate at the date of publication. Neither the publisher nor the authors or the editors give a warranty, express or implied, with respect to the material contained herein or for any errors or omissions that may have been made. The publisher remains neutral with regard to jurisdictional claims in published maps and institutional affiliations.

This Palgrave Macmillan imprint is published by the registered company Springer Nature Switzerland AG
The registered company address is: Gewerbestrasse 11, 6330 Cham, Switzerland

Preface

This book was motivated by a desire to explore the current features of the relationship between Cuba and the Caribbean Community (CARICOM), considering the major changes that Cuba's relations with the United States (U.S.) have undergone since December 17, 2014 (17D). It was born from a project initiated, in 2016, at the Institute of International Relations of The University of the West Indies (UWI), St. Augustine Campus. We dedicated two years to the research for, and writing of, this book. Our aim was to fill a gap in understanding of the potential impact on CARICOM of recent changes in relations between Cuba—the largest Caribbean island—and the United States—a global superpower with various interests in the Caribbean region. Indeed, this had become critical to do in view of the key transformations initiated, in 2014, by the normalizing of Cuba-U.S. relations; and it became an intriguing and exciting research project for us.

The idea for the research project originated from Debbie Mohammed, senior lecturer at the UWI Institute of International Relations (IIR), who invited the other three of us to collaborate on the project with her. Unfortunately, due to unforeseen circumstances, Dr. Mohammed had to step away from the project. Special mention must be made of her late husband, Nizam Mohammed, who provided great moral support to her.

Our hope is that this book is useful and will stimulate discussions on how to understand the Caribbean—from a Caribbean perspective—as a key hemispheric actor that continues to explore avenues for integration and socio-economic development. We also hope that this book results in the promotion of informed debates and policy responses for the benefit of the Caribbean.

St. Augustine, Trinidad and Tobago Jacqueline Laguardia Martinez
February 2019 Georgina Chami
Annita Montoute
Debbie A. Mohammed

Acknowledgments

We are extremely grateful to the interviewees who willingly gave their time and shared their knowledge of the subject matter under study. Our gratitude goes to the School for Graduate Studies and Research of the University of the West Indies, campus St. Augustine, for providing the funding for fieldwork and for the publication of this book. The research assistance of PhD candidate, Samantha Allahar, deserves special mention. She provided substantial support to the research project. Her work was consistently of high quality from the inception of the project to its very end. The project could not have been completed without her help. Samantha, we are very grateful.

Special thanks are owed to Professor Jessica Byron, Director of the Institute of International Relations at the University of the West Indies, for her support of this research.

Many thanks also go to Dr. Kudrat Virk for her assistance with the copy editing of this manuscript, which improved the text significantly. Also, we are grateful to the many scholars in the Caribbean region and beyond who contributed in one form or another to the completion of this book.

Finally, we offer our deepest gratitude to Palgrave Macmillan for working with us to ensure that this book became a reality.

Contents

1	Introduction	1
2	Interrogating Regional Integration Worldwide	5
3	Regional Integration in the Caribbean	19
4	The History and Background of Cuba-U.S. Relations (Until December 17, 2014)	37
5	Advancements in the Cuba-U.S. Relationship	61
6	Limits on the Cuba-U.S. Relationship	93
7	Factors and Actors Impacting Cuba-U.S. Relations	111
8	Background: U.S. Impact on the Cuba-CARICOM Relationship	143
9	Cuba-CARICOM Cooperation	157
10	Cuba-CARICOM Trade and Economic Relations	177
11	Conclusion	195

Appendix A: Interviewee Profiles   215

Appendix B: Interviewees by Region of Operation   217

Appendix C: Interviewees by Areas of Work   219

Index   221

About the Authors

Jacqueline Laguardia Martinez is a lecturer at the Institute of International Relations at The University of the West Indies (UWI) since 2014. She teaches courses on small states in the global system, the international relations of the Caribbean, and the international relations of Latin America. Previously, she was an associate professor at the University of Havana and a research associate at the Cuban Institute for Cultural Research Juan Marinello in Havana, Cuba. Her research areas include Cuban studies, small island developing states (SIDS), Cuba-Caribbean relations, climate change and sustainable development, and creative industries.

Laguardia Martinez was the project leader, in charge of coordinating fieldwork, the production of the final research report, and the internal editing of the manuscript. She also contributed to the conceptual direction of the project and wrote several of the chapters contained in this book, while contributing to others.

Georgina Chami joined the UWI Institute of International Relations as a research fellow in 2014. She lectures on international diplomacy at the diploma and master's levels. She is also the faculty advisor for the Harvard National Model United Nations and the Model United Nations (Model UN) Club at the UWI St. Augustine campus. Chami was the recipient of a Central America/Caribbean Fulbright Visiting Scholars Award in 2010. Her research interests include peace and security, international organizations, global governance, and civil society.

Beyond the writing of substantive chapters and her contribution to others, Chami's knowledge of the academic publishing industry was key to the publication of this book. She liaised with several publishing houses and successfully presented the draft manuscript to them. This was instrumental in helping the research team to select the best publication option.

Annita Montoute is a lecturer at the UWI Institute of International Relations. She has authored peer-reviewed journal articles and book chapters on issues such as civil society, crime and security, EU-Caribbean relations, and China in the Caribbean. She is the co-editor, with Kudrat Virk, of the book, *The ACP–EU Development Partnership: Beyond the North–South Debate*, published by Palgrave Macmillan. She was the lead researcher for the UWI IIR, and European Union-Latin America and Caribbean Foundation study: "The Caribbean in the EU-CELAC Partnership" and was research fellow at the European Centre for Development Policy Management in Maastricht, the Netherlands.

In addition to contributing to the conceptual direction of the project, writing substantive chapters, and contributing to others, Montoute's input was integral to the internal editing and finalization of the manuscript and in ensuring that the research met the required standards of high-quality academic research.

Debbie A. Mohammed is Senior Lecturer in International Trade at the UWI Institute of International Relations. She served as one of the five members of the EU-Latin America and Caribbean (EU-LAC) Foundation Academic Council for the 2013–2015 and 2015–2017 periods. She is a member of the International Studies Association (ISA) and the ISA Committee on the Status of Women as well as the ISA Global South Caucus. She is also a member of the Trinidad and Tobago Transparency Institute and serves as its representative on the National Steering Committee of the Trinidad and Tobago Extractive Industries Transparency Initiative. The work of Mohammed has been published widely in the areas of Caribbean competitiveness and development, and she has served as an independent reviewer for several academic journals. Her research interests include trade policy issues, Caribbean competitiveness, environmental and natural resource sustainability, and governance issues.

Apart from nurturing the initial idea of the research project and from coordinating the initial funding and early aspects of the fieldwork, Mohammed contributed to the conceptual framework of the project and to substantive aspects of the book, mainly through the gathering of fieldwork data.

Abbreviations

17D	December 17, 2014
ACP	Africa, Caribbean, and Pacific group of states
ACS	Association of Caribbean States
ALBA	Bolivarian Alliance for the Peoples of Our America
ALBA-TCP	Bolivarian Alliance for the Peoples of Our America – Peoples' Trade Treaty
AMU	Arab Maghreb Union
AOSIS	Alliance of Small Island States
APEC	Asia-Pacific Economic Cooperation
APS	Action Plan for Statistics
ASEAN	Association of Southeast Asian Nations
AU	African Union
BIS	Bureau of Industry and Security (U.S. Department of Commerce)
BRIC	Brazil, Russia, India, and China
BRICS	Brazil, Russia, India, China, and South Africa
CACR	Cuban Assets Control Regulations (U.S. Department of the Treasury)
CAIC	Caribbean Association of Industry and Commerce
CANF	Cuban American National Foundation
CARICOM	Caribbean Community
CARIFESTA	Caribbean Festival of Creative Arts
CARIFORUM	Forum of the Caribbean Group of ACP States
CARIFTA	Caribbean Free Trade Association
CARIWIG	Caribbean Weather Impacts Group
CCCCC	Caribbean Community Climate Change Centre
CCJ	Caribbean Court of Justice

CDA	Cuban Democracy Act (United States)
CDB	Caribbean Development Bank
CDEMA	Caribbean Disaster Emergency Management Agency
CELAC	Community of Latin American and Caribbean States
CHG	Conference of Heads of Government (CARICOM)
CIA	Central Intelligence Agency (United States)
CLI	Caribbean Law Institute
CLIC	Caribbean Law Institute Centre
COFAP	Council for Finance and Planning (CARICOM)
COFCOR	Council for Foreign and Community Relations (CARICOM)
COHSOD	Council for Human and Social Development (CARICOM)
COMECON	Council for Mutual Economic Assistance
CONSLE	Council for National Security and Law Enforcement (CARICOM)
COTED	Council for Trade and Economic Development (CARICOM)
CRS	Common Reporting Standard
CSCE	Commission on Security and Cooperation in Europe
CSME	CARICOM Single Market and Economy
CTO	Caribbean Tourism Organization
EAR	Export Administration Regulations (U.S. Department of Commerce)
ECCM	Eastern Caribbean Common Market
ECO	Economic Cooperation Organization
ECOWAS	Economic Community of West African States
EDF	European Development Fund
EEC	European Economic Community
EGREM	*Empresa de Grabaciones y Ediciones Musicales* (Cuba)
EJN	*Ejército de Liberación Nacional* (Colombia)
ELAM	Latin American School of Medicine
EPAs	Economic partnership agreements
ETECSA	*Empresa de Telecomunicaciones de* Cuba S.A.
EU	European Union
FAA	Federal Aviation Administration (United States)
FARC	*Fuerzas Armadas Revolucionarias de Colombia* (Colombia)
FBI	Federal Bureau of Investigation (United States)
FCSC	Foreign Claims Settlement Commission (U.S. Department of Justice)
FDI	Foreign direct investment
FIU	Florida International University
GCC	Gulf Cooperation Council
ICAIC	Cuban Institute for Cinema Arts and Industry
IMF	International Monetary Fund

INDER	National Institute of Sports, Physical Education, and Recreation (Cuba)
INSMET	Institute of Meteorology (Cuba)
ISI	Import substitution industrialization
ISIS	Islamic State of Iraq and Syria
JIATF South	Joint Interagency Task Force South
LAIA	Latin American Integration Association
LDCs	Less developed countries
LLDCs	Landlocked developing countries
MDCs	More developed countries
MERCOSUR	Southern Common Market
MFN	Most favored nation
MINCEX	Ministry of Foreign Trade and Investment (Cuba)
MLB	Major League Baseball
MoU	Memorandum of understanding
NAFTA	North American Free Trade Area
NATO	North Atlantic Treaty Organization
NED	National Endowment for Democracy (United States)
NGOs	Non-governmental organizations
NOAA	National Oceanic and Atmospheric Administration (United States)
OAS	Organization of American States
OAU	Organization of African Unity
ODA	Official development assistance
OECS	Organization of Eastern Caribbean States
OFAC	Office of Foreign Assets Control (U.S. Department of the Treasury)
ONHG	National Office of Hydrography and Geodesy (Cuba)
PCC	Communist Party of Cuba
PDCA	Political Dialogue and Cooperation Agreement
SAARC	South Asian Association for Regional Cooperation
SACU	Southern African Customs Union
SADC	Southern African Development Community
SADCC	Southern African Development Coordination Conference
SCCS	Standing Committee of Caribbean Statisticians
SELA	Latin American and Caribbean Economic System
SICA	Central American Integration System
SIDS	Small island developing states
Southcom	United States Southern Command
STZC	Sustainable Tourism Zone of the Greater Caribbean
TECA	Trade and Economic Cooperation Agreement
TPP	Trans-Pacific Partnership

TSRA	Trade Sanctions Reform and Export Enhancement Act (United States)
TTIP	Transatlantic Trade and Investment Partnership
TWEA	Trading with the Enemy Act (United States)
UK	United Kingdom
UN	United Nations
UN ECLAC	United Nations Economic Commission for Latin America and the Caribbean
UNASUR	Union of South American Nations
UNDP	United Nations Development Programme
UNEP	United Nations Environment Programme
UNESCO	United Nations Educational, Scientific, and Cultural Organization
UNWTO	United Nations World Tourism Organization
U.S.	United States
USAID	United States Agency for International Development
USCBC	U.S.-Cuba Business Council
USSR	Union of Soviet Socialist Republics
UWI	University of the West Indies, The
WISA	West Indies Associated States Council of Ministers
WTO	World Trade Organization
ZED Mariel	Mariel Special Development Zone

List of Figures

Fig. 6.1	U.S. exports to Cuba, 2007–2016 (in USD thousands). Source: U.S. Census Bureau (n.d.)	94
Fig. 10.1	Cuban imports of goods from main CARICOM trade partners and the Dominican Republic, 2009–2014 (in USD). Source: Based on figures in ONEI (2015)	185
Fig. 10.2	Cuban exports of goods to main CARICOM trade partners and the Dominican Republic, 2009–2014 (in USD). Source: Based on figures in ONEI (2015)	186
Fig. 10.3	The Caribbean (selected economies): inward FDI, 2015–2016 (millions of USD). Source: UN ECLAC (2018)	188
Fig. 10.4	CARIFORUM visitor arrivals, 2016. Source: CTO (2017a)	190
Fig. 10.5	CARIFORUM visitor arrival increases, from 2015 to 2016. Source: CTO (2017a)	190

LIST OF TABLES

Table 2.1	A contrast of old and new regionalism	7
Table 5.1	Cuba-U.S. dialogue mechanisms	65
Table 5.2	Arrivals in Cuba, 2012–2016	73
Table 5.3	Cuban American arrivals in Cuba, 2014–2016	74
Table 7.1	Top 12 U.S. claims on confiscated property by Cuba (over USD 50 million)	125
Table 9.1	Cuban collaborators working in Caribbean territories by country (December 31, 2016)	159
Table 9.2	Typology of Cuba's medical cooperation actions	162
Table 9.3	Caribbean university graduates in Cuba from 1961 to 2007–2008	165

List of Boxes

Box 6.1   Cost Summary for the United States, According to Engage
         Cuba Report   102
Box 10.1 Key Facts About the Mariel Special Development Zone   179

CHAPTER 1

Introduction

The thawing of relations between Cuba and the United States (U.S.) in 2014 brought fresh thinking to a complicated area in diplomatic relations. The Cuba-U.S. relationship has been plagued by distrust and antagonism since 1959—the year Fidel Castro's movement, together with political and social forces in Cuba, overthrew a U.S.-backed military regime in Havana. The hostility in relations continued in the years that followed, and deepened when Cuba declared itself a socialist state allied with the Union of Soviet Socialist Republics (USSR) and East European socialist countries.

The announcement of the re-establishment of diplomatic relations meant a dramatic shift in hemispheric international relations. The announcement sparked a series of transformations in the Cuba-U.S. bilateral relationship, touching on several areas: foreign policy, cooperation, communication, and travel, among others. The process—slow but steady—aroused interest all around the world, but particularly in Latin America and the Caribbean. A new reality was presented to regional actors, who were uncertain as to what the transformations were and to the nature of their potential impact on the national and international levels. The Donald Trump administration's policy toward Cuba has since added new uncertainties to the future development of the Cuba-U.S. relationship. Some questions being asked include: is a total reversal of the previous Barack Obama administration's policies possible? How all this process might affect the Caribbean?

After almost five years from the initiation of the thaw in diplomatic relations between Cuba and the United States, the end of the two-term Obama presidency, and over two years of the Trump administration, enough time has passed to allow an examination of the nature, scope, and extent of changes in the bilateral Cuba-U.S. relationship and of the impact that the normalization process has on the Caribbean and on Cuba-Caribbean relations. The empirical findings of this book, however, do not cover the entire Caribbean region, but instead are concerned with a subset of the Caribbean—namely, the member states of the Caribbean Community (CARICOM).

Cuba's long and close relationship with CARICOM countries is put in the spotlight, in the context of Cuba's re-establishment of relations with the United States. CARICOM members have embarked on solid cooperation schemes with Cuba, despite the traditional U.S. rhetoric against the island country. Will the re-establishment of relations between the United States and Cuba create a stronger pull toward the North, at the expense of CARICOM countries in the global South? Do Cuba and CARICOM countries have the requisite institutional, financial, legislative, and technical competencies to make timely adjustments in order to be prepared for, and to capture the benefits of, impending changes?

A crucial motivating factor for undertaking this study has been the absence of comprehensive research, from an academic standpoint, which analyzes the changing engagement between the United States and Cuba, and its impacts on CARICOM member states. Moreover, to our knowledge, no research has been undertaken utilizing a Caribbean investigative lens to examine the potential implications of this engagement. From a Caribbean perspective, national governments as well as the private sector and the CARICOM secretariat would benefit from access to comprehensive analyses of this important development in order to advance appropriate responses and strategies. This pioneering research is intended to provide such knowledge to the various stakeholders. It identifies potential areas for enhancing relations between Cuba and the rest of the Caribbean based on the implications of the former's changing relationship with the United States.

The desk review for this research study benefited from approximately 300 sources, including official communiqués, press releases, policy briefs, statistical databases, scholarly journal articles, books, opinion-editorials, and blogs by reputable institutions and contributors. The research also benefited from in-depth elite interviews, which sought the views of experts in the domestic policies and international relations of the three actors under investigation: the United States, Cuba, and CARICOM. Profiles of these interviewees are provided in the Appendixes.

The book is divided into 11 chapters. This brief Introduction (Chap. 1) is followed by Chap. 2, which examines the evolution of regionalism at the global level and thus provides the context for discussing how the recent changes in Cuba-U.S. relations could impact on the CARICOM Caribbean. Chapter 3 then focuses on regionalism in the Caribbean context. It outlines some of the key characteristics of CARICOM and how the regional organization functions, and also explores some of the challenges it faces. Chapter 4 offers an extensive examination of the political and economic history of Cuba and the United States until December 17, 2014 (17D). This chapter provides the background information important for understanding the significance of 17D. Next, Chap. 5 looks at advancements in the Cuba-U.S. relationship and Chap. 6 at the limits on the relationship. In so doing, the two chapters highlight some key developments that have occurred since 17D—including the response of the Trump administration to the Cuban policy adjustments made under President Barack Obama—and evaluate them in terms of whether they are fostering, or obstructing, changes in the bilateral relationship between Havana and Washington. Chapter 7 examines the factors and actors that have been driving the changes in Cuba-U.S. bilateral relations, as well as the limits to these. Chapter 8 presents a historical overview of the relationship between Cuba and CARICOM, and its challenges; and an analysis of the causes of these challenges. Chapter 9 outlines cooperation between Cuba and CARICOM in key sectors such as health, education, climate change, disaster risk reduction, and cultural exchanges. In so doing, it includes data for other Caribbean territories as well. Chapter 10 takes a close-up look at Cuba-CARICOM trade and economic relations and considers the strategies that the two partners have employed in their striving for economic growth and regional development. Chapter 11 concludes with some broad reflections and recommendations for the Caribbean, with the aim of capitalizing on the changing regional dynamics.

The book aims to contribute to the knowledge of Cuba's relations with CARICOM and understanding of the ways in which the Obama administration's efforts to "normalize" relations with Havana may have affected Cuba's role in the Caribbean. It is written from the distinctive perspective of Caribbean stakeholders, who see these developments as part of an ongoing process of shifting geopolitics, not only within the region but globally. We have sought to fill a gap in the literature available in the English language, as Cuba's ties to its neighbors have not been extensively written about by scholars. The book is mainly intended to serve as a resource for university courses offered by institutions in the Caribbean, as students at these institutions are not adequately served by the existing array of publications on Cuba's role in the international arena. Bearing this in mind, we have made a concerted effort to compile the changes that have occurred in Cuba-U.S. relations, not only to facilitate a better understanding of their impacts on the Caribbean, but also to provide accurate information on what has been effectively transformed (e.g. the Caribbean public wrongly believes that the U.S. embargo on Cuba has been lifted and that U.S. tourists can now visit Cuba). It is also hoped that the usefulness of the findings presented here will extend beyond students to a wide and diverse range of scholars, policymakers and strategists, companies, and non-governmental organizations (NGOs), as well as members of the general public, with an interest in U.S. foreign policy, Cuban foreign policy, and Caribbean studies.

The election of Donald J. Trump as U.S. president, in November 2016, rekindled debates over U.S.-Cuba policy. There is growing speculation as to the likely economic, political, social, institutional, and security implications for Cuba, the United States, and the Latin American and Caribbean region of changes brought in by the Trump administration that has returned to invocate the Monroe Doctrine as a valid approach to orientate U.S. foreign policy, for instance. Additionally, in February 2019, a proposal for a new Constitution was voted on and approved in a popular referendum in Cuba. Given Cuba's ongoing political and economic restructuring, alongside the renewal of its relations with the United States (now under a hostile administration that seems to want to step back to the Cold War era), the consequent modifications in the relationship between Cuba and the CARICOM countries must be explored. There is a need, therefore, for wide-ranging studies which track and capture data on these new developments, to provide targeted analyses that answer the questions posed above. We hope that this book makes a valuable contribution to this major purpose of promoting informed debates and policy responses for the benefit of the Caribbean.

CHAPTER 2

Interrogating Regional Integration Worldwide

Regionalism, regional cooperation, regional integration, and regionalization are key terms in the discussion on regional relations in this chapter. Regionalism, as defined by Börzel and Risse (2016, 7), is "a state-led process of building and sustaining formal regional institutions and organizations among at least three states".[1] Regional cooperation is considered to be "inter-governmental relations that do not entail the transfer of authority" (ibid., 8). The complexities and various manifestations of regional integration, though, make it a more challenging phenomenon to define, but simply put, regional integration involves states giving some authority and sovereignty to a regional arrangement (see Lingberg 1963). Nye (1968) expands on this idea by underscoring that integration should be considered by examining its various components: economic, social, and political integration, and how these interact with and are interdependent on one another. While regionalism focuses on "top-down state-led institution building" (Börzel and Risse 2016, 8), regionalization connotes "the pattern of ties between the economies of the region, manifesting themselves

[1] "Institutions are sets of norms, rules and procedures that enable as well as constrain actor behaviour with some predictability over time, and may also constitute their identities and preferences ... organizations are formal institutions 'with a street address', i.e. with at least some degree of actorness. Accordingly, regional organizations are formal and institutionalized cooperative relations among states or sub-state units of different countries and constitute regionalism" (Börzel and Risse 2016, 7).

© The Author(s) 2020
J. Laguardia Martinez et al., *Changing Cuba-U.S. Relations*,
https://doi.org/10.1007/978-3-030-20366-5_2

in trade and migration" as opposed to a focus on intergovernmental relations (Libman and Vinokurov 2011, 469).

This chapter focuses on regionalism in its various forms—regional cooperation and regional integration—and examines the evolution of regionalism at the global level, which helps to establish the foundation for doing the same for the Caribbean, specifically the Caribbean Community (CARICOM), in Chap. 3. This chapter also provides emerging anti-regionalism tendencies in some parts of the world. Altogether the discussion serves to provide the context and background for examining Cuba's changing relations with the United States and the implications for CARICOM and regional integration, which are subsequently discussed. To these ends, this chapter first examines the history and evolution of regionalism, by outlining overarching global trends which have manifested in the different waves of regionalism in the global political economy and then addresses questions concerning the possible shift from regionalism and multilateralism toward nationalism.

GLOBAL TRENDS IN REGIONALISM

Regionalism is not a new phenomenon: early notions of regions and regional communities came in the form of empires, kingdoms, alliances, and unions, among others. The establishment of the earliest and clearest regional configurations can be traced to Europe around discourses of "shared history and political thought" (Börzel and Risse 2016, 18) that go back centuries to ancient Greece. The idea, therefore, of states taking advantage of the common environment with other states existed long before the establishment of regional organizations, but formal regional organizations, as manifested in the European integration project, have their genesis around the end of the Second World War in 1945.

It is also significant to note that most Western European states were colonizers; colonialism influenced regionalism in both Europe and its former colonies, and "these trajectories continue to influence more recent regionalist ideas and projects, not only in the post-colonial world but also in contemporary Europe. European colonial empires were sometimes organized regionally; but anti-colonial struggles also took a regional form" (Börzel and Risse 2016, 18). This can be illustrated by considering specific regional situations. In the case of Africa, where the establishment of early regional groupings was shaped by European colonial rule, for instance, the Southern African Customs Union (SACU) was linked to European natural resource exploitation. In the case of Latin America, regionalism has its roots in the struggle for independence from European rule in the early nineteenth century, which has inspired a vision of pan-Americanism and regionalism up to the twenty-first century. Other pan-continental/regional movements—such as pan-Europeanism, pan-Africanism, pan-Asianism, and pan-Arabism—emerged simultaneously in the nineteenth century and the first half of the twentieth century (Börzel and Risse 2016, 20).

The regionalism that occurred after the Second World War has consequently been placed into two main categories: a wave of "old regionalism", from the 1950s to the end of the 1970s; and "new regionalism", from the mid-1980s onward (Hettne and Söderbaum 1998). It must be noted that the boundaries between these two waves are not absolute and that there are "similarities and continuities" between them as some regional arrangements were established under the previous wave and were simply either renewed, relaunched, or reinvigorated under the new wave (Börzel and Risse 2016, 17). It is generally agreed, however, that these two waves—old and new regionalisms—have differences, not only in substance and content but also in the circumstances under which they occurred (Hettne and Söderbaum 1998). Table 2.1 contrasts old regionalism and new regionalism in this regard.

Table 2.1 A contrast of old and new regionalism

Old regionalism	New regionalism
Dominated by the bipolar Cold War structure, a historical context that is imperative for understanding old regionalism	Occurs in a post-Cold War context, which requires consideration of the interrelated global transformations of the current era, as these are associated with, or influence, new regionalism
Held to specific objectives and content, with a straightforward and limited focus on free trade arrangements and security alliances	Presents as more complex, with a more "comprehensive, multifaceted and multidimensional process" involving a range of considerations of which the most significant include culture, security, economic policies, and political regimes
Was often imposed, either directly or indirectly, from the top and from the Cold War hegemonic powers	Occurs more organically, originating from below and from within the region itself, which more closely reflects the realities and challenges of the region
Was often "inward-oriented" and decidedly restricted in terms of member states	Is more inclusive of external actors, which parallels the interconnected nature of the international political system

Source: Contents of the table drawn from Hettne and Söderbaum (1998, 1–4)

Regionalism was not a popular concept in international relations before the end of the Second World War, but the war eroded the old European order, and as the Cold War took root, the world became split into two camps, each in the sphere of influence of one of the two superpowers. As a result, "[t]he region as a unit of analysis became important not only in a Cold War context, but increasingly as a result of the growing assertiveness and self-consciousness of regions themselves" (Fawcett 1995, 12). This thinking was reflected in the 1945 Charter of the United Nations (UN), with regional organizations regarded as the first point for resolving conflicts among their members. Nonetheless, Cold War politics subverted the role that regional organizations were meant to play in the maintenance of peace and security. In fact, some regional bodies were established specifically to serve the interests of the superpowers—the North Atlantic Treaty Organization (NATO) and the Warsaw Pact were military alliances of the Western bloc and Eastern bloc respectively. Others, such as the Organization of American States (OAS), were conduits for the promotion of the interests of the United States, and the policy of early European institutions was to keep Western Europe in an anti-Soviet alliance (Fawcett 1995).

Organizations such as the Arab League and the Organization of African Unity (OAU)—now the African Union (AU)—faced a different set of problems. These "pan-movements" were not able to keep their members united. For example, Southern coalitions—in particular, the Non-Aligned Movement and the Group of 77, which embraced a structuralist approach to their development challenges and solutions—were unable to adequately keep their members united behind a common agenda (Fawcett 1995).

It should be noted that except for the Inter-American System and the European Economic Community (EEC)—a common market established in 1957—there were not many regional arrangements in existence before the end of the Second World War in 1945. What existed were several public and private associations, such as the General Postal Union and the International Law Association—as well as the League of Nations—which had universal membership. Regionalism, as described above, appears contradictory to the ideals of the collective security system and to the notions of international governance.

In the 1960s, European integration especially was perceived to be a model for the rest of the world, and as a consequence, various common markets sprang up in Africa, the Middle East, the Pacific, and the Americas. However, these did not have similar results to Europe, which, although it experienced challenges, was relatively successful.[2] The 1970s and 1980s, though, saw the establishment of a comparatively more effective set of regional arrangements which tried to overcome the challenges of regionalism of the decade before, and whose agendas were not informed by the dynamics of the East-West conflict. Some instances of these were: the Association of Southeast Asian Nations (ASEAN) in 1967; the Caribbean Community in 1973; the Economic Community of West African States (ECOWAS) in 1975; the Southern African Development Coordination Conference (SADCC) (now the Southern African Development Community [SADC]) in 1980; the Gulf Cooperation Council (GCC) in 1981; and the South Asian Association for Regional Cooperation (SAARC) in 1985. These bodies symbolized serious efforts toward regionalism free from superpower support, but, while they remained on the international radar, the bipolar environment of the Cold War caused their agendas to remain limited in scope. Among the other factors that adversely affected their effectiveness was their reluctance to surrender some measure of their sovereignty in security and non-security matters. What would eventually provide renewed inspiration for regional integration were developments in the European Community in the mid-1980s (Fawcett 1995).

The New Regionalism

Most would agree that in the 1980s, regionalism was on the rise and that the "[t]win late-1980s announcements, by the United States and Canada of negotiations for a free-trade area, and by the [European Economic Community] of an attempt to complete its internal market, ignited a conflagration of regional integration" (Ethier 1998, 1149). The 1980s essentially saw a new set of regional arrangements emerging, as well as the revival of old arrangements (Fawcett 1995). This new wave of regionalism took root even before the end of the Cold War, by which time significant progress in regionalism had already begun in regions such as Western Europe, the Americas, Southeast Asia, and the Middle East (Fawcett 1995). Developments in European integration, together with global political and economic changes, were responsible for this new set of transformations taking place in regional cooperation.

Stallings (1995) has pointed out that the face of world politics in the 1990s was influenced by several factors:

[2] European integration was considered successful until about 2010.

1. The end of the Cold War
2. The changing relations among more advanced capitalist systems
3. The increased globalization of trade and production
4. The changing structures of economic interactions at an international level
5. The changing ideologies that were surfacing at the time

The decreasing tensions in the international system, coupled with the beginning of the phenomenon of globalization, explain why the growth in regionalism continued into the 1990s. The end of the Cold War signaled the collapse of the bipolar system, creating a decentralized multipolar international climate (Fawcett 1995; Hettne and Söderbaum 1998). This shift from the bipolar system also created a positive attitude toward regionalism and international cooperation. NATO and the European Union (EU) expressed a desire to expand their membership and scope of activities as a result of these geopolitical changes, and both superpowers—the United States and Russia—expressed a new attraction to regionalism. Additionally, the governments of Eastern Europe and the former Soviet republics expressed a desire to participate in the cooperation efforts of Western Europe. Developing countries, too, became aware of the idea that as superpower rivalry was ending, issues would be addressed at the regional level rather than at the global level (Fawcett 1995).

While the end of the Cold War had ushered a greater sense of independence in many regions of the world, it had also brought a greater sense of vulnerability. New or more effective regional organizations were perceived to be tools to counter the isolation which was being faced by many countries. Post-Soviet states and Eastern European countries saw regionalism as a potential avenue for countering the economic and security vacuum created by the ending of the Council for Mutual Economic Assistance (COMECON) and the Warsaw Pact. Many developing countries sought regionalism as a method of combating marginalization, as they faced competition for aid, loans, and markets from the newly independent post-Soviet states and Eastern European countries; they saw regional cooperation as a means to establish links with developed countries in order to become more independent and self-reliant (Fawcett 1995). Even in the Asia-Pacific region where, in comparison, the question of marginalization was not as much of an issue, regional cooperation was seen to be an important response to changes in the international system (Fawcett 1995).

In essence, the new regionalism "demonstrates the growing influence of diplomacy and interregional exchanges, political dialogues and development cooperation" (Byron 2015, 150).[3]

Furthermore, this new wave of regionalism in the post-Cold War period is distinct from earlier waves of regionalism in that it covers "all issue areas and has a truly global reach" (Fawcett 1995, 9). Although regionalism made the most progress in its institutionalized form in Western Europe and Latin America, it did have a universal appeal, albeit in very diverse ways (Fawcett 1995, 9). For example, in some instances, members recommitted to a greater level of unity, as in the case of the European Community, ASEAN, OAU (now AU), and the Andean Community. In other instances, countries—for example, several Eastern European countries and former Soviet republics—attempted to join existing economic and security arrangements such as the European Community, NATO, the Commission on Security and Cooperation in Europe (CSCE), or the Nordic Council. Others either established new regional schemes or rejuvenated old ones, such as the Southern Common Market (MERCOSUR) in South America; the Arab Maghreb Union (AMU) in North Africa; the Economic Cooperation Organization (ECO), consisting of Islamic countries of Central and South Asia; and the Visegrad Pact and the Pentagonale Initiative in Central and Eastern Europe. In some cases, countries chose to maintain loose regional arrangements in the form of conferences or discussion fora, such as the Asia-Pacific Economic Cooperation (APEC) forum (Fawcett 1995).

Apart from the changes brought about by the end of the Cold War, other developments fueled the growth of regionalism in both the economic and strategic (political) spheres. Prominent among these events was the deepening of the European integration project. The establishment of the European Single Market in 1992 served as a central source of inspiration to renewed regional efforts globally (Fawcett 1995; Hettne and Söderbaum 1998). This may have even stirred the United States and Canada to choose regionalism over multilateralism, as evidenced by their establishment of the North American Free Trade Agreement (NAFTA) (including Mexico) and support for an Asia-Pacific trading bloc. "[T]his

---

[3] Translated from the original in Spanish: "El regionalismo contemporáneo también manifiesta la creciente influencia de la diplomacia y los intercambios interregionales, de los diálogos políticos y la cooperación al desarrollo."

second wave of European-led integration produced the further launching of ambitious schemes borrowing heavily from the Europe 1992 idea" (Fawcett 1995, 24) in various parts of the world, as can be seen in the examples provided by the AMU, the Andean Community, MERCOSUR, and ASEAN, which aimed to establish common markets within a particular timeframe. In various regions, countries were encouraged by the deepening of Europe's regional integration project to launch, or recommit to, regional cooperation to meet their own development needs (Fawcett 1995). Other factors identified as encouraging regionalism in the 1990s include: the decline of U.S. hegemony; the reconfiguration of the global political economy into major economic blocs; and uncertainty about the future of the multilateral trading system (Hettne and Söderbaum 1998).

An important driver of regionalism in the so-called Third World was the decline of groupings based on collective solidarity among the countries of the developing world, in particular as they become increasingly heterogeneous—economically and politically—by the 1990s. There was, therefore, a movement away from "broad coalitions and towards ... subgroupings of like-minded members" (Fawcett 1995, 27).

Regionalism has not always taken place in the context of traditional geographic spaces, and some groupings from diverse geographic regions have engaged in "regional" cooperation. Regional cooperation defined by geographical boundaries has been complemented by cooperation based on non-geographic considerations. One such example is the African, Caribbean, and Pacific (ACP) group of states, consisting of former European colonies facing similar development challenges in the postcolonial era. The group was established in 1975 to negotiate aid and trade concessions from former colonial powers. The Cotonou Agreement of 2000, the fifth and latest framework governing ACP-EU relations, envisaged trade relations via economic partnership agreements (EPAs) based on geographic regions. The new framework agreement, expected to replace Cotonou in 2020, promises to favor cooperation based on country groupings facing similar issues and common interests; these may transcend common geography and history.

In the case of the ACP group, its establishment and, in particular, its relations with Europe were based on its members' shared status as former European colonies and disadvantaged position in the global political economy. Other more recently established groupings such as the Brazil, Russia, India, China, and South Africa (BRICS) bloc differ in that their rationale for cooperation is not based on shared history, but on similar levels of economic power envisaged at a particular point in time.

Developments in Regionalism in the Twenty-First Century

The twenty-first century has seen a myriad of new trends in regionalism. The first of these is the increasing inclusion of non-state actors, civil society organizations, and multinational corporations with the aim of advancing the development and security needs of regions. Second, the inter-regional relations of the global South are being increasingly diversified to include non-Western partners, like those from the East such as China and India (Fanta et al. 2013). The third, and perhaps most dramatic, trend in regionalism has been the emergence of post-liberal integration schemes, particularly in Latin America (Phillips 2003; Sanahuja 2010; Serbin 2017).[4]

Latin America had been forced to adopt open regionalism since the late 1980s, after closed regionalism became discredited following the Latin American debt crisis and the failure of economic strategies utilizing import substitution industrialization (ISI) (Briceno-Ruiz and Morales 2017). Post-liberal schemes emerged after a decade of neo-liberalism-driven regionalism. These have been characterized by an ideological dimension, which has as its purpose the countering of the effects of neo-liberal globalization and Western influence, particularly that of the United States. As Western powers have been excluded from these schemes, this has enabled the groupings to assert a greater level of autonomy over the political and economic agenda of their regions. Sanahuja (2010) attributes the increase in Latin American and Caribbean South-South regionalism at the start of the twenty-first century—as a consequence of increased South-South cooperation within the region—to a number of factors:

1. It was an outward expression of the growing economic and political strength of emerging countries within the region.
2. It indicated the extending international scope of their national interests.
3. It demonstrated their leadership at the regional and international levels.
4. It was an assertion of their desire to gain more agency in international politics and the global financial system.

---

[4] Phillips (2003) highlights the stages and variations of this new Latin American and Caribbean regionalism by further identifying under the umbrella of new regionalism, not just post-liberal regionalism, but also post-hegemonic regionalism, third-generation regionalism, spaghetti-bowl regionalism, and rhetorical regionalism.

Sanahuja (2010, 19) underscores that "[a] strong discourse of self-legitimisation is being built around South-South cooperation in Latin America as a regional expression of the global debate about the role of such cooperation in the international aid system." Examples of such schemes include: Bolivarian Alliance for the Peoples of Our America (ALBA), Union of South American Nations (UNASUR), and Community of Latin American and Caribbean States (CELAC), established in 2004, 2008, and 2011, respectively. These integration initiatives emerged in sharp contrast to those in the late twentieth century in which the United States was a dominant actor, "physically and ideologically" (Council for Hemispheric Affairs 2013).

Like in previous years, the new developments in regionalism have been happening simultaneously. North-South regionalism continues alongside South-South regional initiatives and post-liberal initiatives have inter-regional relations with more powerful Northern partners, as illustrated by the strategic partnership between CELAC and the EU. The scope of the regional integration agenda also continues to be broad—a characteristic of the new regionalism of the 1990s.

But even as regionalism takes various forms, there are unfavorable developments affecting regional integration and cooperation among some segments of the global community.

Concluding Reflections: A Retreat to Nationalism and Isolationism?

Nationalism is on the rise globally. This is reflected in recent developments, including the policies of Japan's Prime Minister Shinzo Abe, India's Prime Minister Narendra Modi, Turkey's President Recep Tayyip Erdogan, and U.S. President Donald Trump; the election and increasing prominence of far-right parties across Europe; the emergence of a similar trend in Latin America, as evidenced by the election of Mauricio Macri in Argentina, Sebastián Piñera in Chile, and Jair Bolsonaro in Brazil; and the decision of the United Kingdom (UK) to leave the EU—Brexit (Bieber 2018).

Pre-Second World War American isolationist policies of the 1920s and 1930s seem to be resurfacing in that country's foreign policy: President Trump's stance on immigration, his opposition to the Trans-Pacific Partnership (TPP) and the Transatlantic Trade and Investment Partnership (TTIP), and U.S. withdrawal from the Paris Agreement on climate change are all evidence pointing in this direction (Henökl 2017; Krauthammer 2017). A similar trend can be seen in Europe with the withdrawal of the UK—a major power—from the EU and nationalist tendencies in Europe, as mentioned above. By exiting the EU, the UK is indicating its preference to be away from the European regional integration project (Della Ventura 2016). Similarities have been drawn between the 2016 U.S. presidential elections and the 2016 UK referendum on the country's future in the EU (Fukuyama 2016; Murray 2016). Murray (2016) states that these "two political upheavals are united in that both societies include a class of people whose job prospects have been wrecked by the outsourcing of labor, people for whom globalization is a problem rather than an opportunity". Colgan and Keohane (2017) further state that "the two states that had done the most to construct the liberal order—the United Kingdom and the United States—seemed to turn their backs on it. In the former, the successful Brexit campaign focused on restoring British sovereignty; in the latter, the Trump campaign was explicitly nationalist in tone and content".

Since 2008, the EU has been facing various challenges that have put its integration project under immense pressure. These include: the 2008 global financial crisis and the consequent euro crisis; an unsettling of the post-Cold War balance in Europe by Russian military action; as well as the activities of the Islamic State of Iraq and Syria (ISIS) and resulting migration flows into the member states of the EU (Riley and Ghilès 2016).

The economic crisis of 2008 forced an influx of migrants from throughout the eurozone. Since the UK was never part of the eurozone, it was able to stabilize its economy more rapidly than other states after 2008. The large number of people seeking employment in the UK, along with the fear of greater inward migration, has been attributed as a major contributor to the "Leave" victory in the 2016 Brexit referendum (Riley and Ghilès 2016; Friedman 2016). The mindset that viewed immigration to the UK with apprehension and the resultant vote to leave the EU, is indicative of trends of nationalism and the pursuit of greater autonomy over the national agenda taking place around the world. Citizens are disillusioned with institutions which are perceived to have outlived their purposes and which are seen to be robbing nations of control over their affairs, in other words, their sovereignty (Friedman 2016).

These sentiments are evident when one also considers other European countries that share these perspectives, and which are seeking to curb immigration to their countries. Italy, Austria, Hungary, and Poland are all examples of the trend toward right-wing and populist governance.

Brexit has had, and will continue to have, a significant impact on the EU and the global community in general. After the UK referendum, the value of the pound sterling dropped very low, and stock markets around the world fell because of panic selling. Supporters of the EU are wary of the fact that Brexit will "weaken the West as it grapples with Donald Trump's unpredictable U.S. presidency and growing assertiveness from Russia and China" (Reuters 2018).

As is the case with Brexit, developments in the United States are highlighted here because of their direct relevance to the discussions of this book. Recent developments in the United States have implications not only for Cuba-U.S. relations but also for regional integration projects such as CARICOM, whose direction has traditionally been influenced and driven by global developments led by the West.

The idea of nationalism and national sovereignty lies at the heart of President Donald Trump's foreign policy, and the term "nationalist" has stirred up controversy in the United States regarding its meaning and connotation. Elving (2018) explains that in the past, nationalism was often a synonym for patriotism, but over the years, the meaning has changed, especially when the word "white" was added to it. It is this brand of nationalism, which connotes a superiority rooted in racism, that has come to define the term and has caused many to refrain from describing themselves as "nationalists". President Trump, however, has adopted a different meaning of the word and has stated that "[a]ll I want is for our country to be treated well, to be treated with respect, so in that sense I'm absolutely a nationalist, and I'm proud of it" (Trump in Elving 2018). These sentiments are reflective of trends that can be seen not only in Europe but also in Latin America (e.g. in Argentina, Chile, and Brazil).

Although it is too early to come to a definite conclusion, developments in the United States, in particular, hold the promise of impacting the country's relations with Cuba and consequently Cuba's relations with its Caribbean neighbors.

References

Bieber, Florian. 2018. Is Nationalism on the Rise? Assessing Global Trends. *Ethnopolitics* 2 (5): 519–540.
Börzel, Tanja A., and Thomas Risse. 2016. *The Oxford Handbook of Comparative Regionalism*. Oxford: Oxford University Press.

Briceno-Ruiz, José, and Isidro Morales. 2017. *Post-Hegemonic Regionalism in the Americas: Toward a Pacific–Atlantic Divide?* London and New York: Routledge.

Byron, Jessica. 2015. Una perspectiva caribeña sobre el regionalismo: ¿cuál es el rol de la CELAC? In *El ALBA-TCP: origen y fruto del nuevo regionalismo latinoamericano y caribeño*, compiled by Maribel Aponte García and Gloria Amézquita Puntiel and edited by Pablo Gentili, 147–169. Buenos Aires: El Consejo Latinoamericano de Ciencias Sociales (CLACSO).

Colgan, Jeff D., and Robert O. Keohane. 2017. The Liberal Order Is Rigged: Fix It Now or Watch It Wither. *Foreign Affairs* 96 (3) (May/June). Accessed January 5, 2019. https://www.foreignaffairs.com/articles/world/2017-04-17/liberal-order-rigged.

Council for Hemispheric Affairs. 2013. *21st Century Regionalism: Where Is Latin America Headed?* September 3, 2013. Accessed June 7, 2017. http://www.coha.org/21st-century-regionalism-where-is-latin-america-headed/.

Della Ventura, Lucas. 2016. Brexit: The UK's Isolationist Fantasy. *The Hill*, June 30, 2016. Accessed June 9, 2017. http://thehill.com/blogs/pundits-blog/international-affairs/286000-brexit-the-uks-isolationist-fantasy.

Elving, Ron. 2018. What Is a Nationalist in the Age of Trump? *National Public Radio (NPR)*, October 24, 2018. Accessed December 21, 2018. https://www.npr.org/2018/10/24/660042653/what-is-a-nationalist-in-the-age-of-trump.

Ethier, Wilfred J. 1998. The New Regionalism. *The Economic Journal*, 108 (July): 1149–1161. Accessed June 9, 2017. http://www.china-up.com:8080/international/case/case/1431.pdf.

Fanta, Emmanuel, Timothy M. Shaw, and Vanessa T. Tang. 2013. *Comparative Regionalisms for Development in the 21st Century: Insights from the Global South*. London and New York: Routledge.

Fawcett, Louise. 1995. Regionalism in Historical Perspective. In *Regionalism in World Politics: Regional Organization and International Order*, ed. Louise Fawcett and Andrew Hurrell, 9–36. New York: Oxford University Press.

Friedman, George. 2016. 3 Reasons Brits Voted for Brexit. *Forbes*, July 5, 2016. Accessed December 21, 2018. https://www.forbes.com/sites/johnmauldin/2016/07/05/3-reasons-brits-voted-for-brexit/#47650b01f9d6.

Fukuyama, Francis. 2016. US Against the World? Trump's America and the New Global Order. *Financial Times*, November 11, 2016. Accessed December 21, 2018. https://www.ft.com/content/6a43cf54-a75d-11e6-8b69-02899e8bd9d1.

Henökl, Thomas. 2017. Trump, Brexit, Populism – Wither Multilateralism and Liberal World Order? *The Current Column*, January 20, 2017. Accessed June 11, 2018. https://www.die-gdi.de/en/the-current-column/article/trump-brexit-populism-wither-multilateralism-and-liberal-world-order/.

Hettne, Björn, and Fredrik Söderbaum. 1998. The New Regionalism Approach. *Politeia* 17 (3): 6–21.

Krauthammer, Charles. 2017. Trump's Foreign Policy Revolution. *The Washington Post*, January 26, 2017. Accessed June 9, 2017. https://www.washingtonpost.com/opinions/global-opinions/trumps-foreign-policy-revolution/2017/01/26/c69268a6-e402-11e6-ba11-63c4b4fb5a63_story.html?utm_term=.13341128f5bb.

Libman, Alexander, and Evgeny Vinokurov. 2011. Is It Really Different? Patterns of Regionalisation in Post-Soviet Central Asia. *Post-Communist Economies* 23 (4): 469–492.

Lingberg, Leon N. 1963. *The Political Dynamics of European Economic Integration*. Stanford, CA: Stanford University Press.

Murray, Douglas. 2016. From Brexit to Trump: Giving the Elites a Hard Kick. *Foreign Affairs*, November 10, 2016. Accessed January 3, 2019. https://www.foreignaffairs.com/articles/2016-11-10/brexit-trump.

Nye, Joseph S. 1968. Comparative Regional Integration: Concept and Measurement. *International Organization* 22 (4) (Autumn): 855–880. Accessed June 9, 2017. http://www.jstor.org/stable/2705847.

Phillips, Nicola. 2003. The Rise and Fall of Open Regionalism? Comparative Reflections on Regional Governance in the Southern Cone of Latin America. *Third World Quarterly* 24 (2): 217–234.

Reuters. 2018. Explained: What Is Brexit and Why Does It Matter? *New Straits Times*, December 18, 2018. Accessed December 21, 2018. https://www.nst.com.my/world/2018/12/441915/explained-what-brexit-and-why-does-it-matter.

Riley, Alan, and Francis Ghilès. 2016. BREXIT: Causes and Consequences. *Notes Internacionals*, 159 (October). Barcelona Centre for International Affairs (CIDOB). Accessed December 20, 2018. https://www.cidob.org/publicaciones/serie_de_publicacion/notes_internacionals/n1_159/brexit_causes_and_consequences.

Sanahuja, José Antonio. 2010. Post-Liberal Regionalism: S-S Cooperation in Latin America and the Caribbean. *Poverty in Focus*, 20 (April): 17–19. International Policy Centre for Inclusive Growth Poverty Practice, Bureau for Development Policy, United Nations Development Programme (UNDP). Accessed December 17, 2018. http://www.ipc-undp.org/pub/IPCPovertyInFocus20.pdf.

Serbin, Andrés. 2017. When Cuba Went Regional: Latin American Post-Liberal Regionalism and Cuban Foreign Policy. *Pensamiento Propio* 45: 111–142. Accessed December 18, 2018. http://www.cries.org/wp-content/uploads/2017/09/008-serbin.pdf.

Stallings, Barbara, ed. 1995. *Global Change, Regional Response: The New International Context of Development*. Cambridge: Cambridge University Press.

CHAPTER 3

Regional Integration in the Caribbean

Having explored regional trends at the global level in the previous chapter, the foundation has been laid for us to now turn for a closer look at the Caribbean region specifically. The chapter gives an overview of regional integration efforts from the time of the West Indies Federation to the Caribbean Free Trade Association (CARIFTA) and the Caribbean Community (CARICOM). This chapter also examines how the Caribbean Community operates as a regional organization. It provides a general introduction to CARICOM, its objectives, mandate, governance structure, institutions, challenges, and future direction. Finally, the chapter exposes CARICOM's development challenges and reflects on what emerging trends against regional cooperation could mean for Cuba-CARICOM relations.

The nature of Caribbean integration has, for the most part, been externally driven. This can be seen in the rationale for the very first attempt at regional integration, initiated by the British government through the establishment of the West Indies Federation (CARICOM 2017).[1] Established in 1958, the Federation was driven by Britain's long-standing desire to manage its colonies in a more efficient and economical manner. The British felt that cooperation was a necessary precondition for independence, one that was essential to overcome size deficiencies and to

---

[1] The West Indies Federation comprised ten territories: Antigua and Barbuda, Barbados, Dominica, Grenada, Jamaica, Montserrat, the then St. Kitts-Nevis-Anguilla, St. Lucia, St. Vincent, and Trinidad and Tobago. It was established by the British Caribbean Federation Act of 1956.

© The Author(s) 2020
J. Laguardia Martinez et al., *Changing Cuba-U.S. Relations*,
https://doi.org/10.1007/978-3-030-20366-5_3

foster political and economic stability. The Federation lasted only four years and was dissolved in 1962 (CARICOM 2017).

The failure of the West Indies Federation set the tone for the birth of the Caribbean's indigenous regional integration project. At this time, the government of Trinidad and Tobago proposed "a Caribbean Economic Community of all the island territories of the English, French, Spanish and Dutch speaking Caribbean" (Girvan 2012a, 35). This led to the establishment of CARICOM's predecessor, the Caribbean Free Trade Association (CARIFTA), in 1968, as a "loose arrangement for economic cooperation, rather than as a political framework" (Gilbert-Roberts 2013, 62). CARIFTA found impetus in a shift away from notions of "West Indianness" to economic considerations as the basis for regional cooperation. Yet, while Jamaica and Trinidad and Tobago had attained their independence and were thus able to exercise political authority over their territory, their socio-economic circumstances had not improved; ideas of sovereignty and self-governance were subsequently redirected back to the need for regional cooperation (ibid., 51).

As with regional integration schemes in other parts of the world, developments around CARICOM must be understood in the context of larger global processes and developments—specifically the transformation of the European Economic Community (EEC) into the European Union (EU) and the creation of the North American Free Trade Agreement (NAFTA) (McLean et al. 2014). A free trade area in the Caribbean gave way to a common market—the Caribbean Community—and subsequently to plans for a single market and economy. CARICOM was patterned after the European model of regional integration—in particular, the EEC. CARICOM's agenda was based on the development imperatives of its member states rather than the exigencies of East-West politics, as had been the case with many regional groupings in the Cold War era. CARICOM's objectives were to foster economic integration and to coordinate foreign policy in areas such as health, education, culture, and social development.

As the Cold War was ending and globalization was ushered in, Europe transitioned toward a single market and economic space, beginning with the signing of the Single European Act in 1986, which would lead to the completion of the Single Market in 1992. In response to globalization and complementary changes in EU integration, CARICOM took the decision, in 1989, to deepen and widen regional integration. Widening took the form of a move toward expansion of CARICOM's membership and cooperation to include the non-Anglophone Caribbean and Latin American countries with Caribbean coastlines (The West Indian Commission 1993). Haiti's assumption of full membership of CARICOM in 2002 and the formation of the Association of Caribbean States (ACS) in 1994 are concrete manifestations of the widening. The policy move toward further deepening manifested in the decision to launch the CARICOM Single Market and Economy (The West Indian Commission 1993; CARICOM 2011). The CARICOM Single Market and Economy (CSME) was established by the Revised Treaty of Chaguaramas in 2001, with the stated aim of making the Community a stronger and more cohesive force in the face of economic globalization (CARICOM 2011).

At the end of the Cold War, CARICOM relations with Europe and the Americas changed. CARICOM faced the urgency of integration since it feared relegation within the African, Caribbean, and Pacific (ACP) and within Latin America, since most of the EU's trade and investment were directed to the Southern Common Market (MERCOSUR) countries,[2] and other countries in the region.

CARICOM: Overview

CARICOM was established by the Treaty of Chaguaramas, which was signed on July 4, 1973, and came into effect on August 1, 1973. The idea of cooperation has been a long-standing mission for Caribbean countries: beginning with the attempts at political union, leading to the West Indies Federation in 1958, then to "deeper and more structured engagements" through the Caribbean Free Trade Association formed in 1965, and finally, to "more sustained" regional integration through the Caribbean Community established in 1973 (CARICOM org).

CARICOM comprises 15 full member states (14 independent and 1 non-independent) and 5 associate members.[3] The approximately 16 mil-

---

[2] MERCOSUR member states are Argentina, Brazil, Paraguay, Uruguay, and Venezuela. Bolivia is in the process of accession.

[3] Anguilla, British Virgin Islands, Turks and Caicos Islands, Cayman Islands, and Bermuda (CARICOM org).

lion citizens who inhabit CARICOM countries are mainly descendants of the indigenous peoples of the Caribbean, Africans, East Indians, Europeans, Chinese, Portuguese, and Javanese. CARICOM countries are multilingual, having English as the major language as well as French and Dutch and their variations, along with varieties of African and Asian linguistic expressions (CARICOM org).

Although CARICOM countries differ significantly in terms of geography and economic characteristics, they share several common elements, all of which are closely inter-related: small, open economies; narrow export base; heavy reliance on trade preferences that have been increasingly eroded in recent years; and susceptibility to adverse climatic conditions. These characteristics have influenced the rationale for the integration efforts of the region as well as its policy direction. "These characteristics of smallness have shaped the integration process in terms of the provision of administrative and technical capacity at the regional level, special provisions for the less developed countries (LDCs)" (CARICOM 1999, 1). This has also led to CARICOM seeking special and differential treatment for its members through its hemispheric and extra-regional economic relations (CARICOM 1999).

CARICOM: Objectives and Functions

The Revised Treaty of Chaguaramas establishing the Caribbean Community including the CARICOM Single Market and Economy was signed in 2001. The Revised Treaty specifies the objectives of CARICOM (CARICOM Secretariat 2001, 7). According to Article 6 of the Revised Treaty, the objectives are:

1. Improved standards of living and work;
2. Full employment of labor and other factors of production;
3. Accelerated, coordinated, and sustained economic development and convergence;
4. Expansion of trade and economic relations with third states;
5. Enhanced levels of international competitiveness;
6. Organization for increased production and productivity;
7. The achievement of a greater measure of economic leverage and effectiveness in dealing with third states, groups of states, and entities of any description;
8. Enhanced coordination of member states' foreign and (foreign) economic policies; and
9. Enhanced functional cooperation.

The Caribbean Community was established in 1973 on three main pillars: economic integration, functional cooperation, and foreign policy coordination. Considering the increasing security concerns and challenges facing the region, CARICOM's leaders agreed to establish security as a fourth pillar (CARICOM org).

An explanation of each is provided below:

Economic Integration: This was the main objective for the establishment of CARIFTA in 1968 and became the cornerstone of the Treaty of Chaguaramas in 1973. It was further developed and expanded in the Revised Treaty of Chaguaramas and through the CARICOM Single Market and Economy. The CSME views CARICOM as a single economic space, in which trade, business, and labor can work/function (CARICOM org).

Foreign Policy Coordination: This pillar is founded on the recognition that small states are most effective in the international arena when they speak with a united voice. With this in mind,

> the CARICOM, mandated the Council for Foreign and Community Relations (COFCOR) to coordinate the Foreign Policies of Member States; coordinate positions in intergovernmental organizations and on international issues in order to arrive at common positions viz third States, groups of States and international and intergovernmental organizations. (CARICOM Secretariat 2001)

This is also articulated in Article 16 of the Revised Treaty of Chaguaramas.

Traditionally, CARICOM has used a special brand of "small state diplomacy" to advance its interests within the global governance structure. It has leveraged the collective voice of its members to garner credibility and influence and to access fora in which decisions affecting the Caribbean are taken (CARICOM org).

The foreign policy coordination by the region has allowed for some positive accomplishments, including the influential role played by the Caribbean in the formation of the African, Caribbean, and Pacific (ACP) group of states in 1975; the establishment of the Association of Caribbean States (ACS) in 1994; and CARICOM's successful engagement on key issues of global importance such as climate change and non-communicable diseases (CARICOM 2017).

Functional Cooperation: Functional cooperation is considered to be central to regional integration process and a key pillar in the work of CARICOM (CARICOM 2007), with Article 6 (i) of the Revised Treaty of Chaguaramas, identifying enhanced functional cooperation as one of the fundamental objectives of CARICOM. A Community for All: Declaration on Functional Cooperation, issued by the Heads of Government of the Caribbean Community in 2007, recalled:

> the immense contribution that functional cooperation has made so far to the regional integration movement and [noted] that these purposeful, collaborative, coordinated actions have yield[ed] significant, and tangible benefits to the people of the Community, especially in areas such as education, health, sport, culture, sustainable development and security. (CARICOM 2007)

Also, leaders stated that they were:

> fully convinced that functional cooperation, conceived as the body of actions and activities that integrate the Community's political, economic, security and social policy goals with its cultural, scientific, technological and environmental objectives, offers great opportunities for the future and therefore must permeate the work of every council and institution of the Community and in this regard, contribute to the increase in the welfare and security of the Community's citizens. (CARICOM 2007)

Security. The fourth pillar, security, was added in 2005 in response to the "growing threat to citizen security and other regional assets and institutions and as the objectives of the organization were being threatened by the complex security environment of the 21st Century" (Pryce 2013). The CARICOM Crime and Security Strategy (2013) categorizes security threats under four tiers:

> Tier 1 threats consist of the mutually-reinforcing relationship between transnational organised criminal activities involving illicit drugs and illegal guns; gangs and organised crime; cyber-crime; financial crimes and corruption. Tier 2 Threats are Substantial Threats to the Region. They include human trafficking and smuggling, natural disasters and public disorder crimes. Tier 3 Risks consist of Significant Potential Risks and include attacks on critical infrastructure and terrorism. Tier 4 Risks consist of Future Risks, with unknown probabilities and consequences. They include climate change, pandemics and migratory pressure. (CARICOM IMPACS 2013, 5)

CARICOM Governance

The governance of CARICOM is set out in its original treaty, the 1973 Treaty of Chaguaramas, and the Revised Treaty of Chaguaramas establishing the Caribbean Community including the CARICOM Single Market and Economy. The principal organs of the Community are the Conference of Heads of Government (the Conference) and the Community Council of Ministers (the Council). Their work is supported by five organs, three bodies,[4] and the Secretariat (CARICOM org).

The Conference of Heads of Government is the highest organ of the Caribbean Community and determines and provides policy direction to the organization. It is also the final authority for concluding treaties on behalf of the Community and for forging relationships between the Community and International Organizations and States. This organ is additionally responsible for making financial arrangements to meet the expenses of the Community, but this has been delegated to the Community Council. Unanimous decision-making is generally followed by the Conference (CARICOM org). This organ's work is assisted by the Bureau of the Conference, which initiates proposals for development and approval by the Ministerial Councils; assists with getting consensus of member states on issues determined by the Conference; facilitates the implementation of CARICOM decisions efficiently and effectively; and guides the Secretariat on policy issues (CARICOM org).

The Community Council—the second highest organ of the Community—comprises of Ministers responsible for CARICOM Affairs from member countries. According to Article 13 of the Revised Treaty, the Council's main responsibility is "for the development of Community strategic planning and coordination in the areas of economic integration, functional cooperation [Human and Social Development] and external relations" in line with the policy directions of the Conference. The Council also "serves as a preparatory body for the meetings of the Conference including the preparation of the Provisional Agenda". Additionally, the Community Council is responsible for "examin[ing] and approv[ing] the Community budget, as well as mobilis[ing] and allocate[ing] resources for the implementation of Community plans and programmes" (CARICOM org).

---

[4] The Bodies are the following: the Budget Committee which examines the draft work programme and budget of the Secretariat and makes recommendations to the Community Council; the Committee of Central Bank Governors which provides recommendations to the Council for Finance and Planning (COFAP) on monetary and financial matters; the Legal Affairs Committee (LAC), which is comprised of Attorneys-General and Ministers of Legal Affairs and replaces the Standing Committee with responsibility for Legal Affairs. The committee's function is to advise the organs and other bodies of the Community. A new body is being formed—the CARICOM Committee of Ambassadors. Its role is to facilitate the implementation of the Strategic Plan.

The five supportive organs are:

1. The Council for Trade and Economic Development (COTED), which promotes trade and economic development of CARICOM and manages the functioning of the CSME.
2. The Council for Foreign and Community Relations (COFCOR), which determines CARICOM's relations with international organizations and third states. It is also charged with encouraging friendly and mutually beneficial relations among member states.
3. The Council for Human and Social Development (COHSOD), which supports human and social development.
4. The Council for Finance and Planning (COFAP), which oversees matters of economic policy and the financial and monetary integration of member states.
5. The Council for National Security and Law Enforcement (CONSLE), which coordinates efforts relating to the safety and security of the region (CARICOM org).

The Secretariat is the key administrative organ of the Community and has responsibility for providing relevant services in support of, and promoting, the regional integration and related agenda of the Community. The Head of the Secretariat is the Secretary-General, who is the Chief Executive Officer of the Community. The Secretary-General is appointed by the Conference of Heads of Government (on the recommendation of the Council) for no more than five years and may be reappointed (CARICOM org).

CARICOM has adopted a political culture which relies heavily on the personal authority of heads of government. This structure impedes other regional organs, such as the various ministerial organs and the Secretariat from exercising their decision-making authority and discourages the participation of non-political stakeholders. In brief, Caribbean leaders have been unwilling to sacrifice their right to political independence and self-determination in pursuit of regional goals. Rather, as guardians of sovereignty, they have used the regional decision-making process to preserve as much national autonomy and control as possible (Bishop and Payne 2010).

In this context—characterized by unanimity—a decision-making process controlled by heads of government, ineffective legislation, and insufficient regional executive authority for implementation—the overall CARICOM governance framework has focused largely on procedures of governance rather than on intended outcomes (CARICOM 1973). CARICOM has, however, acknowledged the need to follow-up with members and monitor national compliance with regional initiatives more effectively.

INSTITUTIONS OF CARICOM

Globally, economic integration has become a key response to the changing international economic environment and is the primary way in which Caribbean countries too have adapted to this environment. In this context, the extent to which the Caribbean region is able to improve its prospects for broad-based economic growth, job creation, and poverty reduction will be heavily influenced by the progress it can make toward the successful implementation of its regional integration project.

Furthermore, CARICOM has sought to strengthen and make full use of regional and sub-regional mechanisms in order to assist countries to develop and adapt to the evolving global landscape. As a result, select institutions share a special relationship with CARICOM and provide direct technical support to member states in a range of areas. While an integral part of the CARICOM system, these Community Institutions exist as separate legal entities with differing governance arrangements. The CARICOM Community sees the strengthening of existing and emerging regional institutions, and the formalizing of the relationship between these institutions, as essential for making more effective, the CARICOM Single Market and Economy policy framework (CARICOM org). These Institutions are classified into three categories: Community Institutions,[5] Associate Institutions,[6] and Functional Cooperation Institutions[7] (CARICOM 2007).

---

[5] Community Institutions: Caribbean Agricultural Development Institute (CARDI); Caribbean Agricultural Health and Food Safety Agency (CAHFSA); Caribbean Aviation Safety and Security Oversight System (CASSOS); Caribbean Center for Renewable Energy and Energy Efficiency (CCREEE); Caribbean Centre for Development Administration (CARICAD); Caribbean Community Climate Change Centre (CCCCC); Caribbean Court of Justice (CCJ); Caribbean Disaster Emergency Management Agency (CDEMA); Caribbean Examinations Council (CXC); Caribbean Institute for Meteorology and Hydrology (CIMH); Caribbean Meteorological Organisation (CMO); Caribbean Public Health Agency (CARPHA); Caribbean Regional Fisheries Mechanism (CRFM); Caribbean Telecommunications Union (CTU); CARICOM Competition Commission (CCC); CARICOM Development Fund (CDF); CARICOM Implementing Agency for Crime and Security (IMPACS); and CARICOM Regional Organization for Standards and Quality (CROSQ).

[6] Associate Institutions: Caribbean Development Bank (CDB); Caribbean Law Institute (CLI)/Caribbean Law Institute Centre (CLIC); University of Guyana (UG); and The University of the West Indies (UWI).

[7] Functional Cooperation Institutions: Caribbean Export and Investment Agency (CaribExport); Caribbean Regional Information and Translation Institute (CRITI); Caribbean Tourism Organization (CTO); and Council of Legal Education (CLE).

Challenges Facing CARICOM

CARICOM faces three main challenges, and several other problems also. The first deals with the restructuring of its own integration process, in order to make it more sustainable and relevant in a rapidly changing regional and international context. The second-related challenge is to adequately monitor, analyze, and meaningfully participate in the various regional integration processes that are taking place in Latin America and the Caribbean; chief among them being the Community of Latin American and Caribbean States (CELAC).[8] The third challenge is to adjust national and regional external policies to CARICOM's development strategies.

With regard to the structure of CARICOM itself, many challenges have been identified as inhibitors of the regional integration process. Girvan (2012a) attributes some of these challenges to "faulty implementation of agreed integration schemes, or to inappropriate design of the schemes themselves, or ... inherent limits in the capacity of economic integration (...) to drive development in these economies". More specifically, some of the challenges facing CARICOM include a reluctance to surrender or pool sovereignty, diversion from its original mandate, increasing fragmentation, inadequate political will, asymmetric benefits across member states, and economic and financial difficulties. It is worth discussing these challenges in greater detail here.

First, CARICOM suffers from challenges related to sovereignty. Progress toward one of CARICOM's main objectives—to pool the sovereignties of member states for increased strength against economic instability and external threats—has been lagging. CARICOM territories are relatively "young" in the international system. Having gained independence less than only 50 years ago, states are not eager to relinquish their sovereignty; this has been a hindrance to regional cooperation (Gilbert-Roberts 2013). These territories continue to protect their sovereignty,

---

[8] CELAC is a valuable mechanism for coordinating the positions of Latin America and the Caribbean on a wide range of global governance issues, and a firm platform from which to speak in multilateral and bilateral fora. For the grouping of very small and developing states of CARICOM, it provides additional visibility and a new forum for interaction with both emerging and traditional global powers. CELAC offers diplomatic opportunities not only for CARICOM but also for those close neighbors like Cuba, and much diplomatic capital has been invested in its success. It also supports the exchange of experiences and the development of procedures to maximize the benefits of cooperation programs.

autonomy, and independence. However, as Sanders (2011) states: "[a]s long as CARICOM countries continue to see their economic and social development through the narrow lens of 'national sovereignty', their conditions will deteriorate still further."

Second and closely linked to the previous challenge, it has been asserted that CARICOM has "wandered from its purposes" (Sanders 2016, 3). This situation perhaps reflects a shift in the priorities of CARICOM toward greater concern with the status quo, as opposed to deeper integration (Knight 2016). In addition to sovereignty, questions of nationalism hinder the integration process within the region. Having experienced a measure of economic success during the 1980s, individual member states assumed that the preferential access they had obtained to European and North American markets—at a time when the Caribbean was of strategic importance during the Cold War—would last; this, however, was not the case (Sanders 2016). Today it appears that individual CARICOM states are welcoming alliances with other regional groups, which, like CARICOM, aim to ensure the sustainable development of their members. While this is understandable, and permissible under CARICOM legislation, it ultimately detracts from the obligations that CARICOM members have to the Community in terms of their commitment to the regional integration project.

This then leads to the third challenge: fragmentation within the CARICOM configuration. CARICOM is becoming increasingly fragmented as individual member states participate in diverse alternate regional arrangements. This characterizes, to some extent, the current phase of regional integration: not only is there more diversity in the groups that aim to achieve regional cooperation, but there is a notable increase in the number of groups that include members from both the Anglophone Caribbean and Latin American regional configurations (Byron 2015, 152). For example, Guyana and Suriname participate in the Union of South American Nations (UNASUR); Antigua and Barbuda, St. Vincent and the Grenadines, St. Kitts and Nevis, Grenada, and Dominica in the Bolivarian Alliance for the Peoples of Our America—Peoples' Trade Treaty (ALBA-TCP); Belize in the Central American Integration System (SICA); and all CARICOM countries—except for Trinidad and Tobago, and Barbados—participate in PetroCaribe.

McLean and Khadan (2015) speak to the notion that this complementarity between the different groups seems to be a common practice, and evidently would not be pursued as an option among the countries involved if they did not acquire benefits from the economic arrangements. While this could augur well for the development of the individual member states of CARICOM, it is a fair deduction, for the purpose of the current discussion, that participation in these arrangements signifies that "economic integration in CARICOM is no longer at the forefront" (Girvan 2012b).

More recently, there have been concerns about the continued membership of one of CARICOM's largest member states, Jamaica, and a possible repetition of history—Jamaica's withdrawal from the West Indies Federation in 1961, the decisive development, which led to the demise of the Federation. The rethinking of Jamaica's membership in CARICOM is due to events, in 2016, involving Trinidad and Tobago's denial of entry and alleged mistreatment of some Jamaican nationals. This was in contravention of the main objective of the CARICOM Single Market and Economy: to facilitate the free movement of nationals within the Caribbean Community even if, at the moment, only skilled nationals are allowed to move freely. Jamaica's withdrawal could possibly further weaken CARICOM economically and politically (Jamaica Observer 2013).

Fourth, regional integration is affected by the lack of political will on the part of regional leaders. The 1973 Treaty of Chaguaramas establishing the Caribbean Community "envisaged a significant degree of government initiative" (Girvan 2012a, 41), with Article 4 stating that member states "shall facilitate the achievement of the objectives of the Common Market" (CARICOM 1973). However, according to former Commonwealth Secretary-General, Shridath Ramphal, one of CARICOM's weaknesses is the lack of determination on the part of political leaders to implement decisions. There is evidence of a genuine interest in advancing the regional integration project; however, this is not matched by concrete action to implement requisite decisions (Guyana Chronicle 2009). Sanders (2011) offers that CARICOM leaders "should be strengthening and sharpening the regional integration process", but

> the process has to start with a willingness by leaders to talk with each other frankly, openly and with empathy, and the dialogue has to be infused with an acknowledgment that the regional integration process has been side-tracked and must put be back on a main track because their countries need it. The conversation has to be underlined by a desire to reach collective decisions which take account of the circumstances of each in trying to achieve benefits for all.

Unless the leaders of CARICOM member states tangibly demonstrate political will to undertake the necessary measures for facilitating and advancing the region's integration project, then the process will remain stagnant and ultimately lose its relevance.

Fifth, the benefits of regional integration have not been equitably distributed. According to Girvan (2012a), the benefits from CARICOM and the CSME are seemingly limited and unequal, thus subverting the aim of fostering equality among member states. McLean et al. (2014) highlight the fact, for instance, that it is the more developed countries (MDCs)[9] within the CARICOM arrangement who dominate intra- and extra-regional trade, and consequently, their benefits, with Jamaica the leading importer and Trinidad and Tobago the leading exporter.

Sixth, CARICOM faces financial and economic challenges which ultimately affect the prospects of the integration project. McLean et al. (2014, 9) state that "the decline in regional and extra-regional demand for major goods and services exports of many Caribbean economies" has in part contributed to these challenges. Girvan (2012a) further points out that CARICOM essentially confronted financial difficulties as soon as it was formed. Oil price shocks in 1973 created unexpected economic upsets for those CARICOM member states who imported energy. Subsequent actions taken by the CARICOM oil importers had a negative impact on intra-regional trade. The debt crisis which followed led countries to take loans from the international financial institutions which forced them to adopt the accompanying neoliberal structural adjustment conditionalities in the 1980s. This further cemented the financial challenges and posed an obstacle to the advancement of the CARICOM's development efforts.

Seventh, it has been observed in relation to the CSME that there are the "gaps in coverage of the free movement regime with respect to the treatment of goods produced in free zones, free circulation of goods within the Community, an electronic commerce regime and a government procurement regime" (Girvan 2012a, 37). It is important to underscore here that

---

[9] The member states of the Caribbean Community (CARICOM) are further divided into more developed countries (MDCs) and less developed countries (LDCs). The MDCs are Barbados, Guyana, Jamaica, Suriname, and Trinidad and Tobago. The LDCs are Antigua and Barbuda, Belize, Dominica, Grenada, Montserrat, St. Kitts and Nevis, St. Lucia, and St. Vincent and the Grenadines. Economic agreements involving CARICOM typically make special provisions for the LDCs to ensure that trade liberalization does not place them at a further economic disadvantage (Trade Wins 2006).

there are indeed some advances in trade integration that CARICOM can attest to. However, despite these, there are areas which demand attention.

Furthermore, the region did not escape the consequences of the 2008 global economic collapse. One salient example in this regard was the collapse of the biggest financial conglomerate in the Caribbean—CL Financial—which had repercussions not only on private citizens but also on specific economies within the region, and ultimately on the region as a whole (Byron 2015).

Concluding Reflections

What do the CARICOM's own internal challenges as well as global trends, particularly those emanating from developments in the United States, the United Kingdom, and the EU, mean for the Caribbean's regional integration project and CARICOM's relations with Cuba? The challenges and developments indicate a need for reflection on the future direction of CARICOM. Taken together, the changed relationship between Cuba and the United States (since December 17, 2014) and the recent rise of nationalism in the United States, the United Kingdom, and several EU member states present an opportune moment to engage in this reflection. Is this a moment to expand and strengthen CARICOM cooperation? Or instead adopt protectionist policies? Or perhaps prioritize national objectives over regional agendas? In the Conclusion (Chap. 11), we reflect more profoundly on the implications of changing Cuba-U.S. relations for the Caribbean regional integration project. Here we engage in this discussion, in the context of developments in the United Kingdom and the EU.

First, Brexit may have resonance with individual countries, which already have misgivings about the utility and value-added of CARICOM for achieving their development objectives. CARICOM was established to help meet the development needs of its members, but today, as discussed in this chapter, CARICOM member states are engaged in a myriad of other arrangements and relationships which seemingly serve those same needs. If member states perceive that their development needs are being met through other channels, then CARICOM may seem to be less relevant to them than it was in the past (see, e.g. Montoute 2015). This signals the need to reinvigorate the economic dimensions of the regional integration project, that is, to work on the added value of CARICOM as a framework for realizing the socio-economic needs of its member states.

Second, although a powerful country leaving a regional grouping may weaken the arrangement, a lone country exiting the European Union does not provide enough evidence that the EU is disintegrating. Additionally, it will be challenging for a Caribbean country to advance economically, independent of the CARICOM market.

Third, if the United Kingdom ceases to contribute to EU funding sources, this could mean less EU funding for Caribbean countries, for example, through the European Development Fund (EDF). It could also mean less diplomatic support for CARICOM in negotiations with Brussels.

Fourth, the EU has been a major promoter and supporter of Caribbean integration, through the EDF. With the upsurge of right-wing politics and nationalist policies in several EU member states, support for Caribbean regional integration may not receive the attention that it previously did.

These Brexit-related challenges do not by any means indicate that the CARICOM project should be abandoned, or that a protectionist stance should be adopted; neither does it provide support against the expansion of CARICOM and, by extension, the strengthening of the arrangement. On the contrary, Brexit provides an example of the effects of nationalism and an example of what CARICOM member states should guard against in the future.

It also points to the need for an indigenous turn in the nature, direction, and speed of Caribbean integration as well as the need for the region to find independent ways of funding and supporting its own integration project(s). The current environment in which Cuba finds itself in its relations with the United States presents a window of opportunity to explore and reflect on these and other issues related to regional integration.

References

Bishop, Matthew Louis, and Anthony Payne. 2010. *Caribbean Regional Governance and the Sovereignty/Statehood Problem*. CIGI Caribbean Paper No 8, Series: The Caribbean Papers, January 29.

Byron, Jessica. 2015. Una perspectiva caribeña sobre el regionalismo: ¿cuál es el rol de la CELAC? In *El ALBA-TCP: origen y fruto del nuevo regionalismo latinoamericano y caribeño*, compiled by Maribel Aponte García and Gloria Amézquita Puntiel and edited by Pablo Gentili, 147–169. Buenos Aires: El Consejo Latinoamericano de Ciencias Sociales (CLACSO).

Caribbean Community (CARICOM). 1973. *Treaty Establishing the Caribbean Community*. Accessed June 9, 2017. https://caricom.org/documents/4905-original_treaty-text.pdf.

———. 1999. Communique of the Seventh Special Meeting of the Conference of Heads of Government of the Caribbean, October 28, 1999. Accessed May 31, 2019. https://caricom.org/media-center/communications/communiques/communique-of-the-seventh-special-meeting-of-the-conference-of-heads-of-gov.

———. 2007. A Community for All: Declaration on Functional Cooperation, Issued by The Heads of Government of the Caribbean Community on the Occasion of the Twenty-Eighth Meeting of the Conference, 1–4 July 2007, Needham's Point, Barbados. Accessed May 12, 2019. https://caricom.org/media-center/communications/statements-from-caricom-meetings/a-community-for-all-declaration-on-functional-cooperation-issued-by-the-hea.

———. 2011. *The History of the Caribbean Community (CARICOM)*. Accessed June 3, 2017. http://archive.caricom.org/jsp/community/history.jsp?menu=community.

———. 2017. *UN SG Lauds CARICOM Leadership on Global Issues*, 21 July 2017. Accessed May 31, 2019. https://caricom.org/communications/view/un-sg-lauds-caricom-leadership-on-global-issues1.

CARICOM Implementation Agency for Crime and Security (IMPACS). 2013. *CARICOM Crime and Security Strategy 2013. Securing the Region*. Accessed May 31, 2019. https://www.caricomimpacs.org/Portals/0/Project%20Documents/CCSS_STRAT.pdf.

CARICOM org. *CARICOM Official Website*. Accessed May 31, 2019. https://caricom.org.

CARICOM Secretariat. 2001. *Revised Treaty of Chaguaramas Establishing the Caribbean Community Including the CARICOM Single Market and Economy*. Accessed June 9, 2017. https://caricom.org/about-caricom/who-we-are/our-governance/the-revised-treaty/.

Gilbert-Roberts, Terri-Ann. 2013. *The Politics of Integration: Sovereignty Revisited*. Kingston: Ian Randle Publishers.

Girvan, Norman. 2012a. Caribbean Community: The Elusive Quest for Economic Integration. In *Regional Integration: Key to Caribbean Survival and Prosperity*, ed. Kenneth Hall and Myrtle Chuck-A-Sang, 34–67. Printed in the United States of America: Trafford Publishing.

———. 2012b. *The Caribbean and Cuba: Cuba and the Caribbean: A Reflection*. Panel Discussion at the Havana International Book Fair, Havana, Cuba, February 11, 2012.

Guyana Chronicle. 2009. *Lack of Political Will at Root of CARICOM's Troubles*. July 5, 2009. Accessed June 3, 2017. http://guyanachronicle.com/2009/07/05/lack-of-political-will-at-root-of-caricoms-troubles.

Jamaica Observer. 2013. *Who Should Lead CARICOM?* December 26, 2013. Accessed June 8, 2017. http://www.jamaicaobserver.com/editorial/Who-should-lead-Caricom-_15697734?profile=&template=PrinterVersion.

Knight, Andy. 2016. CARICOM Is in Danger of Losing Relevance. *The Caribbean Camera*, July 17, 2016. Accessed June 8, 2017. http://www.thecaribbeancamera.com/community-events/caricom-is-in-danger-of-losing-relevance/.

McLean, Sheldon, and Jeetendra Khadan. 2015. *An Assessment of the Performance of CARICOM Extraregional Trade Agreements: An Initial Scoping Exercise.* Santiago: United Nations Economic Commission for Latin America and the Caribbean (UN ECLAC). Accessed July 19, 2017. https://repositorio.cepal.org/bitstream/handle/11362/37612/5/lcarl455_rev1.pdf.

McLean, Sheldon, Machel Pantin, and Nyasha Skerrette. 2014. *Regional Integration in the Caribbean: The Role of Trade Agreements and Structural Transformation.* Santiago: UN ECLAC.

Montoute, Annita. 2015. *CARICOM's External Engagements: Prospects and Challenges for Caribbean Regional Integration and Development.* Policy Brief. German Marshall Fund of the United States and OCP Policy Center. Accessed June 9, 2017. http://www.gmfus.org/publications/caricoms-external-engagements.

Pryce, Murphy George. 2013. *Security: The Fourth Pillar of the Caribbean Community: Does the Region Need a Security Organ?* Technical Report, 1 August 2015, 10 June 2016. Accessed May 31, 2019. https://apps.dtic.mil/docs/citations/AD1020347.

Sanders, Ronald. 2011. *CARICOM: It's Leadership That's Needed.* February 11, 2011. Accessed December 28, 2017. http://www.sirronaldsanders.com/viewarticle.aspx?ID=219.

———. 2016. *Clouds Gather over CARICOM: Where's the Umbrella?* Address to the Annual General Meeting of the St Lucia Hotel and Tourist Association, St Lucia, May 19, 2016. Accessed June 9, 2017. http://www.sirronaldsanders.com/Docs/Clouds%20gather%20over%20CARICOM,%20where%20is%20the%20Umbrella.pdf.

The West Indian Commission. 1993. *Time for Action.* 2nd ed. Kingston: University of the West Indies Press.

Trade Wins. 2006. The CARICOM/Cuba Trade and Economic Co-Operation Agreement Explained. *Critical Issues for Business* 2 (1) (November). Accessed July 18, 2017. http://www.carib-export.com/login/wp-content/uploads/2010/01/Final%20TradeWins%20revised.pdf.

CHAPTER 4

The History and Background of Cuba-U.S. Relations (Until December 17, 2014)

Introduction

To appreciate the nature of contemporary relations between Cuba and the United States, it is necessary to understand how these relations began and have evolved. This chapter examines the history of relations between Cuba and the United States and the conflicts originating from U.S. economic and geostrategic interests in the Caribbean and particularly in Cuba. The chapter identifies key features of the bilateral relationship, to set the stage for the discussion (in later chapters) on the implications of more recent developments for future engagement between the two sides.

Cuba-U.S. relations have been antagonistic since the time of Cuba's independence in 1898. This is due to several factors, including their proximity to each other and the asymmetries between them, and since 1959 their ideological differences. On one side exists the U.S. conviction that Cuba, or "that infernal little Cuban republic" as President Theodore Roosevelt called it in 1906 (Schoultz 2009), due to the law of political gravitation and the Manifest Destiny, is a logical extension of the United States—a key element of U.S. national security—and incapable of exercising its independence. The very existence of Cuba has been imagined in correlation to U.S. needs (Pérez 2008). From the Cuban perspective, on the other hand, there is resistance to being considered as an appendage to the United States, and there is the determination to act as an independent nation in governing its own domestic affairs and exercising its sovereignty in the multilateral arena.

© The Author(s) 2020
J. Laguardia Martinez et al., *Changing Cuba-U.S. Relations*,
https://doi.org/10.1007/978-3-030-20366-5_4

Former U.S. Secretary of State, James Buchanan, stated that a Cuba annexed to the United States would relieve the nation "from the apprehensions which we can never cease to feel for our own safety and the security of our commerce, whilst it shall remain in its present condition" (Buchanan 1909, 94). The Ostend Manifesto of 1854 explicitly articulated this national consensus: "[t]he Union can never enjoy repose, nor possess reliable security, as long as Cuba is not embraced within its boundaries" (Pérez 2008, 27). According to the American historian, Lou A. Pérez Jr., the idea of a secure U.S. nationhood depended upon the possession of Cuba. If Cuba seemed to have no destiny other than belonging to the United States it was because, for the United States, there was no secure future without having Cuba (Pérez 2008).

Pérez underscores the U.S. fixation on Cuba by offering the rationale for the underpinning assumptions upon which the United States considered Cuba. Cuba was of strategic importance to the United States in terms of military strength and security which made the U.S. conviction to control the island a logical one. As a country, the United States felt it could not be whole and that it possessed a vulnerability if Cuba was not a part of it (Pérez 2008, 26): "We must have Cuba. We can't do without Cuba," insisted James Buchanan (Buchanan 1909, 361).

Colonial Cuba-U.S. Relations

Even though Cuba cannot surpass other states in valuable natural resources, it showed its economic possibilities when, after the Haitian Revolution, it became the largest sugarcane producer and exporter in the Caribbean. The ties between Cuba and the United States stemmed from economic interactions centered primarily on sugar production and trade. By the mid-1800s Cuba was producing 25 percent of the world's sugar with over 1500 sugar plantations (Copeland et al. 2011), and the United States provided a natural market for the product.

The collapse of the international sugar market in 1884 meant bankruptcy for many sugar mills in Cuba, but U.S. investors purchased these sugar mills, pouring capital back into Cuba (Le Riverend 1971). During the nineteenth century, the United States consolidated its position as the main market for Cuba's sugar exports: while Spain remained the political colonial power that controlled Cuba, the island became an economic colony of the United States (Le Riverend 1971; Loyola Vega 2003; Pérez 2015).

In the U.S. mindset, the importance of Cuba was not limited to commercial exchanges. Its wish to extend its borders, coupled with the concern that European powers would try to regain the region after the end of the Napoleonic Wars, set the context for the Monroe Doctrine of 1823[1]—a doctrine that supported U.S. presence and policy in Latin America and Cuba (Domínguez 1997).

The relationship between the United States and Cuba stimulated ideas of annexation. Most Cubans, however, felt that the better option would be either to remain a Spanish dependency or to fight for full independence (Loyola Vega 2003; Torres Cuevas and Loyola Vega 2002; Molina Molina 2007). The second option prevailed: the Cuban Independence War began in 1868 and, after an interruption from 1878 to 1895, ended in 1898 in the context of the so-called Spanish-American War.

U.S. intervention in the Cuban Independence War came when President William McKinley, through a resolution sent to the U.S. Congress, requested a declaration of war on Spain, asserting that the conflict in Cuba posed a threat to the United States and to peace. This resulted in a diplomatic end to the war in December 1898 and saw Cuba become a protectorate of the United States. The U.S. military occupied the island until 1902 to help create an economic, political, and sociocultural environment favorable to the United States in the island (Loyola Vega 2003; Holmes 2009).

After elections were held in Cuba in 1902, the Cuban Constitutional Convention was forced to include, as part of the Constitution, the Platt Amendment (Dye and Sicotte 1999) as a requisite for the United States to withdraw their troops and end the military occupation. The Platt Amendment impacted heavily on Cuba-U.S. relations from 1903 to 1934. The amendment gave the United States legal support for its direct and indirect interventions in Cuban political affairs up until the revolution in 1959, even though it was officially revoked in 1934 (Mendes 2015). It allowed the U.S. control over Cuba without actual annexation.

---

[1] The introduction to the Monroe Doctrine states: "the occasion has been judged proper for asserting, as a principle in which the rights and interests of the United States are involved, that the American continents, by the free and independent condition which they have assumed and maintain, are henceforth not to be considered as subjects for future colonization by any European powers" (Monroe 1823).

Cuba-U.S. Relations in the First Half of the Twentieth Century

Cuban historians (Le Riverend 1971; Torres Cuevas and Loyola Vega 2002; López Civeira 2003) refer to the period from 1902 to 1959 as the "Neocolonial Period", due to the kind of relations Cuba established with the United States. The United States assisted Cuba financially, militarily, and politically in exchange for Havana acting in the best interests of Washington. For the United States to ensure its control over Cuba, a series of treaties and agreements was signed during the first decades of the twentieth century to ensure the application of the Platt Amendment and to strengthen the Cuban economy's dependence on the United States.

Sugar continued to be the strategic economic good for Cuba and the main link between the U.S. financial sector, the Cuban sugar bourgeoisie, and businesspersons in both countries (Le Riverend 1971; López Civeira 2003; Molina Molina 2007). The United States used sugar as a key instrument of control over Cuba's economy, always considering first its own domestic circumstances and national interests (García Molina 2005).

The Cuban sugar market initiated a notable wave of emigration to Cuba from other islands in the region, especially at the start of the twentieth century. A large number of these migrants came from Jamaica and Haiti (Glennie and Chappell 2010; Perusek 1984). The sugar market required a large labor force, and as the U.S. occupation government from 1898 to 1902 had forbidden the immigration of non-whites to Cuba, a worker shortage persisted. In 1912, however, the United Fruit Company obtained a special permit from President José Miguel Gómez, to allow Haitians into Cuba for sugar harvesting. When the First World War started, the Cuban sugar market required more workers. Between 1914 and 1918, about 27,000 Haitians and 23,000 Jamaicans entered Cuba (Perusek 1984). These figures do not account for the illegal migration that was also occurring.

During the first half of the twentieth century, U.S. corporations invested in Cuban sugar and nickel production; owned most of the arable land; and invested in the utilities, transport, and real estate sectors. In the 1930s, Cuba was the first recipient of U.S. investments in Latin America, with preference given to agriculture (sugar), transport, utilities, and land (López Civeira 2003). By 1933, the Chase National Bank of New York, First National Bank of Boston, and First National City Bank of New York were the principal institutions of the financial system in Cuba (García

Molina 2005). These economic investments essentially endorsed U.S. action to intervene militarily in Cuba whenever these institutions perceived their interests to be under threat due to political animosity or social protests, and whenever President Howard Taft's Dollar diplomacy did not work.[2]

In 1933, President Franklin D. Roosevelt announced his Good Neighbor policy as a new mechanism for subtle intervention in the hemisphere. Consequently, in 1934, the Platt Amendment was eliminated, and a new agreement was signed which opened possibilities for agricultural and industrial development in Cuba while widening U.S. access to Cuban markets. This new agreement resulted in an increased Cuban dependency on trade to the United States. In 1942, the island had 84 percent of its imports coming from the United States (Rodríguez 1983). By the late 1950s, U.S. companies represented 95 percent of the foreign direct investment (FDI) in Cuba; and in 1958, U.S. direct investment in the country amounted to USD 1000 million (García Molina 2005).

The United States supported those in Cuba who reinforced its political and economic interests, including the dictatorship of Fulgencio Batista from 1952 to 1959, during which time the United States had almost complete control over the Cuban economy. While Havana was depicted as a vibrant and modern city, the rest of the country—except for a few urban centers in Santa Clara, Camagüey, and Santiago de Cuba—was subject to rampant poverty and instability, unemployment, and human rights violations.

Consequently, Fidel Castro's 26 de Julio Movement became the leader among resistance organizations and popular forces fighting against Batista and the unfavorable social conditions. In addition to the economic crisis, this revolutionary movement identified several other key challenges that needed to be addressed in order to guarantee the welfare of the Cuban people—problems of land, industrialization, housing, unemployment, education, and health—along with the restoration of civil liberties and political democracy in the country (Castro 1975).

---

[2] Cuba has been an exemplary tests case for U.S. policies toward Latin America and the Caribbean. Depending on the historic period, context, and particular circumstances, U.S. policies toward Cuba have been inspired by the Monroe Doctrine (since 1823); Manifest Destiny (since 1845); Big Stick Diplomacy (since 1901); Roosevelt Corollary (since 1904); Dollar Diplomacy (since 1909); Moral/Missionary Diplomacy (since 1913); Good Neighbor Policy (1930–beginning of the Cold War) or a combination of these.

Cuba-U.S. "Relations" After the Revolution in 1959

The 26 de Julio Movement triumphed in 1959, initializing a series of events that contributed to a steady decline in diplomatic relations between Cuba and the United States. Initially, Washington supported the Castro-led government; this support, however, changed very soon into a posture of caution since the revolutionary government's agenda of national development worked in opposition to U.S. interests in Cuba. The situation deteriorated further when it "became clear that Castro's socioeconomic project for Cuba and a good relationship with Washington were irreconcilable" (Mendes 2015, 6).

In March 1959, the revolutionary government intervened in the Compañía Cubana de Teléfono—affiliated to the International Telephone and Telegraph Corporation—and ordered a reduction of between 30 and 50 percent on landline rental fees. In April, all Cuban beaches were declared public property. In August, electricity tariffs were reduced by 30 percent, affecting the incomes of the Compañía Eléctrica that actually belonged to the American Foreign Power Company. The real confrontation, however, started upon the approval of the First Agrarian Reform Law that affected large U.S. land properties and changed class structure and property tenure in Cuba (Silva León 2005; Franklin 2015). In January 1960, the Cuban government expropriated 70,000 acres from U.S. companies, including 35,000 acres from the United Fruit Company. As a result, President Dwight D. Eisenhower started maneuvering to cancel Cuba's sugar quota (Franklin 2015).

Cuba started looking for alternatives for its sugar exports as well as many of its imports, since the bilateral relation with its key trade partner was deteriorating rapidly. In February 1960, Anastas Mikoyan, Vice Prime Minister of the USSR, visited Cuba and signed the first trade agreement between Cuba and the Soviet Union. Cuba would import oil and oil by-products, wheat flour, fertilizers, iron, and heavy machinery; and, in exchange, the USSR would buy Cuban sugar. The Soviets also agreed to facilitate credit of USD 100 million at an interest rate of 2.5 percent. Havana and Moscow re-established diplomatic relations later that year, on May 7. In addition, later in July, Cuba signed its first agreement with China, by which the Asian nation would buy 500,000 sugar tons from Cuba (Silva León 2005; Franklin 2015).

Tensions between Havana and Washington rose when Esso and Texaco refineries, together with the British Shell refinery, refused to refine Russian oil, and Cuba nationalized these refineries for their refusal. Days later, in July 1960, Cuba authorized the nationalization of all U.S. property on Cuban soil and President Eisenhower canceled Cuba's sugar quota. In January 1961, the United States closed its embassy in Havana, severed diplomatic ties, and began a secret campaign to overthrow the Castro government (Silva León 2005; Franklin 2015). Since that time "successive U.S. administrations pursued policies intended to isolate the country economically and diplomatically" (Felter and Renwick 2018).

The growing engagement of Cuba with the USSR renewed the fears of the United States of an adversary establishing itself so closely to its territory and now in a context of combating communism to penetrate the Western Hemisphere. The missile crisis of October 1962 and the Soviet center in Lourdes, among other examples, served as confirmation of the expanding Cuba-USSR ties.

Besides the U.S. will of keeping the "red menace" out of its "backyard", in the United States existed "a proprietary sentimentality toward Cuba" (Pérez n.d., 17). U.S. public opinion considered that the U.S. people had sacrificed their lives and resources to free Cuba. They felt that Cuba had aligned itself with the USSR, and this was perceived as an act of betrayal and ingratitude. U.S. policy aims focused on the leaders in Cuba, especially Fidel Castro, and evolved into an obsession. *The New York Times* editor, Thomas Friedman, was correct when suggesting that the U.S. position on Cuba was "not really a policy. It's an attitude— a blind hunger for revenge against Mr. Castro" (Pérez 2003, 272).

Washington used economic exclusion, isolation, and paramilitary strikes (with the direct involvement of the Central Intelligence Agency [CIA]) to try and depose Cuba's revolutionary government. However, Fidel Castro's administration proved more resistant than anticipated, and U.S. policy objectives were redefined to punish Cuba and of making it an example to dissuade other Latin American countries from following Cuba's example (Leogrande 2015).

The United States also responded to the Cuban situation by encouraging pressure from Latin American neighbors to isolate the island. In the months of February and March 1960, President Eisenhower emphasized, among the governments of Latin America, the necessity of having in place "democratic systems", in order to create a common front against "communist infiltration" in the region. In August, at the Seventh Meeting of Consultation of Ministers of Foreign Affairs of the Organization of American States (OAS) in San José, Costa Rica, the final declaration condemned the intervention of "extra-continental power in the affairs of the American republics", a clear updating of the Monroe Doctrine, and clearly rejected "the attempt of the Sino-Soviet powers to make use of the political, economic, or social situation of any American state" (OAS 1960).

In response to the Declaration of San José, Cuba issued the First Declaration of Havana, adopted on September 2, 1960. In this latter document, the revolutionary government announced the ending of the military aid agreement between Cuba and the United States, and its intention to establish diplomatic relations with the People's Republic of China. It stated that the support of the USSR in the event of foreign aggression should be taken as an act of solidarity and never as an intrusion in domestic affairs. The Declaration of Havana also condemned the Monroe Doctrine and "hypocritical Pan-Americanism", as well as U.S. military interventions in Latin America (Republic of Cuba 1960).

The use of the OAS as a foreign policy tool to isolate Cuba continued. At the Eighth Meeting of Consultation of Ministers of Foreign Affairs, in Punta del Este, Uruguay, in February 1962, Cuba was excluded from participating in the Inter-American System since "[t]he ... Government of Cuba ... identified itself with the principles of the Marxist-Leninist ideology, ... established a political, economic, and social system based on that doctrine, and [accepted] military assistance from extracontinental communist powers" (OAS 1962). The ministerial declaration added that "this situation [demanded] unceasing vigilance on the part of the member states of the Organization of American States" and that "any fact or situation that could endanger the peace and security of the hemisphere" would be reported to its Permanent Council (OAS 1962).

In July 1964, during the Ninth Meeting of Consultation of Ministers of Foreign Affairs in Washington, D.C., a resolution concerning the application of measures to the present government of Cuba was adopted. It stated that American states would not continue having diplomatic or consular relations with Cuba; that their trade with Cuba, whether this was done directly or indirectly, would halt[3]; and that all sea transportation between American states and Cuba would be suspended, except for humanitarian reasons (OAS 1964).

Cuba reacted to the new OAS actions first with the Second Declaration of Havana in February 1962 followed by the Declaration of Santiago de

---

[3] This excluded trade in foodstuffs, medicines, and medical equipment needed as part of humanitarian efforts.

Cuba in July 1964. In the Second Declaration of Havana, the Cuban government denounced the OAS as the "Yankee Ministry of Colonies, a military alliance, and an apparatus of repression against the liberation movements of the Latin American peoples" (Republic of Cuba 1962).

In the Declaration of Santiago de Cuba, the Cuban government warned that if pirate attacks carried out by the United States and other countries in the Caribbean Basin were not stopped, if the training of mercenaries to carry out acts of sabotage against the Cuban Revolution persisted, and if the United States continued dispatching agents, weapons, and explosives to the territory of Cuba, then the people of Cuba would understand that they were entitled to help the revolutionary movements, with the resources available to them, in all those countries that joined Washington in meddling in Cuba's internal affairs (Republic of Cuba 1964).

Along with diplomatic pressure, the United States appealed to open violence to overthrow the Cuban government. In 1960, there were several air strikes against Cuban sugar plantations and mills. In March 1960, the French freighter *La Coubre* exploded in the harbor of Havana, while it was unloading 76 tons of Belgian munitions. About 100 people died and many more were injured (Silva León 2005; Franklin 2015).

April 1961 saw the Bay of Pigs (*Bahía de Cochinos*) invasion—a fruitless attempt organized by the CIA to overthrow Fidel Castro by training Cuban exiles for a ground attack. Just prior to the invasion, on April 15, airplanes attacked airports in Havana and Santiago de Cuba. The following day, during the burial of the victims of the bombings, Castro declared the Cuban Revolution to be a socialist revolution. On April 17, the invasion forces disembarked, and by April 19, they had been defeated (Silva León 2005; Franklin 2015): the invasion lasted three days. Although the United States, under President John F. Kennedy at the time, initially denied any involvement in the invasion, "the world immediately understood that the entire operation had been organized and funded by the U.S. government. The invaders had been trained by CIA officers and supplied with American equipment, and the plan had been approved by the Joint Chiefs of Staff and the President of the United States" (Rasenberger 2011).

President Kennedy, though, cannot be held solely responsible for the invasion, as his predecessors had set the stage for it. The year before, for instance, in 1960, President Dwight Eisenhower approved a security document—*A Program of Covert Action Against the Castro Regime*—which aimed to remove the Castro government from power (5412 Committee 1960).

The Cuban victory over the U.S.-sponsored invasion worsened bilateral relations by deepening the embarrassment of the United States, resulting in U.S. policy acquiring one of its persistent features: punitive purpose. The Bay of Pigs catastrophe seemed to harden the resolve of the U.S. National Security Council, which aimed to continue "all kinds of harassment to punish Castro for the humiliation he has brought to our door" (U.S. Department of State n.d.) People participating in the post-Bay of Pigs discussions recalled the mood of the Kennedy White House as being "[e]motional, almost savage" (Pérez n.d.), and it stands to reason that it was President Kennedy who institutionalized the embargo policy.

After the Bay of Pigs invasion came Operation Mongoose, which included a series of attempts to end Fidel Castro's life. From 1961 to 1963, there were at least five plots to assassinate, injure, or disgrace Castro, ranging from the use of exploding seashells to the use of chemicals to make Castro's beard fall out (Silva León 2005; Suddath 2009).

What is of major significance about the Bay of Pigs invasion, though, is that it led to Cuba strengthening its ties with the USSR. This ultimately led to the Cuban Missile Crisis of 1962, an event which held severe implications for the rest of the world as the threat of nuclear warfare loomed. On October 15, 1962, U.S. spy planes confirmed that the USSR was building missile bases in Cuba. Soviet Premier Nikita Khrushchev's decision to send missiles to Cuba was probably based on satisfying Fidel Castro's requests for Soviet protection and to thrust the USSR power onto the Western Hemisphere (Hilsman 1996).

President Kennedy refrained from military action, issuing instead a public demand for the missiles to be removed. The United States placed a naval blockade around Cuba to prevent Soviet military support from entering the country. Days later, on October 28, Khrushchev agreed to remove the missiles from Cuba and to not replace them in the future, on the condition that the United States would not make any future attempts at invasion and that it would remove U.S. missiles in Turkey (Silva León 2005; Suddath 2009; Franklin 2015).

Despite this understanding between Washington and Moscow, after the Missile Crisis, for the former not to attack Cuba, the United States continued its aggressive strategy, now by supporting Cuban exiles in conducting violent actions against Cuba. Even though this mechanism started in the early years of the Cuban Revolution, it intensified after the Missile Crisis, with the CIA supporting armed opposition in the Escambray Mountains and executing terrorist actions (Franklin 2015).

Another noteworthy factor in the history of Cuba-U.S. relations was the Cuban Adjustment Act of 1966. This law allowed anyone who fled from Cuba and managed to reach the United States the opportunity, after a year, to seek U.S. residence. This policy was later linked to the 1986 Immigration Reform Act and another migration agreement in 1994 which, combined, led to the "wet foot, dry foot" policy. This allowed Cuban migrants who were able to arrive on dry land in the United States to stay, while those who were found in the ocean between the United States and Cuba were compelled to return.

Meanwhile, the attacks against Cuba never ceased, and some form part of the collective Caribbean memory. On October 6, 1976, Cuban exiles placed a bomb on a Cuban plane which exploded near the coast of Barbados, causing the death of the 73 people on board. CIA and Federal Bureau of Investigation (FBI) documents identified two Cuban exiles with links to the CIA as the perpetrators of the sabotage (Franklin 2015; Alzugaray Treto 2010; Kornbluh 2010; Silva León 2005).

Bombs were also placed at the Cuban Mission to the United Nations in New York and at diplomatic representations of countries that maintained relations with Cuba. Cuban citizens were murdered as well, among them: Eulalio Negrín, a member of the Comité de los 75, in New Jersey in 1979; Félix García Rodríguez, a Cuban diplomat, in New York in 1980; and Águedo Morales Reina, a Cuban teacher, in Nicaragua in 1981. In 1980, sabotage against the biggest kindergarten center in Cuba was carried out (Franklin 2015). From 1959 to 1997, the United States made no fewer than 5789 terrorist attacks against Cuba that cost the lives of 3478 people and caused 2099 others to fall ill. Fidel Castro himself was a target of 637 assassination attempts (Lamrani 2014).

In 1997, a series of bombings damaged several Cuban hotels. One attack on Hotel Copacabana resulted in the death of an Italian tourist, Fabio di Celmo. Other targets included the hotels Sol Palmeras, Tritón, Chateau Miramar, Capri, Hotel Nacional de Cuba, and Meliá Cohiba (Alzugaray Treto 2010).

One of the biggest definers of Cuba-U.S. relations has been the embargo, which has evolved in harshness over the years. The U.S. embargo began when President Eisenhower split relations in 1961, under the Trading with the Enemy Act (TWEA), which allowed the U.S. president to impose economic sanctions on a hostile country during wartime "or any other period of national emergency declared by the President" (U.S. Department of State 1917, sec. 5[b]). A few months later, Congress passed the Foreign Assistance Act proscribing aid to communist countries (Gordon 2012). On February 7, 1962, immediately after ordering a batch of 1200 Cuban cigars for himself, President Kennedy instituted the embargo.

The U.S. president's capacity to remove or alter the terms of the embargo was limited when Congress passed the Cuban Democracy Act (CDA)[4]—also known as the Torricelli Act—and the Cuban Liberty and Democratic Solidarity Act[5]—more commonly known as the Helms-Burton Act—which tightened the embargo in the 1990s (Franklin 2015; Gordon 2012; Suddath 2009; Silva León 2005).

The 1992 Cuban Democracy Act "declare[d] that the President should encourage countries that conduct trade with Cuba to restrict their trade and credit relations with Cuba in a manner consistent with this Act" (U.S. Congress 1992). It also gave the U.S. government the authority to impose sanctions on countries that provided any assistance to Cuba, and considered this as a way of discouraging other foreign governments from offering any assistance to the island. It is useful to note here that the CDA gave rise to objection and debate over its place in international law, and a few countries enforced blocking orders as they considered the CDA to be an infringement of their own sovereignty and in contradiction to their own economic interests (Wong 1994).

In 1996, the Helms-Burton Act was passed into U.S. federal law. This act claims the right for the United States to decide on domestic policies in Cuba and to set a political and economic system to the liking of the United States (Domínguez 1997). It came as a reaction to Cuba's shooting down of two civilian aircraft belonging to a Cuban exile group, *Hermanos al Rescate* (Brothers to the Rescue). The act served to reinforce what was already in place, as it "impose[d] additional sanctions on the Cuban

---

[4] The 1992 Cuban Democracy Act (CDA) reinforced the embargo by prohibiting trade by subsidiaries of U.S. companies in third countries and prohibiting ships visiting Cuba from U.S. ports for 180 days. It lifted sanctions on medical sales, although it imposed such tough certification requirements that few sales have actually being materialized (The Cuba Consortium 2016, 21).

[5] The Cuban Liberty and Democratic Solidarity Act of 1996 codified in law the economic sanctions against Cuba in the U.S. Department of Treasury's Cuban Assets Control Regulations (CACR). The regulations established that they be lifted once Cuba becomes a democracy with a market economy and political parties. It also codified the executive authority of the U.S. president to license exceptions to the embargo (The Cuba Consortium 2016, 21).

regime, mandate[d] the preparation of a plan for U.S. assistance to transitional and democratically elected Cuban governments, create[d] a cause of action enabling U.S. nationals to sue those who expropriate or 'traffic' in expropriated properties in Cuba, and denie[d] such traffickers entry into the United States" (Clinton 1996).

U.S. policy toward Cuba has always been rationalized as being for the "freedom" of the Cuban people. However, as Hoffmann (1998, 20) notes: "If Washington's policy of confrontation is a decisive element of legitimacy for the Castro government, the Helms-Burton law renewed it, contributing thus to a tightening and stabilization of the political status quo, not to its opening up." Once again, as with the CDA, foreign governments, as well as humanitarian groups, questioned the legality of the act and expressed concern over the humanitarian consequences of U.S. sanctions.

Another noteworthy example of the tensions between the two countries came in 1998 when five Cubans, who became known as the Cuban Five or *Los Cinco*—Gerardo Hernández, Ramón Labañino, Fernando González, Antonio Guerrero, and René González—were arrested in Miami and accused of conspiracy to commit espionage. The case drew international attention as some protested what appeared to be biased court proceedings against these Cuban agents, based in Florida, who were gathering information on terrorist activities against Cuba and organized on U.S. soil. The release of the prisoners on 17D proved to be an important gesture in subsequent developments in Cuba-U.S. relations under President Barack Obama.

The embargo denies Cuba access to U.S. markets and goods and restricts its trade with third countries. The embargo bans Cuba and Cuban citizens to conduct transactions in U.S. dollars, forbids U.S. companies or their foreign subsidies from selling equipment to Cuban organizations and pose great difficulties to conduct scientific and cultural exchanges between both countries. Other actions had made the embargo more profound, such as limiting the selling of technology to countries which the United States considers to be "state sponsors of terrorism" (Gordon 2012, 64). The United States had Cuba included in that list from 1982 until 2015. In 2019, the Trump administration announced that Cuba may be reintroduced to the list mainly due to the island's support to President Maduro. U.S. measures "have had a far greater impact on Cuba's economy and society than would ordinarily be expected of a unilateral trade embargo, for the simple fact that it is extraterritorial: it interferes in Cuba's trade with companies located in third countries" (Gordon 2012). It is for this reason that it is called "blockade" instead of "embargo" by Cubans.

In 2000, the U.S. Congress passed the Trade Sanctions Reform and Export Enhancement Act (TSRA) providing partial exemptions from the embargo, by allowing U.S. companies to trade in agricultural and medical goods with Cuba under certain limitations.

Until 2014, the bilateral relationship maintained its adversarial nature. This does not mean that there had not been occasions that required some level of diplomatic interaction: maritime issues, the release of political prisoners, and, in the 1970s and again in the 1990s, migration agreements. These socio-political issues affected both countries and needed to be addressed with some degree of collaboration. Some positive steps were taken by the United States in the 1970s when, for instance, soon after he was inaugurated in 1977, President Jimmy Carter lifted the travel ban entirely, and this remained so until President Ronald Reagan reinstated the restrictions in 1982 for business and tourist travel. In 1999, President Bill Clinton permitted travel to Cuba for reasons including humanitarian, religious, cultural, and educational purposes. He also created the category of people-to-people educational travel. President George W. Bush reinstated restrictions on Cuban American family travel and educational travel in 2007, making them stricter by eliminating the people-to-people category (The Cuba Consortium 2016, 26).

Attempts at Re-establishing Bilateral Relations

Before President Obama, it was President Carter who made the most advances toward normalizing relations with Cuba (Morales Domínguez and Ramírez Cañedo 2015; Badella 2014). However, it is worth pointing out that before this, in 1975, President Gerald Ford relaxed the U.S. embargo by permitting U.S. subsidiaries in third countries to sell products to Cuba. In March 1977, President Carter signed Presidential Directive/NSC-6, which stipulated that the United States should attempt a normalization of relations with Cuba (Brenner and Scribner 2016; Leogrande and Kornbluh 2015). This approach accepted the Cuban government and, together with the non-renewal of the ban on travel to Cuba by U.S. citizens, altered the rationale for the embargo imposed during the Kennedy administration on the alleged grounds that Cuba posed a threat to the United States.

This approach was consistent with the recommendations of the Commission on United States-Latin American Relations, whose 1974 report argued that to improve relations with Latin America, the United

States had to stop treating Cuba as a pariah (Brenner and Scribner 2016). A similar spirit can be found in President Obama's strategy that opted for fully recognizing the legitimacy of Cuba's government and institutions, and advanced the normalization of bilateral relations as a possibly better approach to promote regime change in Cuba, in light of the fact that previous hostility had not brought about the expected results (Morales Domínguez and Ramírez Cañedo 2015).

According to Morales Domínguez and Ramírez Cañedo (2015), during Carter's administration, some U.S. sectors believed in approaching Cuba and offering a normal relationship with the United States, in exchange for Cuba abandoning its international activism in Africa as well as its close ties to the USSR; and, by doing so, promote the rejection of socialist ideology and a transition to capitalism.

Since Cuba continued its involvement in Africa and in the Grenadian and Nicaraguan Revolutions, and also as a consequence of the Mariel Boatlift in 1980, the re-establishment of diplomatic relations was not achieved at the time. According to Brenner and Scribner (2016), normalization under the Carter administration also failed because of Cuba's close relationship with the USSR; a determined opponent close to the U.S. president (Zbigniew Brzezinski, National Security Advisor), who relentlessly framed events involving Cuba in terms of the Cold War superpower rivalry; the clash resulting from Cuba and the United States pursuing incompatible foreign policy interests; and the fact that the U.S. presidency's initial rationale for the policy change no longer made sense. Leogrande and Kornbluh (2015) stated that President Carter aspired to be the first post-Cold War president in an era in which the Cold War was not yet over. President Carter oscillated between his hopes for world peace and his fears of Soviet aggression. These authors highlight that, looking back, Carter felt he missed an opportunity to cut the Gordian knot of Cuba-U.S. hostility. Morales Domínguez and Ramírez Cañedo (2015), though, established that the main reason behind the failure of Carter's attempts to normalize relations with Havana was the unchanging colonial intention of the U.S. government of being a key actor in Cuba's domestic and foreign policies. Leogrande has stated that the Carter initiative—as well as the one promoted by then Secretary of State, Henry Kissinger—was unsuccessful because Cuba's ties with the USSR proved to be firm and not easily broken. It was because of this that Washington considered Cuba's decision to send troops to Angola and Ethiopia, with Soviet logistical support, as an extension of the Cold War, and why it returned to its policy of isolation and economic restriction (Leogrande 2015).

Nevertheless, major improvements under the Carter administration were attained. Initiated by President Fidel Castro, negotiations on fishing and maritime boundaries accords were held, and in September 1977, Cuba and the United States began to use their own diplomats to staff their sections at the Swiss and Czech embassies in Havana and Washington, D.C., respectively. The United States also agreed to cease overflights (Brenner and Scribner 2016; Franklin 2015; Morales Domínguez and Ramírez Cañedo 2015).

The end of the Cold War meant an end to the justification of the U.S. national security policy in relation to Cuba. The historical shift likewise provoked that the Cuban armed forces transformed essentially into a home defense force, unable to extend force in the international sphere, as they were now operating without Soviet support (Leogrande 2015).

Nonetheless, after the fall of the USSR and European socialism, the U.S. government decided to tighten sanctions to kill off the Cuban Revolution and, with the approval of the 1992 Cuban Democracy Act—discussed in the previous section—foreign subsidiaries of U.S. firms were forbidden to trade with Cuba. The CDA also denied foreign ships entry into U.S. ports within six months of having docked in Cuba and tightened restrictions on travel and cash remittances (U.S. Congress 1992).

Before President Obama, the most recent attempt at bringing both nations closer was made during the Clinton administration—this effort was at its most determined during President Clinton's second term despite the ambivalence shown in his policy toward Cuba (Brenner and Scribner 2016; Leogrande and Kornbluh 2015; Morales Domínguez and Ramírez Cañedo 2015). President Clinton relaxed U.S. policy toward Cuba by taking some measures allowed by the Track Two program of the CDA, which also supported anti-Castro groups within Cuba. In 1994, as a result of the Cuban Rafter Crisis, both governments agreed to a memorandum to regularize migration from Cuba to the United States and, in 1995, a new understanding was reached regarding the admittance of Cuban migrants detained at Guantánamo Bay Naval Base into the United States (Morales Domínguez and Ramírez Cañedo 2015; Domínguez 2010).

In 1998 and 1999, the U.S. Department of the Treasury updated licensing systems for U.S. and Cuban citizens traveling between both countries and approved charter flights to Cuba. The U.S. Department of State allowed for more cultural, educational, journalistic, religious, humanitarian, and sport exchanges (Brenner and Scribner 2016).

Unlike President Carter, President Clinton never intended to normalize relations with Cuba, although he introduced changes to the hardline approach followed by his predecessor, President George H. W. Bush. During his presidential term, relations between the two countries navigated through periods of ups and downs (Morales Domínguez and Ramírez Cañedo 2015). According to Brenner and Scribner (2016), among the factors that motivated Clinton's decision to engage Cuba in a less hostile manner was the presence of new groups—in particular, business leaders and former government officials provided political cover by calling for a re-evaluation of U.S. policy toward Cuba. International pressures also acted as incentives for the president to move forward. These included Pope John Paul II's 1998 visit to Cuba during which he condemned the embargo, and calls by European allies to void the extraterritorial aspects of the Helms-Burton Act.

The Obama Administration Before 17D

President Barack Obama, while campaigning as a presidential candidate, stated that he would facilitate relations between Cuban Americans and Cubans and disregard the guidelines established by the George W. Bush administration (Domínguez 2010). During the run-up to the 2008 presidential election, the expectations on both sides of the Florida Strait were that, if elected, Obama would hit the diplomacy reset button and revisit the contours of the decades-old relationship forged by Cold War realities (Casells 2017; Leogrande 2015; Badella 2014).

When elected, Obama pursued what may be considered an ambivalent policy toward Cuba—similar to that of President Clinton. On one hand, he persisted in the approach expressed during his campaign and, in his remarks at the Fifth Summit of the Americas in Port of Spain, Trinidad and Tobago, affirmed that:

> The United States seeks a new beginning with Cuba. I know there's a longer journey that must be traveled to overcome decades of mistrust, but there are critical steps we can take toward a new day … Over the past 2 years, I've indicated, and I repeat today, that I'm prepared to have my administration engage with the Cuban Government on a wide range of issues … Now, let me be clear: I'm not interested in talking just for the sake of talking. But I do believe that we can move U.S.-Cuban relations in a new direction. (Obama 2009)

Until 17D, President Obama had rolled back to the Clinton presidency and allowed Cuban Americans to travel more easily to Cuba and to send remittances to relatives, as well as allowed U.S. citizens to visit the island for educational travel (Obama 2009). He had even gone beyond this by promoting more bilateral cooperation on multilateral issues such as drug interdiction in the Caribbean Sea, joint responses to humanitarian emergencies and extreme climatological events in the region, and fighting Ebola in Africa (Laguardia Martinez 2016). He also liberalized regulations on telecommunications and sending packages, and proposed to resume bilateral migration talks which President George W. Bush had suspended in 2003. The first talks on migration under the Obama administration took place in July 2009 and discussion on postal services later in September that year (Domínguez 2010).

At the same time, however, under President Obama, the U.S. Department of the Treasury fined several non-U.S.-based companies dealing with Cuba in accordance with its Cuban Assets Control Regulations (CACR) (Badella 2014). During his administration, the United States continued to invest a significant amount of money in financing the promotion of liberal democracy on the island. According to the Common Reporting Standard (CRS), from 1996 to 2012, the U.S. Congress appropriated some USD 225 million in funding for promoting democracy in Cuba. This included USD 45.3 million for 2008 and USD 20 million for each year from 2009 through 2012. The administration's requests for 2013 and 2014 were for USD 15 million per year, but an estimated USD 19.3 million was ultimately allocated for 2013 and USD 17.5 million for 2014 (Badella 2014).

However, at the end of his second term, President Obama risked a policy change toward Cuba. In pursuit of coherence with his foreign policy vision for Latin America and the Caribbean, President Obama ventured a different strategy to engage with Cuba in a post-Cold War scenario. The following chapters explore more on how, why, and what was done after 17D.

Concluding Reflections

This chapter has highlighted the salient areas of interest concerning relations between Cuba and the United States before 17D. This is a necessary step in understanding the present-day Cuba-U.S. bilateral relationship, since it sets the context, first, for the processes established and advancements made because of 17D, and second, for the more recent reversals that have taken place under the Trump administration. Understanding the history that these two countries share is imperative to formulating insight into their future interactions.

Cuba occupies a special place in the history of U.S. imperialism. It has served as a sort of laboratory for testing U.S. policies to secure hemispheric and global domain. The methods used constitute a scaled-down version of the U.S. experience of dominance: armed intervention and military occupation; drafting of constitutions; foreign direct investment and cultural saturation; puppet regimes; formation of a clientelistic system and akin political institutions; establishment of subordinated armies; obligation to commit to binding treaties; establishment of permanent military bases; economic assistance and trade preferences; and diplomatic acceptance, depending on the circumstances. Since 1959, the United States has applied trade sanctions, political isolation, and covert operations against Cuba. In essence, "[a]ll that defines U.S. imperialism has been practiced in Cuba" (Pérez 2008, 1).

Cuba's importance to the United States, besides the security concerns and the conviction of possession, lies in economic interests. Cuba, the largest island in the Caribbean, is less than 100 miles from the United States and has various harbors of strategic significance—harbors that were especially appreciated in times when navy ships were more important than airplanes to fight wars.

The rationale for Washington's traditional antagonism against the Cuban Revolution lies in historical reasons linked to national security and economic concerns. As a partner of the USSR, Cuba engaged in a foreign policy that diverged from U.S. interests in the context of the Cold War. In addition, the support given by Havana to guerrilla movements in Latin America and to independence movements in Africa was completely against Washington's interests.

The Cuban revolutionary government understood the high cost to be paid for not maintaining diplomatic and economic relations with the United States and sought to undertake various initiatives to approach different U.S. administrations, in order to re-establish relations. Nevertheless, before President Obama, all attempts at normalization ended badly (Brenner and Scribner 2016; Franklin 2015; Leogrande and Kornbluh 2015; Morales Domínguez and Ramírez Cañedo 2015), in spite of the seeming determination of some prior U.S. administrations to re-establish relations with Cuba.

From the time of his candidacy, there was much anticipation that an Obama administration would significantly shift U.S. relationships with the rest of the world. Unlike his immediate predecessor, President Obama sought to halt hemispheric neglect and attempted to redirect and reassert U.S. presence in the region. In the case of Cuba, he inherited the fractious policy of ten predecessors and was able to break through with a fresh look into Cuba-U.S. relations.

References

5412 Committee. 1960. *A Program of Covert Action Against the Castro Regime.* Accessed July 30, 2016. https://history.state.gov/historicaldocuments/frus1958-60v06/d481.

Alzugaray Treto, Carlos. 2010. La seguridad nacional de Cuba frente a los Estados Unidos: conflicto y ¿cooperación? *Revista Temas,* 62–63 (April–September): 43–53.

Badella, Alessandro. 2014. Between Carter and Clinton: Obama's Policy Towards Cuba. *Caribbean Journal of International Relations & Diplomacy* 2 (2): 29–31. Accessed June 12, 2017. http://libraries.sta.uwi.edu/journals/ojs/index.php/iir/article/view/483/409.

Brenner, Philip, and Colleen Scribner. 2016. Spoiling the Spoilers: Evading the Legacy of Failed Attempts to Normalize U.S.-Cuba Relations. In *Cuba-US Relations: Normalization and Its Challenges,* ed. Margaret E. Crahan and Soraya M. Castro Mariño, 385–419. New York: Institute of Latin American Studies, Columbia University.

Buchanan, James. 1909. *The Works of James Buchanan, Comprising His Speeches, State Papers, and Private Correspondence, Volume VIII: 1848–1853.* Collected and edited by John Bassett Moore. Philadelphia and London: J.P. Lippincott Company.

Casells, Elsada Diana. 2017. Las relaciones entre Cuba y el Caribe tras el 17D: del optimismo a la incertidumbre. In *Cuba en sus relaciones con el Caribe después del 17D,* ed. Jacqueline Laguardia Martinez, 129–142. Buenos Aires: El Consejo Latinoamericano de Ciencias Sociales (CLACSO).

Castro, Fidel. 1975 [1953]. *La historia me absolverá.* Translated by Pedro Álvarez Tabío and Andrew Paul Booth. Havana: Editorial de Ciencias Sociales. Accessed April 10, 2017. https://www.marxists.org/history/cuba/archive/castro/1953/10/16.htm.

Clinton, William J. 1996. Statement on Signing the Cuban Liberty and Democratic Solidarity (LIBERTAD) Act of 1996. March 12, 1996. Online by Gerhard Peters and John T. Woolley, American Presidency Project. Accessed June 9, 2017. http://www.presidency.ucsb.edu/ws/?pid=52532.

Copeland, Cassandra, Curtis Jolly, and Henry Thompson. 2011. The History and Potential of Trade Between Cuba and the US. *Journal of Economics and Business*. Fox School of Business, Temple University, Philadelphia, PA, United States. Accessed April 13, 2017. http://www.auburn.edu/~thomph1/cuba-history.pdf.

Domínguez, Jorge I. 1997. U.S.-Cuban Relations: From the Cold War to the Colder War. *Journal of Interamerican Studies and World Affairs* 39 (3) (Fall): 49–75. Accessed April 11, 2017. http://www.jstor.org/stable/166485.

———. 2010. Reconfiguración de las relaciones de los Estados Unidos y Cuba. *Revista Temas* 62–63 (April–September): 4–15.

Dye, Alan, and Richard Sicotte. 1999. U.S.-Cuban Trade Cooperation and Its Unraveling. *Business and Economic History* 28 (2): 19–31.

Felter, Claire, and Danielle Renwick. 2018. U.S.-Cuba Relations. Council on Foreign Relations. Last updated April 23, 2018. Accessed June 9, 2017. https://www.cfr.org/backgrounder/us-cuba-relations.

Franklin, Jane. 2015. *Cuba-Estados Unidos: cronología de una historia*. Havana: Editorial de Ciencias Sociales.

García Molina, Jesús M. 2005. La economía cubana desde el siglo XVI al XX: del colonialismo al socialismo con mercado. *CEPAL Serie Estudios y Perspectivas* 28. Accessed April 18, 2017. http://archivo.cepal.org/pdfs/2005/S050273.pdf.

Glennie, Alex, and Laura Chappell. 2010. Jamaica: From Diverse Beginning to Diaspora in the Developed World. June 16, 2010. Migration Policy Institute. Accessed November 24, 2018. https://www.migrationpolicy.org/article/jamaica-diverse-beginning-diaspora-developed-world.

Gordon, C. Joy. 2012. The U.S. Embargo Against Cuba and the Diplomatic Challenges to Extraterritoriality. *Fletcher Forum of World Affairs* 36 (1) (Winter): 63–79. Accessed June 12, 2017. http://digitalcommons.fairfield.edu/cgi/viewcontent.cgi?article=1019&context=philosophy-facultypubs.

Hilsman, Roger. 1996. *The Cuban Missile Crisis: The Struggle over Policy*. Westport, CT: Praeger Publishers.

Hoffmann, Bert. 1998. *The Helms-Burton Law and Its Consequences for Cuba, the United States and Europe*. Paper presented at the meeting of the Latin American Studies Association, Palmer House Hilton Hotel, Chicago, IL, United States, September 24–26, 1998. Accessed June 9, 2017. http://lasa.international.pitt.edu/lasa98/hoffmann.pdf.

Holmes, Ann-Marie. 2009. The United States and Cuba 1898–1959. Master's thesis, Hawai'i Pacific University, Honolulu, HI, United States. Accessed June 9, 2017. https://www.hpu.edu/CHSS/History/GraduateDegree/MADMSTheses/files/Ann_Marie_Holmes.pdf.

Kornbluh, Peter. 2010. El terrorismo y el acuerdo anti-secuestros en las relaciones de Cuba con los Estados Unidos. *Revista Temas* 62–63 (April–September): 54–58.

Laguardia Martinez, Jacqueline. 2016. *CARICOM and Cuba in a Changing Hemispheric Environment: A Balance Since 17D.* Henricus Heidweiller Memorial Lecture, Anton de Kom University, Paramaribo, Suriname, May 18, 2016.
Lamrani, Salim. 2014. *Cuba, the Media, and the Challenge of Impartiality.* New York: Monthly Review Press.
Le Riverend, Julio. 1971. *Historia económica de Cuba.* Havana: Instituto Cubano del Libro.
Leogrande, William M. 2015. El 17D: secuencias y consecuencias (primera entrega). *Catalejo: el blog de Temas,* January 5, 2015. Accessed March 3, 2019. http://www.cubadebate.cu/especiales/2015/01/07/el-17d-secuencias-y-consecuencias-william-leogrande/.
Leogrande, William M., and Peter Kornbluh. 2015. *Back Channel to Cuba: The Hidden History of Negotiations Between Washington and Havana.* Chapel Hill, NC: University of North Carolina Press.
López Civeira, Francisca. 2003. La república (1899–1959). In *Cuba y su historia.* Havana: Editorial Félix Varela, edited by Francisca López Civeira, Oscar Loyola Vega and Arnaldo Silva León.
Loyola Vega, Oscar. 2003. La sociedad criolla. In *Cuba y su historia.* Havana: Editorial Félix Varela, edited by Francisca López Civeira, Oscar Loyola Vega and Arnaldo Silva León.
Mendes, Isa. 2015. Mending Bridges: The Unfinished Business of the US and Cuba. *BPC Policy Brief* 5 (6) (April–May). BRICS Policy Centre. Accessed May 28, 2017. http://bricspolicycenter.org/homolog/uploads/trabalhos/6909/doc/2132751521.pdf.
Molina Molina, Ernesto. 2007. *El pensamiento económico de la nación cubana.* Havana: Editorial de Ciencias Sociales.
Monroe, James. 1823. Message to Congress. December 2, 1823. Gilder Lehrman Institute. Accessed May 28, 2017. http://www.digitalhistory.uh.edu/disp_textbook.cfm?smtID=3&psid=161.
Morales Domínguez, Esteban, and Elier Ramírez Cañedo. 2015. *Aproximaciones al conflicto Cuba-Estados Unidos.* Havana: Editora Política.
Obama, Barack. 2009. Remarks to the Summit of the Americas in Port of Spain, Trinidad and Tobago. April 17, 2009. Accessed May 28, 2017. https://www.gpo.gov/fdsys/pkg/PPP-2009-book1/pdf/PPP-2009-book1-Doc-pg511.pdf.
Organization of American States (OAS). 1960. Final Act of the Seventh Meeting of Consultation of Ministers of Foreign Affairs. August 22–29, 1960, San José, Costa Rica. Accessed April 19, 2017. http://www.oas.org/council/MEETINGS%20OF%20CONSULTATION/Actas/Acta%207.pdf.

———. 1962. Final Act of the Eight Meeting of Consultation of Ministers of Foreign Affairs. January 22–31, 1962, Punta del Este, Uruguay. Accessed April 19, 2017. http://www.oas.org/consejo/meetings%20OF%20consultation/actas/acta%208.pdf.

———. 1964. Final Act of the Night Meeting of Consultation of Ministers of Foreign Affairs. July 21–26, 1964, Pan American Union, Washington, DC, United States. Accessed April 19, 2017. http://www.oas.org/council/MEETINGS%20OF%20CONSULTATION/Actas/Acta%209.pdf.

Pérez, Louis A. 2003. *Cuba and the United States: Ties of Singular Intimacy*. 3rd ed. Athens, GA: University of Georgia Press.

———. 2008. *Cuba in the American Imagination: Metaphor and the Imperial Ethos*. Chapel Hill, NC: University of North Carolina Press.

———. 2015. *Cuba: Between Reform and Revolution*. 5th ed. New York: Oxford University Press.

———. n.d. Cuba as an Obsessive Compulsive Disorder. University of North Carolina at Chapel Hill. Accessed June 12, 2017. http://www.socsci.uci.edu/uc-cuba/webdocs/Cuba_as_an_obsessive_compulsive_disorder.pdf.

Perusek, Glenn. 1984. Haitian Emigration in the Early Twentieth Century. *The International Migration Review* 18 (1) (Spring): 4–18. Accessed November 24, 2018. https://www.jstor.org/stable/2545999.

Rasenberger, Jim. 2011. *The Brilliant Disaster: JFK, Castro, and America's Doomed Invasion of Cuba's Bay of Pigs*. New York: Simon & Schuster.

Republic of Cuba. 1960. *The First Declaration of Havana*. August 28, 1960. Accessed April 19, 2017. http://www.walterlippmann.com/fc-09-02-1960.html.

———. 1962. *The Second Declaration of Havana*. February 4, 1962. Accessed April 19, 2017. http://www.walterlippmann.com/fc-02-04-1962.pdf.

———. 1964. *Declaración de Santiago de Cuba*. July 26, 1964. Accessed April 19, 2017. http://www.fidelcastro.cu/es/documentos/declaracion-de-santiago-de-cuba.

Rodríguez, Carlos Rafael. 1983. *Letra con filo*. Havana: Editorial de Ciencias Sociales.

Schoultz, Lars. 2009. *That Infernal Little Cuban Republic: The United States and the Cuban Revolution*. Chapel Hill, NC: University of North Carolina Press.

Silva León, Arnaldo. 2005. La revolución en el poder (1959–1995). In *Cuba y su historia*. Havana: Editorial Félix Varela, edited by Francisca López Civeira, Oscar Loyola Vega and Arnaldo Silva León.

Suddath, Claire. 2009. A Brief History of U.S.-Cuba Relations. *Time*, April 15, 2009. Accessed April 18, 2017. http://content.time.com/time/nation/article/0,8599,1891359,00.html.

The Cuba Consortium. 2016. *The Opening to Cuba: Annual Report of the Cuba Consortium*. October 3, 2016. Accessed June 3, 2017. http://files.thecubaconsortium.org/media/TheCubaConsortiumAnnualReport11.3.16.pdf.

Torres Cuevas, Eduardo, and Oscar Loyola Vega. 2002. *Historia de Cuba 1492–1898: formación y liberación de una nación.* Havana: Editorial Pueblo y Educación.
U.S. Congress. 1992. *Cuban Democracy Act.* Accessed April 13, 2017. https://www.treasury.gov/resource-center/sanctions/Documents/cda.pdf.
U.S. Department of State. 1917. *Trading with the Enemy Act.* Accessed June 9, 2017. https://www.gpo.gov/fdsys/pkg/USCODE-2011-title50/pdf/USCODE-2011-title50-app-tradingwi.pdf.
———. n.d. Notes on the 479th Meeting of the National Security Council. Foreign Relations of the United States, 1961–1963, Volume X, Cuba, January 1961–September 1962. Documentaliste 184. Accessed June 9, 2017. https://history.state.gov/historicaldocuments/frus1961-63v10/d184.
Wong, Kam S. 1994. The Cuban Democracy Act of 1992: The Extraterritorial Scope of Section 1706(a). *Journal of International Law* 14 (4): 651–682.

CHAPTER 5

Advancements in the Cuba-U.S. Relationship

After 18 months of private negotiations, on December 17, 2014 (17D), U.S. President Barack Obama and Cuban President Raúl Castro announced their intention of normalizing relations between their two countries. This announcement was unexpected and caught the world by surprise, but presented a new course in relations between the United States and Cuba. This chapter provides the substantive and procedural changes which have been taking place since December 2014 ranging from the re-establishment of diplomatic relations until President Obama ending the "wet foot, dry foot" policy. The chapter identifies the concrete ways in which these changes have been manifested, especially on promoting joint dialogue and cooperation between Cuba and the United States.

Most of the initial changes after 17D were made through revisions, announced by the U.S. Departments of the Treasury and Commerce, to their Cuban Assets Control Regulations (CACR) and Export Administration Regulations (EAR) respectively. Five sets of revisions were made in 2015–2016:

1. The first set of revisions, announced in January 2015, eased regulations related to travel, remittances, transactions between financial institutions, telecommunications, and trade (U.S. Department of the Treasury 2015a).
2. Announced in September 2015, the second set of revisions similarly addressed travel and telecommunications, but also allowed the

establishment of a business presence in Cuba, the opening of bank accounts on the island, and other activities such as the provision of legal services, as well as educational activities (U.S. Department of the Treasury 2015b).
3. The third set of revisions was announced in January 2016, and further eased U.S. sanctions on Cuba. The amendments included the removal of limits on exports of non-agricultural items; a further easing of travel restrictions; and the allowing of further transactions related to professional meetings, disaster preparedness and response ventures, and information and informational materials (U.S. Department of the Treasury 2016a).
4. The fourth set of revisions was announced in March 2016, ahead of President Obama's trip to Cuba. These sought to further ease travel by U.S. citizens to Cuba, in order to engage directly with the Cuban people; to expand Cuba and Cuban nationals' access to U.S. financial institutions and to the U.S. dollar; and to extend the means through which Cubans legally present in the United States could earn stipends and salaries beyond their living expenses (U.S. Department of the Treasury 2016b).
5. Announced in October 2016, the fifth set of revisions sought to increase economic opportunity for Cubans and U.S. Americans. The changes focused on scientific collaboration, improving Cuban living conditions, expanding humanitarian reach, and people-to-people interaction (U.S. Department of the Treasury 2016c).

Besides these five packages of measures, there were two other significant changes initiated by the United States in its policy toward Cuba. In May 2015, the U.S. Secretary of State, John Kerry rescinded Cuba's designation on the State Sponsors of Terrorism List (Rathke 2015), and this has remained so under the Donald Trump administration. For Cuba, this has not only led to the reversal of restrictions that previously influenced decisions concerning the provision of U.S. financial support, but also removed the obligation for the U.S. government to oppose loans to Cuba from international financial institutions. Therefore, Cuba's removal from the list, in principle, created an avenue for the country to regain access to the International Monetary Fund (IMF) and to join other multilateral organizations (Tvevad 2015). However, it should be noted that U.S. policy toward Cuba at the IMF is effectively determined by the Helms-Burton Act.

Just before the end of his second term in January 2017, President Obama announced that the U.S. Department of Homeland Security was ending the "wet foot, dry foot" policy. This meant that any Cuban national, who now attempted to enter the United States illegally and was not eligible for humanitarian relief would be subject to deportation, consistent with U.S. law. The Department of Homeland Security also put an end to the Cuban Medical Professional Parole Program (The White House Office of the Press Secretary 2017), a program that encouraged Cuban medical professionals working in third countries to defect. Both steps on the part of the United States demonstrated its readiness to treat Cuban migrants like any other migrant from other countries is treated. This is another aspect of the newer policies that has remained unaffected by President Trump's stance on Cuba.

Acknowledging these major changes made by the United States, the following sections discuss the specific areas in which adjustments have occurred, and the key factors involved in the process of normalization of the Cuba-U.S. bilateral relationship. It is here that some attention must now be paid to examining the changes, and their reversals, that have taken place since 17D.

Settling Institutional Channels

The formal re-establishment of diplomatic relations between Cuba and the United States was accomplished with the reopening of their embassies. The Cuban embassy reopened in Washington, D.C., on July 20, 2015, while the embassy of the United States reopened in Havana on August 14 of the same year (The White House n.d.). In September 2017, however, President Trump removed all non-essential staff from the U.S. embassy in Havana, accusing Cuba of attacks on the health and well-being of the personnel stationed there. In October 2017, the U.S. government expelled 17 Cuban diplomatic officials working at the embassy in Washington, D.C., because of these unexplained health incidents, sometimes referred to as "sonic attacks", affecting U.S. diplomats (Representaciones Diplomáticas de Cuba en el Exterior 2018; Piccone 2018). Furthermore, all U.S. consular services in Havana have been suspended since late 2018 (In Focus 2018).

After 17D, different mechanisms were established to enable permanent dialogue on issues of mutual interest, especially those on which major disagreements remain, such as compensation for nationalized U.S.

companies, embargo-associated losses, and the Guantánamo Bay Naval Base, among others. Several rounds of negotiations and technical meetings were held on issues such as immigration, cultural and academic exchanges, the environment, natural disasters, the Internet, drug interdiction, air safety, remittances, humanitarian aid, democracy, human rights, and cyber security, among others (Laguardia Martinez 2016). These are outlined and explained chronologically in Table 5.1.

High-Level Visits

As of January 2017, 25 official delegations (including six high-level delegations) from Cuba had visited Washington, D.C., and 47 official delegations (including 13 high-level delegations) from the United States had visited Havana (Cabañas 2017). This section presents an overview of the visits, including the high-level personnel involved in them.

As a starting point, it is worthwhile to take note of the number of U.S. Cabinet members who have visited Cuba. John Kerry, Secretary of State in the Obama administration, visited Havana for the reopening of the U.S. embassy in August 2015—he was the first U.S. Secretary of State to visit Cuba in 70 years (Cabañas 2017; Engage Cuba 2016). Other such visits to the island included those made by Secretary of Transportation, Anthony Foxx, and Secretary of Health and Human Services, Sylvia Burwell, in 2016; and Secretary of Agriculture, Thomas J. Vilsack, and Secretary of Commerce, Penny Pritzker, in 2015.

In October 2015, Deputy Secretary of the U.S. Department of Homeland Security, Alejandro Mayorkas, visited Cuba. He was followed, in January 2016, by Deputy Assistant Secretary of State and U.S. Coordinator for International Communications and Information Policy, Daniel A. Sepulveda. Then, in October 2016, U.S. Trade Representative, Michael Froman, made an official two-day visit to Havana (Engage Cuba 2016). In January 2017, President of the U.S. Chamber of Commerce, Thomas Donohue, visited Cuba (Frank 2017).

There were also several visits by U.S. state governors to the island. In 2015, Texas Governor, Greg Abbott; Arkansas Governor, Asa Hutchinson; and New York Governor, Andrew Cuomo visited Cuba. They were followed in 2016 by West Virginia's Earl Ray Tomlin, Virginia's Terry McAuliffe, and Louisiana's John Bel Edwards (Cabañas 2017; Engage Cuba 2016). Since President Trump assumed office in January 2017,

Table 5.1   Cuba-U.S. dialogue mechanisms

Date	Event
January 2015	U.S. Assistant Secretary of State for Western Hemisphere Affairs and Top Negotiator, Roberta Jacobson, traveled to Havana for the first round of diplomatic conversations between the United States and Cuba (Engage Cuba 2016)
February 2015	General Director of the U.S. Division in the Cuban Ministry of Foreign Affairs and Cuba's Top Negotiator to the United States, Josefina Vidal, traveled to Washington, D.C., for the second round of diplomatic talks between the two countries (Engage Cuba 2016)
March 2015	In Washington, D.C., the United States and Cuba held the first planning session for a Human Rights Dialogue at which both governments raised issues to pursue (The White House n.d.)
April 2015	Presidents Barack Obama and Raúl Castro met at the Summit of the Americas in Panama. It marked the first time that the two nations' top leaders sat down for substantive talks in more than 50 years (Engage Cuba 2016)
September 2015	Presidents Obama and Castro met for a second round of talks at the United Nations General Assembly (The Cuba Consortium 2016, 4)
March 2016	Presidents Obama and Castro met for a third round of talks, during the former's visit to Cuba (The Cuba Consortium 2016, 4)
September 2015	The United States and Cuba established the U.S.-Cuba Steering Committee or Bilateral Commission, the primary vehicle for advancing normalization (The White House n.d.), addressing unresolved issues, and facilitating talks on bilateral and multilateral matters with the aim of fostering cooperation in areas of mutual interest. Discussions have focused on property claims, drug trafficking, human trafficking, telecommunications, and environmental protection. As at December 2018, the Committee had met seven times (Whitefield 2018a)
October 2015	The United States and Cuba held the inaugural Regulatory Dialogue to discuss more effective implementation of U.S. regulatory policies toward Cuba (The White House n.d.)
November 2015	The United States and Cuba held their first bilateral Law Enforcement Dialogue, which focused on an extensive range of areas of cooperation "including counter-terrorism, counter-narcotics, transnational crime, cyber-crime, secure travel and trade, and fugitives" (The White House n.d.)
December 2015	The United States and Cuba held the first round of discussions on mutual property claims (Engage Cuba 2016)
September 2016	The United States and Cuba held the inaugural Economic Dialogue in Washington, D.C., at which the negotiators discussed "trade and investment, labor and employment, renewable energy and energy efficiency, small business, intellectual property rights, economic policy, regulatory and banking matters, and telecommunications and internet access" (Engage Cuba 2016)

Mississippi Governor, Phil Bryant, and Colorado Governor, John Hickenlooper, have visited Cuba (Cubadebate 2017).

Similarly, high-level official visits have been made by senior members of the Cuban government. Among the Cuban ministers who traveled to the United States to meet with their counterparts are Bruno Rodríguez Parrilla (Foreign Affairs); Rodrigo Malmierca Díaz (Foreign Trade and Investment); Roberto Morales Ojeda (Public Health); and Gustavo Rodríguez (Agriculture). Former President of Cuba's National Institute of Sports, Physical Education, and Recreation (INDER), Eduardo Becali, has also visited the United States (Prensa Latina 2016). Furthermore, in January 2017, a delegation of government officials and port leaders from Cuba participated in a tour of maritime centers along the U.S. Gulf Coast (Guzzo 2017a).

The high-level visit that has received the most public attention to date was President Barack Obama's trip to Cuba in March 2016. He was accompanied on this state visit by 39 members of the U.S. Congress (Cabañas 2017). One of the highlights of the visit was President Obama's speech at the National Theater in Havana, which was broadcast on Cuban national television and radio (Engage Cuba 2016).

Communications

Various provisions in the five packages of measures, authorized in 2015–2016, were related to the telecommunications sector. For instance, a general license to establish telecommunications facilities for the provision of services within Cuba, between the United States and Cuba, and between Cuba and third countries was approved in January 2015. Additionally, and also in January 2015, it became possible for individuals to obtain licenses for the sale or donation of personal communication devices. In September 2015, this authorization was extended to U.S. individuals or firms to establish a business presence in Cuba, including through joint ventures, to provide specific telecommunications and Internet-based services. Finally, as of September 2015, it became possible to import mobile applications of Cuban origin and to hire Cuban nationals to develop them, with the March 2016 amendments expanding this to include software (The Cuba Consortium 2016).

In March 2015, the United States and Cuba established direct calling capability between the two countries for the first time in 15 years. Given how many Cubans and Cuban Americans reside in the United States, calls emanating from the United States to Cuba benefit U.S. telecommunications providers (Engage Cuba 2017). Since 2016, the four largest telecommunications companies in the United States—AT&T, Verizon, T-Mobile, and Sprint—have offered mobile roaming on the island (Engage Cuba 2017).

Technology providers and networks were also able to capitalize on the diplomatic developments taking place. Notably, Google entered into an agreement with the major Cuban telecommunications provider, *Empresa de Telecomunicaciones de* Cuba S.A. (ETECSA), in December 2016, to allow for faster and easier access to its services (Engage Cuba 2017). In addition, Google commenced operation of its installed rack servers in Cuba (Frenkel 2017); Twitter began allowing users in Cuba to select their location in their account settings, an option which was previously unavailable (Franceschi-Bicchierai 2015); and Apple removed Cuba from its restricted country list for foreign trade (Hughes 2015).

Moreover, in March 2016, direct mail service between the United States and Cuba resumed (Engage Cuba 2016); and since 17D, as at January 2017, 1667 American journalists had visited Cuba, and many others had traveled from third countries (Cabañas 2017).

Security

Despite the tension in overall bilateral relations, Cuba and the United States have quietly built a cooperative relationship to face common regional security threats. Given the two countries have shared waters, shared airspace, and shared threats, Thale and Jiménez (2018) note that despite their deep political and ideological differences, there have been "modest" levels of cooperation on matters related to security. Even during the most difficult diplomatic periods of Cuba-U.S. relations, the need for cooperation in security, precisely because of the geopolitical positioning of both countries, has been recognized and addressed with some degree of success, making it easier for it to continue through the latest changes in the bilateral relationship.

Even before the announcement of normalization of relations in 2014, security cooperation between the two countries had expanded under the Obama administration since 2009 and accelerated in 2012 when John Kerry assumed the position of U.S. Secretary of State (Thale and Jiménez 2018).

Broadly understood, security cooperation between Cuba and the United States implies "a network of institutional relations that both link and crisscross connections between the Cuban and U.S. militaries and various civilian agencies" (Bach et al. 2017, 17). "Security" covers a range of transborder issues that affect either the United States or Cuba, or both. Some of the issues that must be considered in this regard are drug interdiction, human trafficking maritime safety, environmental disasters, migration, and military-to-military relations (Peters 2009; Thale and Jiménez 2018).

One key example illustrates cooperation on environmental issues. In the Caribbean, environmental risks have become major security challenges. Climate change is exacerbating existing environmental events such as hurricanes and drought. Cuba, like parts of the United States, suffers from these and other like events, which have negative effects on agriculture, food and water security, tourism, health, and economic growth. For years, the U.S. National Hurricane Center and Cuba's Institute of Meteorology (INSMET) and National Forecasting Center have maintained good relations and have shared information. This has also been linked to cooperation between the U.S. Federal Aviation Administration (FAA) and the Cuban Aeronautics Board: U.S. hurricane-hunting planes have crossed Cuba's airspace, with the Cuban authorities' permission, to gather climatic data (Bach et al. 2017). Despite the passing of the Cuban Democracy Act in 1992, which further strengthened the U.S. blockade of Cuba, and the Helms-Burton Act codifying the U.S. embargo in 1996, cooperation in weather and aviation expanded throughout the 1990s (Thale and Jiménez 2018).

Additionally, both countries recognized the importance of jointly combating illicit drug trafficking. In this regard, there has been robust counter-narcotics cooperation between the two countries, with both sides benefitting from such cooperation. Following exchange of information about several drug shipments destined for the United States in the mid-1990s, both countries agreed to the installation of a Coast Guard liaison officer at the then U.S. Interest Section in Havana (now the U.S. Embassy) (Lee 2009). Cuba has also aided U.S. agencies by providing documentation and witnesses for drug trafficking cases (Jorgensen 2018).

To this end, in January 2016, Cuban officials were invited to the headquarters of the Joint Interagency Task Force South (JIATF South)—a U.S. initiative for the detection and monitoring of regional narcotics shipments—and participated for the first time as observers at an annual

United States Southern Command (Southcom)[1] sponsored Caribbean Nations Security Conference (Thale 2016). Later, in July 2016, the United States and Cuba held the third Counter-Narcotics Dialogue (Bach et al. 2017; U.S. Department of State 2016). Through this dialogue, the two governments seek to increase counter-narcotics cooperation and information exchange (U.S. Embassy in Cuba 2016). At this meeting, Cuba and the United States signed an agreement on operational cooperation to combat narcotics trafficking (The Cuba Consortium 2016).

Furthermore, both countries established protocols for search-and-rescue operations in the Florida Straits. An initiative for including a Regional Security Officer at the then U.S. Interest Section in Havana, tasked with managing case-by-case law enforcement issues, was also negotiated. Both countries successfully worked on new security arrangements to support airline passenger screening and safety. Cooperation has extended to cyber-crimes with Cuba's cyber-crime agency sharing information with the U.S. Department of Homeland Security about attempts to hack Cuban computer systems originating in the United States (Thale and Jiménez 2018) and intelligence about cyber-crime cases involving the United States.

Other examples are related to U.S. and Cuban military medical cooperation in Haiti—in 2015, with the visit of the U.S. naval ship *Comfort* to the country, and before that, during the response to the 2010 Haiti earthquake. The U.S. and Cuba's coast guards work together on the open seas to rescue shipwreck victims and to protect borders, and "fence line" dialogues have been taking place monthly since 1995 at the Guantánamo Bay Naval Base fence line between Cuban and U.S. officers about emergency response and other issues related to the presence of U.S. facilities, personnel, and operations in Guantánamo (Alzugaray Treto and Quainton 2011; Klepak 2010; Alzugaray Treto 2010; Domínguez 2010; Bach et al. 2017). Cooperation has also extended to the signing of two migration accords in 1994 and 1995 to ensure safe, legal, and orderly immigration (Rusin et al. 2015).

In March 2016, the U.S. National Oceanic and Atmospheric Administration (NOAA) and Cuba's National Office of Hydrography and

---

[1] Southcom is the U.S. military's operational command group for the Caribbean and the south of Mexico. Southcom's key missions are counter-terrorism, countering transnational organized crime, and contingency responses, all of which require regional cooperation (Rosetti and Holland 2015).

Geodesy (ONHG) signed a memorandum of understanding (MoU) to improve maritime navigation safety and to protect lives and property at sea. The MoU calls for cooperation in "the areas of hydrography, oceanography, geodesy, and related services of mutual interest". One of the major focuses is "to improve maritime navigation safety – including efforts to ensure the accuracy of both electronic and paper charts, eliminate charting overlaps, and fill in gaps in navigational chart coverage" (NOAA 2016).

In May 2016, an MoU between the U.S. Department of Homeland Security and the Cuban Ministry of the Interior and Customs Office was signed (U.S. Department of Homeland Security 2016), with the aim of improving security in trade and travel (U.S. Chamber of Commerce 2016). What the renewing of diplomatic relations between the United States and Cuba offered, therefore, were new opportunities for both nations to enhance security within a framework of cooperation in the Caribbean region.

As previously mentioned, in 2015, the U.S. Department of State removed Cuba from its list of state sponsors of terrorism, and a series of bilateral talks were conducted in the areas of counter-terrorism, law enforcement, drug interdiction, human trafficking, and migration. The dialogues resulted in 23 bilateral agreements, with nine of them focused on national security. In 2016, when many feared a change in U.S. migration policy toward Cuba, 5396 Cubans were rescued by the U.S. Coast Guard (Gámez Torres 2017). In 2017, when the end of the "wet foot, dry foot" policy was announced, there was a notable fall in the number of Cubans apprehended (U.S. Department of State 2018).

In January 2017, in a marathon of initiatives intended to solidify the new policy toward Cuba, various MoUs were signed. A major security-related agreement was reached when U.S. Ambassador-at-Large to Monitor and Combat Trafficking in Persons, Susan Coppedge, met with Cuban officials and others to discuss the country's initiatives to address human trafficking (The White House n.d.). An MoU was signed at this meeting for cooperation in matters of enforcement and enforcement of the Law (Representaciones Diplomáticas de Cuba en el Exterior 2017), whereby both countries agreed to establish working groups to exchange information, share best practices and coordinate operations in specific cases. These areas cover counter-terrorism, human trafficking and immigration fraud, counter-narcotics, cyber security and cyber-crime, and legal cooperation in criminal investigations (Thale and Jiménez 2018). Mention must be made of the fact that earlier, in its *2015 Trafficking in Persons Report*, the U.S. Department of State had upgraded Cuba from Tier 3 to Tier 2, closing that the Cuban government was making noteworthy actions "to meet minimum standards of fighting human trafficking" (The Cuba Consortium 2016, 10).

Other initiatives included: an MoU to strengthen cooperation in the field of maritime and aeronautical search-and-rescue, to enhance effectiveness and efficiency in assisting persons in distress, and to act in continuance of obligations under international law (U.S. Embassy in Cuba 2016); an MoU to delimit the only part of the Cuba-U.S. maritime boundary that had not been agreed on, covering an area of continental shelf in the Gulf of Mexico (U.S. Department of State 2017); and an MoU for cooperation in the field of animal and plant health, complementing a previous MoU (March 2016) on cooperation in the field of agriculture and other related areas (U.S. Department of Agriculture 2017).

As Cuba opens up to greater foreign tourism, trade, and foreign investment, it faces growing pressures to ensure national security and to align its security practices with those of the international and regional community. For instance, port security will take on a much different nature if the links between the Panama Canal and the port at Mariel, with its connections to Europe, become entangled with expanding foreign interests in the Caribbean region. Both countries—Cuba and the United States—also face common security threats related to illegal trade, terrorism, and extreme meteorological events (Bach et al. 2017).

For the United States, working closely with Cuba on cooperation initiatives on security could be beneficial in various ways. The United States would be providing humanitarian support to a near neighbor, and in so doing, be contributing to a reduction of environmental or public health risks that might emanate from Cuba or the Caribbean region. Events surrounding emergencies like the 2010 Haiti earthquake demonstrate the need to anticipate risks and to prepare collective and regional responses (Bach et al. 2017). Cuba has already identified this need and the island works with other Caribbean countries on disaster risk reduction programs and receives support from the EU and international organizations (Bach et al. 2017).

The Caribbean is a critical region for U.S. security. Questions of regional security, particularly transnational crime and disaster risk reduction, demand increased coordination. Cuba is the largest and most populated nation in the Caribbean, and the lack of an established security cooperation framework between Cuba and the United States weakens U.S. ability to respond to regional and national security issues. Having a major regional actor such as Cuba outside regional security cooperation frameworks also limits the ability of the United States and its partners to adequately address security challenges. Cooperation with Cuba would help the United States to maintain security more effectively while bringing with it potential economic opportunities. Additionally, improving security cooperation could serve to reduce risks for U.S. investment and trade relations in the areas of agriculture, energy, and pharmaceuticals, among others (Rosetti and Holland 2015).

According to Bach et al. (2017), for the United States and Cuba to enhance and deepen cooperation on security threats, it is necessary to go beyond technical groups. A complementary, parallel strategic engagement should be developed in order to facilitate information exchanges, identify new opportunities and areas for joint action, and perhaps, transcend longstanding antagonisms. Bach et al. point to the convenience of undertaking regional actions and moving beyond "contingency planning" to build infrastructure capacities that focus on building resilience in the Caribbean, including Cuba.

Flow of People Between the Two Countries

U.S. Citizens Traveling to Cuba

The President of the United States is the final licensing authority with regard to travel to Cuba, except when it concerns tourism. As it currently stands, travel to Cuba for tourism purposes is forbidden for U.S. citizens by the 2000 Trade Sanctions Reform and Export Enhancement Act (TSRA). However, in March 2016, the Obama administration authorized travelers to organize their own individual trips under the people-to-people travel category. Furthermore, in October 2016, the USD 400 limit was lifted on the amount of Cuban goods that travelers could bring back to the United States, for personal use (The Cuba Consortium 2016).

Under the Obama reforms, U.S. citizens falling under the 12 categories of authorized travel[2] could visit the island and therefore the "statutory

---

[2] Tourism is defined as travel not authorized by any of the 12 categories that cover traveling to Cuba: activities of private foundations or of research or educational institutes; authorized export transactions; educational activities; exportation, importation, or transmission of

prohibition of tourism appeared to be notional as the categories of persons and permissible travel-related activities normally fell within the definition of tourism" (CaPRI 2016, 9). The growing interest in Cuba and the rush to visit it "before Americans arrive" triggered tourist arrivals, and after 17D until 2017, a significant increase in visits was reported from travelers to Cuba coming from the rest of the world as well.

As Table 5.2 indicates, even if Canada retains its leading position as the main tourist market for Cuba—accounting for more than 40 percent of the tourism to the island—the United States showed a significant increase in 2015 and 2016. In 2015, U.S. Americans traveling to Cuba represented an almost 50 percent increase from 2014. By 2016, approximately 70 percent more U.S. citizens visited Cuba compared to 2014.

Table 5.2 does not include the figure of Cubans living in the United States since they are not considered to be "foreign visitors". However, when examining the number of Cuban Americans traveling to Cuba after 17D—see Table 5.3—there is an evident increase in the visits made by them to the island as well.

Table 5.2 Arrivals in Cuba, 2012–2016

Foreign visitors	*2012*	*2013*	*2014*	*2015*	*2016*
Canada	1,071,692	1,105,726	1,175,077	1,295,597	1,198,917
Germany	108,709	115,546	139,136	174,415	241,246
United Kingdom	153,731	149,513	123,910	155,626	194,391
Italy	103,287	95,536	112,076	137,288	189,165
France	101,521	96,636	103,475	138,267	186,376
United States	98,051	92,346	91,254	160,811	282,621
Spain	81,354	73,057	77,099	107,193	152,216
China	18,836	22,218	28,291	31,530	40,383
Argentina	94,691	90,083	68,849	84,879	94,164
Russia	86,940	70,398	69,237	42,973	64,891
Rest of the world	535,361	567,502	653,113	806,829	943,592
TOTAL	2,454,173	2,478,561	2,641,517	3,135,408	3,587,962

Source: Perelló Cabrera (2017a, 68–71)

information or information materials; family visits; journalism; humanitarian projects; official government engagements; professional research and meetings; public performances, exhibitions, athletic, and other competitions; religious activities; and support for the Cuban people (The Cuba Consortium 2016).

Table 5.3 Cuban American arrivals in Cuba, 2014–2016

	2014	2015	2016
Cuban Americans	258,814	292,692	344,522

Source: Perelló Cabrera (2017a, 68–71)

Cuban Citizens Traveling to the United States

With regard to illegal migration from Cuba to the United States, according to Admiral Paul Zukunft, Commandant of the U.S. Coast Guard, the number of Cuban migrants stopped at sea on the Florida coast has decreased significantly since January 2017—due in large part to President Obama terminating the "wet foot, dry foot" policy. Since then, the U.S. Coast Guard has apprehended less than 100 migrants, as compared to figures from 2016, of over 10,000 detainees from off the coast of Florida. In April 2017, there were no Cuban migrants intercepted by the U.S. Coast Guard (Cubadebate 2017b). Anticipation of Obama changing the policy, resulted in a noted increase in the number of migrants. Before the decision was announced, the Coast Guard reported intercepting 3376 migrants off the coast of Florida in 2014, of these 2059 came from Cuba, with migrants from the Republic of Haiti and the Dominican Republic comprising most of the rest (Lamothe 2017).

With regard to Cubans visiting the United States, despite the normalization process started in 2014, Cuba holds the highest rate of U.S. B visa (tourism or business) refusals worldwide. According to U.S. Department of State data, 81.9 percent of all applications made by Cuban nationals in 2016 were denied (McCarthy 2017). As part of the reversal of 17D-related policies under the Trump administration, on March 2019, it was announced that B2 visa validity for Cuban nationals was reduced from five years with multiple entries to three months with a single entry (U.S. Embassy in Cuba 2019).

Transport

In February 2016, an MoU was signed to restore scheduled air services between the United States and Cuba (The White House n.d.; Cabañas 2017). Later, in August 2016, the first U.S. passenger flight to Cuba in over 50 years, JetBlue Airways Flight 387, landed in Santa Clara (Engage

Cuba 2016). Currently, the U.S. airlines with services to Cuba are American Airlines, Delta Air Lines, JetBlue, Southwest Airlines, and United Airlines (Engage Cuba 2017). Before January 2018, this list also included Alaska Airlines, Frontier Airlines, Silver Airways, Spirit Airlines, and Sun Country Airlines.

Since U.S. airlines were authorized to travel to Cuba, an increase of about 100,000 passengers was registered from 2015 to 2016. However, the remaining ban on engaging in U.S. tourist activity in Cuba has hindered a further increase, and as a result of the over-supply of about three million seats representing the 110 daily flights to Cuba, three of the five U.S. airlines with services to Cuba—Delta Air lines, Southwest Airlines, and United Airlines—have reduced the frequency of their service or changed the type of airplane in service in favor of others with smaller passenger capacities. The exceptions are American Airlines and JetBlue, which announced, in December 2017, their intent to increase the frequency of their flights to Cuba (Prensa Latina 2017).

In May 2016, Carnival Cruise Line's ship, *Adonia*, became the first cruise ship to dock in Cuba in nearly 40 years (Engage Cuba 2016). The U.S. cruise lines with service to Cuba are Carnival Cruises, Norwegian Cruises, Pearl Seas Cruises, Royal Caribbean, and Viking Cruises (Engage Cuba 2017). According to Perelló Cabrera (2017b), until the end of October 2017, Cuba had received 28 cruise ships that year. In 2016, the gross income of Norwegian Cruises Carnival, and Royal Caribbean totaled USD 28,800 million.

In May 2015, the companies Havana Ferry Partners of Fort Lauderdale, Baja Ferries of Miami, United Caribbean Lines Florida of Greater Orlando, and Airline Brokers Company of Miami and Fort Lauderdale were notified of approvals by the U.S. Departments of Treasury and Commerce to operate ferries from the United States to Cuba (Hemlock and Satchell 2015). However, as at February 2019, ferry operations had not yet started.

Several MoUs have been signed between Cuba Ports Authority and U.S. ports and port authorities including the Ports of Mobile in Alabama, Pascagoula and Gulfport in Mississippi, and New Orleans and South Louisiana in Louisiana; as well as Alabama's port authority (EFE 2017). The American Association of Port Authorities signed an MoU with its Cuban counterpart in February 2017 (Guzzo 2017b).

Remittances

As many Caribbean economies, remittances are an important component of Cuba's economy and a main avenue for receiving financial resources from abroad. In 2016, cash remittances to the island amounted to USD3444.68 million, while goods remittances amounted to an estimated USD 3 billion. In total, the Cuban population received a total of USD 6444.68 million. Specifically, cash remittances have grown steadily since 2008 when they reached USD 1447.06 million, generating an average annual growth of USD 221.96 million (Morales 2018).

Remittances to Cuba benefit the U.S. economy in general as well. U.S. money transfer companies charge an average of 8 percent in commission on wire transfers to Cuba. Current remittances to Cuba generate up to USD 320 million annually for U.S. money transfer companies, totaling USD 1.2 billion over four years. A rough estimate of American jobs supported by remittances to Cuba at the largest money transfer companies is 782 (Engage Cuba 2017).

As part of the reversal of 17D-related policies, in June 2017, President Trump signed a memorandum on strengthening Cuban policy, which, though as yet ambiguous, could effectively restrict the remittances received by more than one million Cubans: the number of persons employed by the Cuban Ministry of Defense (Whitefield 2017).

According to the Havana Consulting Group—one of the main cited sources of remittance estimates—an increase in remittances from the United States to Cuba is associated with an increase in Cuban migrants to the United States. The Group estimated a loss of about USD 1 billion in remittances during 2017, as a result of the reduced number of migrants from President Obama's ending of the "wet foot, dry foot" policy. The estimate was generated under the assumptions that the Trump administration would not reverse Obama's decision and that it would continue to abide by the Migration Accord by allowing between 20,000 and 25,000 permanent migrants a year into the United States. Both assumptions are consistent with the formal announcement of Trump's normalization policy on June 16, 2017 (Morales 2017).

In June 2016, Western Union introduced Cuba-U.S. money transfers. Consumers in the United States who use the website wu.com or the Western Union mobile app can select the new "Send to Cuba" option to send money transfers and can track the transfer until they are paid out to the recipients at Western Union's network of 420 locations in Cuba. Western Union has also created the opportunity for their consumers in 29 countries to send money transfers to Cuba (Western Union 2016).

Scientific and Cultural Collaboration

In June 2016, the U.S. Department of Health and Human Services and the Cuban government signed an MoU to encourage cooperation on health matters (Scott 2016). In January 2017, the University of Illinois Hospital and the Cuban Ministry of Health launched a two-year initiative aimed at sharing best practices in providing community-based care. The goal was to reduce infant mortality rates, as well as to improve maternal health and cancer screening by having Cuban personnel practice in some of Chicago's most impoverished neighborhoods (Ross Johnson 2017). Additionally, the Roswell Park Cancer Institute in Buffalo, New York, has begun intensive cancer research collaboration with Cuba and is preparing for clinical trials of the Cuban-origin therapeutic lung cancer vaccine, CIMAvax-EGF (Engage Cuba 2017). The U.S. Food and Drug Administration approved this first clinical trial to test a Cuban drug in the United States. Lung cancer is the leading cause of cancer deaths in the United States, with a five-year survival rate of only 18.6 percent (*American Lung Association* 2019).

In terms of cultural collaborations between the two countries, from November 2016 to August 2017, the American Museum of Natural History of New York hosted *¡Cuba!*—one of the largest exhibitions on Cuba's biodiversity, natural resources and culture ever presented in the United States. It was also the museum's first fully bilingual show (Tugend 2016).

In September 2015, a global licensing agreement was signed between Sony Music Entertainment and Cuba's Empresa de Grabaciones y Ediciones Musicales (EGREM) (Industria Musical 2015). The multi-year agreement allows access to a multinational, for the first time, to all EGREM's recordings. This agreement means that Cuban music can now be accessed globally (Cobo 2015).

In June 2015, Sirius XM Radio's show *The Black Eagle*, hosted by Joe Madison, aired live from Taíno Studios in Havana, becoming the first national American radio talk show broadcast from Cuba after 17D. The broadcast included guests spanning the worlds of academia, culture, entertainment, and social activism (Sirius XM Holdings Inc. 2015).

Furthermore, artists and intellectuals from both countries have increased their visits and have embarked on different joint initiatives. In April 2016, a delegation led by the directors of the National Endowment for the Arts, the National Endowment for the Humanities, and the Smithsonian

Institution went on a three-day mission to Cuba with the purpose of expanding cultural exchanges with the island country (Montgomery 2016). Visits by U.S. artists and celebrities to Havana have increased exponentially since 17D as well. Matt Dillon, Alex Gibney, Annie Leibovitz, Rihanna, Hanif Kureshi, Ethan Hawke, Helen Hunt, and Don Cheadle (Grant 2016) have visited the island; and several U.S. TV shows and films—such as *House of Lies*, *The Fast and the Furious*, *Keeping Up with the Kardashians*, *Conan O'Brien*, and *Cuban Chrome*—have chosen Havana as a location for filming (Diaz 2015; WSVN 2016). Cultural interchange was also seen in November 2016 when Misty Copeland, the American Ballet Theatre's first black Principal Dancer, traveled to Cuba to conduct master classes and for speaking engagements there (P. Frank 2016).

Interactions in different sporting fields have also been part of the cultural connections made since 17D. In June 2015, the New York Cosmos soccer team went to Cuba for a friendly match with the Cuban national soccer team. The New York Cosmos were the first professional team to visit the island since the two countries began their detente effort (AP 2015). In June 2016, basketball player Shaquille O'Neal traveled to Cuba for a Sports Envoy Program aimed at engaging young people in Havana. The program was the first in which the U.S. Embassy in Havana partnered with Cuba's INDER.

In December 2018, after three years of negotiation, U.S. Major League Baseball (MLB) and the Cuban Baseball Federation signed an agreement that would allow Cuban players the opportunity to sign with U.S. baseball teams without having to defect. Though President Trump partially reversed some of the post-17D arrangements, these negotiations were able to continue as—according to the revised regulations of the U.S. Department of the Treasury's Office of Foreign Assets Control (OFAC)—MLB teams are able to transfer money to the Cuban Baseball Federation since it is not a government agency (Trotta and Marsh 2018). Unfortunately, as part of Trump's administration Cuba policy's setback, the Major League Baseball agreement with the Cuban Baseball Federation that would have allowed Cuban baseball players to be signed and play in the United States was cancelled in April 2019 (DeYoung 2019).

In the sphere of education, dozens of universities from around the United States have initiated educational exchange programs with Cuba and embarked on joint research projects with academics on the island. The programs range from study-abroad programs, to training in sports and fine arts, to sending English language specialists to the island (Engage Cuba 2017).

Agriculture and Environment

Cooperation in terms of environmental protection is another realm in which progress has been achieved (Garea Moreda and Pichs Madruga 2016; Sagebien and Leenson 2016). In November 2015, the U.S. and Cuban governments signed an MoU to establish a relationship dedicated to cooperation in the science, conservation, and management of co-protected marine areas. The accord will protect nearby fish and marine life living off the coasts of both countries and allow U.S. and Cuban scientists to collaborate on research. This was the first environmental protection instrument agreed between the two countries after 17D. In November 2015, a second MoU was signed addressing areas that include the protection of coasts and biodiversity, natural disasters, climate change, and marine pollution (The White House n.d.; Engage Cuba 2016; Cabañas 2017; On Cuba 2016; Sato 2016). In March 2016, both countries signed an MoU for setting a broad framework to share ideas and research on issues like nutrition, water safety, and the agricultural problems caused by climate change (Scott 2016).

In December 2016, three MoUs related to environmental issues were signed. The first is related to the conservation of wildlife and protected land areas; the second to seismology and cooperation in the exchange of information on seismic registers and related geological information, especially in matters related to events occurring in the Caribbean Sea and the Gulf of Mexico; and the third to meteorology and climate, covering forecast areas, models for atmospheric and climate conditions, the expansion and integration of meteorological observation and vigilance networks, and hurricane analyses and forecasts (On Cuba 2016).

Soon after, in January 2017, Cuba and the United States signed an MoU to jointly prevent, contain, and clean up oil and other toxic spills in the Gulf of Mexico, as they hurried to conclude deals before President Trump took office (M. Frank 2017). In that same month, the two countries also signed a twinning agreement between Ciénaga de Zapata National Park and Everglades National Park, aimed at contributing to the betterment of the environmental management through the exchange of information, the promotion of modern practices for the sustained management of their resources, and the sharing of scientific expertise (MINREX 2017).

Trade, Finance, and Foreign Direct Investment

The normalization policy that the Obama administration brought with it not only the anticipation of greater opportunities for U.S. companies to access the Cuban market. Despite the permanence of the embargo, a few fissures opened in U.S. trade policy toward Cuba could act as first steps to implement a normal bilateral trade regime and boost commerce between both countries.

In September 2015, the U.S. Chamber of Commerce launched the U.S.-Cuba Business Council (USCBC) for a better use of the open opportunities for trade, investment, and economic cooperation between the United States and Cuba (Tvevad 2015). In January 2017, the U.S. Department of the Treasury removed from its list of sanctions 28 companies and individuals that acted as intermediaries in trade with Cuba. Its Office of Foreign Assets Control decided to eliminate bans on companies and individuals in Mexico, Argentina, Panama, Japan, the United Kingdom, and the Netherlands (U.S. Department of the Treasury 2017).

Also, in January 2017, the first legal Cuban export to the United States in five decades arrived at Port Everglades. It corresponded to the sale of 40 tons of artisanal hardwood charcoal derived from marabou—a woody plant—and made by Cuban cooperatives for a value of around USD 17,000. Cuba exports up to 80,000 tons of charcoal per year (Reuters 2017; LaBash 2017).

In February 2016, the Obama administration approved the establishment of the first U.S. factory in Cuba by allowing a company from Alabama to build a USD 5 million to USD 10 million plant, assembling as many as 1000 small tractors a year for sale to private farmers in Cuba (Padgett 2016).

New facilities to enable financial relations between the two countries had been announced in the different packages of measures announced by the Obama administration after 17D, though from a practical standpoint there have not been any major changes in this area due to the persistence of the embargo. According to the Cuba Consortium (2016), among these facilities were the following:

1. The authorization of U.S. financial institutions to open accounts with Cuban banks, in order to facilitate sanctioned transactions and to allow for U.S. credit and debit cards to be accepted by Cuban merchants (January 2015)

2. The removal of restrictions on the terms of payment and financing for sanctioned exports (January 2016)[3]
3. The redefinition of "cash in advance" from "cash before shipment" to "cash before transfer of title to, and control of" the exported items, with the aim of simplifying and encouraging agricultural exports (January 2015)
4. The approval given to U.S. financial organizations to manage international financial transactions between Cuba and foreign entities that are done in USD denominations (termed "U-turn transactions") (March 2016)
5. The permission granted to U.S. banks to open and maintain accounts for Cuban nationals in Cuba, in order to facilitate their receipt of payments for authorized transactions and to remit these payments back to Cuba (March 2016) (The Cuba Consortium 2016, 22)

Doing Businesses in Cuba

Various provisions in the five packages authorized by the Obama administration, as outlined at the start of this chapter, are intended to facilitate U.S. business in Cuba. According to the Cuba Consortium (2016), these include the following:

1. The provision of "a general license for travel to conduct market research, commercial marketing, sales or contract negotiation, accompanied delivery, installation, leasing, or servicing in Cuba of items licensed for export (January 2016)"
2. The authorization to establish "a physical presence in Cuba (e.g., offices, retail outlets, warehouses) for news bureaus; authorized exporters; providers of mail, parcel, or cargo transportation services; providers of telecommunications or Internet-based services; entities organizing or conducting educational activities; religious organizations; and providers of travel services (September 2015)"
3. The authorization of "the permanent export of items for use in scientific, archeological, cultural, ecological, educational, historic preservation, sporting activities, or in the traveler's professional research and meetings (September 2015)"

[3] This excludes agricultural commodities and agricultural items (for which cash in advance payment is required by the 2000 Trade Sanctions Reform and Export Enhancement Act).

4. The authorization of "travel and other transactions related to the production of media programs (such as movies and television programs), music recordings, and the creation of artworks in Cuba, including employment of Cuban nationals (January 2016)"
5. The provision of "a general license to organize professional meetings; sports competitions; and public performances, clinics, workshops, other competitions and exhibitions in Cuba (January 2016)" (The Cuba Consortium 2016, 22–23).

Regarding specific U.S. companies in Cuba, in February 2015, Netflix began offering a streaming service for USD 7.99 per month (The Cuba Consortium 2016, 23). The Priceline Group, a major provider of online travel services, agreed to make Cuban hotel rooms available to U.S. customers via one of its subsidiaries, Booking.com, becoming the first U.S. online travel agency to make arrangements with the island. Booking.com operated initially only in Havana but has expanded, working with foreign firms already established on the island, such as France's Accor, Meliá Hotels International SA, NH Hotel Group SA, as well as with government-operated Cuban chains (Dwyer 2016).

On March 2016, Starwood Hotels and Resorts signed hotel contracts in Cuba. The deals include the Hotel Inglaterra, a Havana icon that will become part of Starwood's Luxury Collection, and Hotel Quinta Avenida, which became Four Points by Sheraton Hotel (Mufson 2016). Major U.S. travel and hospitality website companies—including Airbnb, Expedia, and TripAdvisor—now also offer their services in Cuba (Engage Cuba 2017). In March 2016, the U.S. Department of the Treasury licensed Airbnb to accept reservations for Cuba from non-U.S. travelers (The Cuba Consortium 2016).

According to the former U.S. Secretary of Commerce, Penny Pritzker, in 2015, the Department of Commerce issued 490 authorizations, worth USD 4.3 billion, to do business in Cuba. Approval from the Departments of Commerce and the Treasury is needed to do business on the island (Cubatrade 2016).

Apart from those already mentioned, some other well-known U.S. companies that obtained licenses to operate in Cuba include General Electric, Caterpillar, John Deere, Sprint, Mastercard International, Nestle Nespresso USA, Verizon, FedEx, AT&T, and T-Mobile (U.S.-Cuba Trade and Economic Council, Inc. n.d.).

In 2016, 229 U.S. business delegations with 2428 members visited Cuba. Twenty-three trade agreements have been finalized and, at the time of the 2016 U.S. presidential elections, several more were about to be finalized. Relationships have been maintained with 25 business associations, especially the U.S. Chamber of Commerce. Ninety American companies with 240 entrepreneurs attended, and four states were represented, at the Havana International Fair in November 2016 (Cabañas 2017). However, if the numbers present an accurate indication, the changing winds in the Cuba-U.S. relationship under Trump presidency are causing a decline in the business interest being shown in Cuba: in 2016, 33 U.S. companies set up booths at the fair. This number dropped to 17 in 2017, and 16 in 2018 (Marsh 2017; Knobloch 2018; Whitefield 2018b).

Provisions in the five 2015–2016 packages of measures authorized endeavors to promote and facilitate engagement with the Cuban private sector. These included, for instance, the authorization of microfinance for small private businesses (January 2015); the authorization of the import of certain goods and services produced by Cuban private businesses to the United States (January 2015); the authorization of the export of tools, equipment, and supplies to private farmers and businesses, and building materials and tools to private businesses to construct or renovate private buildings (January 2015); the authorization of U.S. businesses to hire Cuban nationals to work and perform in the United States, provided that the beneficiary is not subject to any special taxation in Cuba (March 2016) (The Cuba Consortium 2016).

Concluding Reflections

Immediately after 17D, several changes began reshaping bilateral relations between Cuba and the United States. As of January 2017, the two countries had signed 22 bilateral instruments covering areas such as health, environmental protection, and law enforcement (Cabañas 2017; Representaciones Diplomáticas de Cuba en el Exterior 2017). This chapter has identified positive trends, including the settling of institutional channels, the increase in high-level visits and signatures of MoUs, and charted positive developments in the bilateral relationship across various issues areas, notably communications, security, people flows, transport, remittances, scientific and cultural collaboration, agriculture, and environment.

Most of the changes analyzed correspond to modifications of U.S. policy toward Cuba. It must be noted here that as Cuba has no aspect of its foreign policy to change as it pertains to the United States, the assessment of Cuba's performance is based on the reactions to the steps being taken by the United States and their impacts on Cuba's internal dynamics. As was analyzed in Chap. 4, economic and geopolitical relations between Cuba and the United States have been, and remain, asymmetrical. Therefore, a quid pro quo focus cannot be applied: there are many more factors to contemplate on the U.S. side than on the Cuban side, as advances are made toward normalization. For instance, unlike the behavior of the United States toward Cuba over the years, Cuba does not apply sanctions against U.S. companies or citizens, or occupies U.S. territory; nor does release radio or television broadcasts conceived in Cuba and against the U.S. government and U.S. institutions.

With regard to the U.S. embargo against Cuba, the Obama administration's sentiments were reflected in voting, at the United Nations (UN) General Assembly, on the resolution calling for an end to it. In October 2016, the United States changed its vote to an abstention. By a vote of 191 to zero with two abstentions—the United States and Israel—the UN voted in favor of the resolution (Roth 2016).

It is precisely in economic relations where change has not occurred, despite the packages of measures announced by the Obama administration. The embargo imposes numerous regulations and prohibitions that continue to make it more expensive and more difficult for U.S. business persons and companies to engage in trade or investments with Cuban counterparts.

References

Alzugaray Treto, Carlos. 2010. La seguridad nacional de Cuba frente a los Estados Unidos: conflicto y ¿cooperación? *Revista Temas* 62–63 (April–September): 43–53.

Alzugaray Treto, Carlos, and Anthony Quainton. 2011. Cuba-U.S. Relations: The Terrorism Dimension. *Pensamiento Propio*, 34 (July–December). Accessed April 14, 2017. http://www.cries.org/wp-content/uploads/2012/01/34.pdf.

American Lung Association. 2019. Lung Cancer Fact Sheet. Accessed 3 February 2019. https://www.lung.org/lung-health-and-diseases/lung-disease-lookup/lung-cancer/resource-library/lung-cancer-fact-sheet.html.

Associated Press (AP). 2015. New York Cosmos Beat Cuba 4-1 on Historic Soccer Visit to Havana. *ESPN*, June 2, 2015. Accessed June 5, 2017. http://www.espn.com/soccer/story/2476996/new-york-cosmos-beat-cuba-historic-visit-to-havana.

Bach, Robert, Ralph Espach, and William Rosenau. 2017. *From Threat to Partner? A Regional Security Framework for Engaging Cuba*. CNA Occasional Paper series. Accessed December 27, 2018. https://www.cna.org/cna_files/pdf/COP-2016-U-014218-1Rev.pdf.

Cabañas, José Ramón. 2017. Hitos de las relaciones Cuba-Estados Unidos en el 2016. *Cubadebate*, January 29, 2017. Accessed June 2, 2017. http://www.cubadebate.cu/especiales/2017/01/29/hitos-de-las-relaciones-cuba-estados-unidos-en-el-2016/#.WTG8yuvhDIU.

Caribbean Policy Research Institute (CaPRI). 2016. *The Opening Up of Cuba: Implications for Jamaica of United States Policy Changes Towards Cuba*. October. Accessed June 3, 2017. http://www.capricaribbean.com/sites/default/files/public/documents/report/the_opening_up_of_cuba.pdf.

Cobo, Leila. 2015. Sony Enters Historic Agreement to License Egrem's Catalog of Cuban Music. *Billboard*, September 15, 2015. Accessed June 5, 2017. http://www.billboard.com/articles/news/6699585/sony-egrem-cuban-music-catalog-agreement.

Cubadebate. 2017. Gobernador de Misisipi en visita de trabajo en Cuba. April 20, 2017. Accessed June 2, 2017. http://www.cubadebate.cu/noticias/2017/04/20/gobernador-de-misisipi-en-visita-de-trabajo-en-cuba/#.WTHVFevhDIU.

———. 2017b. Ni un solo balsero cubano se registró el mes pasado, por vez primera en una década. *Cubadebate*, May 11, 2017. Accessed June 3, 2017. http://www.cubadebate.cu/noticias/2017/05/11/ni-un-solo-balsero-cubano-se-registro-en-una-decada-el-mes-pasado/#.WTLHe-vhDIU.

Cubatrade. 2016. Let's Put the US$4.3 Billion in 2015 U.S. Commerce Department Licenses in Perspective … Politics Versus Reality. March 14, 2016. Accessed June 3, 2017. https://www.cubatrade.org/blog/2016/3/13/nidtwnqhvdtl3nmkj8s9l3w7it6xb1.

DeYoung, Karen. 2019. "Trump administration cancels Major League Baseball deal with Cuba", *The Washington Post*, April 8, in https://www.washingtonpost.com/world/national-security/trump-administration-cancels-mlb-deal-with-cuba/2019/04/08/99c7d9be-5a2f-11e9-842d-7d3ed7eb3957_story.html?noredirect=on&utm_term=.c5c10dcf5273. Accessed May 28, 2019.

Diaz, Johnny. 2015. Cuba a New Setting for U.S. TV Productions. *Sun Sentinel*, November 25, 2015. Accessed June 4, 2017. http://www.sun-sentinel.com/features/fl-cuba-tv-american-programs-20151125-story.html.

Domínguez, Jorge I. 2010. Reconfiguración de las relaciones de los Estados Unidos y Cuba. *Revista Temas*, 62–63 (April–September), 4–15.

Dwyer, Mimi. 2016. Priceline Strikes Deal with Cuba to Let Americans Book Hotels. *Reuters*, March 21, 2016. Accessed June 9, 2017. http://www.reuters.com/article/cuba-usa-priceline-group-idUSL2N16T039.

EFE. 2017. Autoridades de Cuba y el puerto de EE.UU. firman un pacto para promover los negocios. October 7, 2017. Accessed June 8, 2018. https://www.efe.com/efe/america/economia/autoridades-de-cuba-y-el-puerto-ee-uu-firman-un-pacto-para-promover-los-negocios/20000011-3401543.

Engage Cuba. 2016. A Timeline of the U.S.-Cuba Relationship Since the Thaw December 17, 2014–Present. December 19, 2016. Accessed June 2, 2017. https://cubacentral.files.wordpress.com/2017/01/0badf-2016-12-19-time-linesincethethaw.pdf.

———. 2017. The Economic Impact of Tightening U.S. Regulations on Cuba. May 31, 2017. Accessed June 2, 2017. https://static1.squarespace.com/static/55806c54e4b0651373f7968a/t/592f36dbdb29d6c96a19e3ea/1496266459829/Economic+Impact+of+Tightening+U.S.+Regs+on+Cuba.pdf.

Franceschi-Bicchierai, Lorenzo. 2015. Twitter Adds Iran, Cuba and 20 Other Countries to Location Options. *Mashable*, January 27, 2015. Accessed June 5, 2017. http://mashable.com/2015/01/27/twitter-iran-cuba/#dZn8ct2w8OqA.

Frank, Priscilla. 2016. Misty Copeland Visits Cuba, Where Brown Ballerinas Are the Norm. *Huffington Post*, December 20, 2016. Accessed June 2, 2017. https://www.huffingtonpost.com/entry/misty-copeland-cuba-ballet_us_58585de4e4b0b3ddfd8e61f7.

Frank, Marc. 2017. Cuba's Raul Castro Meets with U.S. Chamber of Commerce President. *Reuters*, January 13, 2017. Accessed June 2, 2017. http://www.reuters.com/article/us-cuba-usa-commerce-idUSKBN14Y02R.

Frenkel, Sheera. 2017. Google Just Became the First Foreign Internet Company to Launch in Cuba. *CNBC*, April 26, 2017. Accessed June 5, 2017. http://www.cnbc.com/2017/04/26/google-just-became-the-first-foreign-internet-company-to-launch-in-cuba.html.

Gámez Torres, Nora. 2017. No más balseros cubanos, dice Guardia Costera. *El Nuevo Herald*, May 12, 2017. Accessed June 9, 2018. https://www.elnuevoherald.com/noticias/mundo/america-latina/cuba-es/article150156192.html.

Garea Moreda, Bárbara, and Ramón Pichs Madruga. 2016. Developing Regional Capacities to Face Climate Change: Spaces for a Common Cuba-U.S. Agenda. In *Cuba-US Relations: Normalization and Its Challenges*, ed. Margaret E. Crahan and Soraya M. Castro Mariño, 241–258. New York: Institute of Latin American Studies, Columbia University.

Grant, Will. 2016. How Havana Became a Celebrity Magnet – Again. *BBC News*, March 25, 2016. Accessed June 4, 2017. http://www.bbc.com/news/world-latin-america-35866651.

Guzzo, Paul. 2017a. Cuban Port Delegation to Seek Deals in Tampa, Along Gulf Coast. *Tampa Bay*, January 13, 2017. Accessed June 7, 2017. http://www.tampabay.com/news/politics/cuban-port-delegation-to-seek-deals-in-tampa-along-gulf-coast/2309568.

———. 2017b. Port of Alabama Signs Agreement with Cuba That Florida Ports Can't. *Tampa Bay*, February 2, 2017. Accessed June 7, 2017. http://www.tampabay.com/news/politics/port-of-alabama-signs-agreement-with-cuba-that-florida-ports-cant/2311863.

Hemlock, Doreen, and Arlene Satchell. 2015. At Least Four Florida Companies Approved for Ferry Service to Cuba. *Sun Sentinel*, May 5, 2015. Accessed June 5, 2017. http://www.sun-sentinel.com/business/tourism/fl-havana-ferry-approval-20150505-story.html.

Hughes, Neil. 2015. Apple Removes Cuba from Restricted Country Trade List Following Changes by US Government. *Apple Insider*, February 18, 2015. Accessed June 5, 2017. http://appleinsider.com/articles/15/02/18/apple-removes-cuba-from-restricted-country-trade-list-following-changes-by-us-government.

In Focus. 2018. Cuba: U.S. Policy Overview. Congressional Research Service. Updated October 26, 2018. Accessed December 27, 2018. https://fas.org/sgp/crs/row/IF10045.pdf.

Industria Musical. 2015. Sony Music distribuirá el catálogo de EGREM, el más importante de música cubana. December 18, 2015. Accessed February 4, 2019. https://industriamusical.es/tag/empresa-de-grabaciones-y-ediciones-musicales-de-cuba/.

Jorgensen, Gabrielle. 2018. The Dangers of U.S. Withdrawal from a Post-Castro Cuba. *Engage Cuba*, April 16, 2018. Accessed December 27, 2018. https://static1.squarespace.com/static/55806c54e4b0651373f7968a/t/5adbf66803ce64c6836f0c25/1524364904467/The+Dangers+of+US+Withdrawal+from+a+Post-Castro+Cuba.pdf.

Klepak, Hal. 2010. Cuba y los Estados Unidos en las esferas de la defensa y la seguridad. *Revista Temas* 62–63 (April–September): 30–42.

Knobloch, Andreas. 2018. Havana Trade Fair: Cuba Looking East Again. *Deutsche Welle*, October 29, 2018. Accessed January 26, 2019. https://www.dw.com/en/havana-trade-fair-cuba-looking-east-again/a-46055175.

LaBash, Cheryl. 2017. U.S. Ports Welcome Cuban Delegation. *Workers World*, February 4, 2017. Accessed June 7, 2017. http://www.workers.org/2017/02/04/u-s-ports-welcome-cuban-delegation/#.WTiuVes1_IU.

Laguardia Martinez, Jacqueline. 2016. US-Cuba Reviewed Relationship: What Future Is There for the Rest of the Caribbean? *The Pelican*, 14 (January–June): 49–53. The University of the West Indies. Accessed May 27, 2017. https://issuu.com/uwimarketing/docs/uwipelicanissue14.

Lamothe, Dan. 2017. Cuban Migration at Sea Has Plummeted Since Obama Ended 'Wet-Foot, Dry-Foot' Policy, Top Coast Guard Officer Says. *The Washington Post*, April 12, 2017. Accessed June 3, 2017. https://www.washingtonpost.com/news/checkpoint/wp/2017/04/12/cuban-migration-at-sea-has-plummeted-since-obama-ended-wet-foot-dry-foot-policy-top-coast-guard-officer-says/?utm_term=.bbcb1ad75f8b.

Lee, Rensselaer. 2009. Cuba, Drugs, and U.S.-Cuban Relations. *Foreign Policy Research Institute*, April 14, 2009. Accessed February 4, 2019. https://www.fpri.org/article/2009/04/cuba-drugs-and-u-s-cuban-relations/.

Marsh, Sarah. 2017. Blooming U.S. Business Interest in Cuba Wilts Under Trump. *Reuters*, November 10, 2017. Accessed January 18, 2019. https://uk.reuters.com/article/us-cuba-usa-trade/blooming-us-business-interest-in-cuba-wilts-under-trump-idUKKBN1DA1VJ.

McCarthy, Nial. 2017. The Countries with the Highest Refusal Rates for U.S. Visas. *Forbes*, March 24, 2017. Accessed June 7, 2017. https://www.forbes.com/sites/niallmccarthy/2017/03/24/the-countries-with-the-highest-refusal-rates-for-u-s-visas-infographic/#5081af2b13d1.

Ministerio de Relaciones Exteriores de Cuba (MINREX). 2017. Cuba and the United States Signed Twinning Agreement Between Ciénaga de Zapata and Everglades National Parks. Accessed June 9, 2017. http://www.minrex.gob.cu/en/cuba-and-united-states-signed-twinning-agreement-between-cienaga-de-zapata-and-everglades-national.

Montgomery, David. 2016. Smokey Robinson and Other U.S. Artists Hail New 'Love' with Cuba. *The Washington Post*, April 21, 2016. Accessed June 4, 2017. https://www.washingtonpost.com/world/the_americas/smokey-robinson-and-other-us-artists-hail-new-love-with-cuba/2016/04/21/8f7ed6d4-07de-11e6-bfed-ef65dff5970d_story.html?postshare=6861461276496135&tid=ss_tw&utm_term=.55e66486dfe0.

Morales, Emilio. 2017. Remittances to Cuba in 2016 Grow by 2.7%. *The Havana Consulting Group and Tech*, July 20, 2017. Accessed June 9, 2018. http://www.thehavanaconsultinggroup.com/Rejected-By-UrlScan/Articles/Article/30?AspxAutoDetectCookieSupport=1.

———. 2018. La importancia de las remesas en la economía cubana. *The Havana Consulting Group and Tech*, August 26, 2018. Accessed December 9, 2018. http://www.thehavanaconsultinggroup.com/(X(1)S(0uyeasjnvl5wr4og2perng4a))/es-es/Articles/Article/68.

Mufson, Steven. 2016. Starwood Signs Historic Deals in Cuba for Three Havana Hotels. *The Washington Post*, March 19, 2016. Accessed June 4, 2017. https://www.washingtonpost.com/business/economy/starwood-signs-deals-in-cuba-for-three-havana-hotels/2016/03/19/4eb2e9c6-ee1e-11e5-b0fd-073d5930a7b7_story.html?utm_term=.1bbb5afb6575.

National Oceanic and Atmospheric Administration (NOAA). 2016. U.S., Cuba Agree on Efforts to Improve Maritime Navigation Safety, March 21, 2016. Accessed May 28, 2019. https://www.noaa.gov/media-release/us-cuba-agree-on-efforts-to-improve-maritime-navigation-safety.

On Cuba. 2016. Cuba and United States in Favor of Protecting Nature. December 23, 2016. Accessed June 9, 2017. http://oncubamagazine.com/science/cuba-and-united-states-in-favor-of-protecting-nature/.

Padgett, Tim. 2016. Cuba Rejects Ballyhooed Plan for a U.S. Factory on the Island. *WRLN*, November 4, 2016. Accessed June 9, 2017. http://wlrn.org/post/cuba-rejects-ballyhooed-plan-us-factory-island.

Perelló Cabrera, José Luis. 2017a. El turismo internacional en Cuba y sus implicaciones en el Caribe ante un escenario de relaciones diplomáticas con los Estados Unidos. In *Cuba en sus relaciones con el resto del Caribe: continuidades y rupturas tras el restablecimiento de las relaciones diplomáticas entre Cuba y los Estados Unidos*, ed. Jacqueline Laguardia Martinez, 63–77. Buenos Aires: El Consejo Latinoamericano de Ciencias Sociales (CLACSO).

———. 2017b. Exitoso desempeño del turismo de cruceros en Cuba. *Excelencias News Cuba*, November 17, 2017. Accessed December 21, 2017. https://www.excelenciascuba.com/noticia/exitoso-desempeno-del-turismo-de-cruceros-en-cuba.

Peters, Philip. 2009. Diplomacy with Cuba and U.S. National Security. *Lexington Institute*, April 29, 2009. Accessed November 24, 2018. https://www.lexingtoninstitute.org/diplomacy-with-cuba-and-u-s-national-security/.

Piccone, Ted. 2018. U.S.-Cuban Relations Are About to Get Worse. *Brookings*, April 16, 2018. Accessed January 3, 2019. https://www.brookings.edu/blog/order-from-chaos/2018/04/16/u-s-cuban-relations-are-about-to-get-worse/.

Prensa Latina. 2016. Ministerial Visits Encourage Bilateral Exchange Between Cuba and USA. *Escambray*, July 19, 2016. Accessed June 4, 2017. http://en.escambray.cu/2016/ministerial-visits-encourage-bilateral-exchange-between-cuba-and-usa/.

———. 2017. American Airlines and JetBlue for More Flights to Cuba. December 13, 2017. Accessed January 5, 2018. http://plenglish.com/index.php?o=rn&id=22204&SEO=american-airlines-and-jetblue-for-more-flights-to-cuba.

Rathke, Jeff. 2015. Rescission of Cuba as a State Sponsor of Terrorism. Press statement. *U.S. Department of State*, May 29, 2015. Accessed June 2, 2017. https://2009-2017.state.gov/r/pa/prs/ps/2015/05/242986.htm.

Representaciones Diplomáticas de Cuba en el Exterior. 2017. Bilateral Instruments Adopted Between Cuba and the United States After 12/17/14. Accessed January 3, 2019. http://misiones.minrex.gob.cu/en/articulo/bilateral-instruments-adopted-between-cuba-and-united-states-after-121714.

———. 2018. The US State Department Uses the Granting of Visas to Affect Diplomatic Relations with Cuba. Accessed January 3, 2019. http://misiones.minrex.gob.cu/en/articulo/us-state-department-uses-granting-visas-affect-diplomatic-relations-cuba.

Reuters. 2017. Charcoal Becomes First Cuban Export to United States in Half a Century. January 5, 2017. Accessed June 2, 2017. http://www.reuters.com/article/us-cuba-usa-export-idUSKBN14Q0DB.

Rosetti, Philip, and Andrew Holland. 2015. Potential Areas of Cooperation Between the United States and Cuba. American Security Project, June. Accessed December 27, 2018. https://www.americansecurityproject.org/wp-content/uploads/2015/06/Ref-0193-Potential-Areas-of-Cooperation-US-and-Cuba.pdf.

Ross Johnson, Steven. 2017. Cuban Doctors Could Offer Best Practices on Improving Community Health in Chicago. *Modern Healthcare*, January 17, 2017. Accessed June 2, 2017. http://www.modernhealthcare.com/article/20170117/NEWS/170119941.

Roth, Richard. 2016. US Changes Vote on UN Resolution Against Cuba Embargo. *CNN*, October 26, 2016. Accessed June 4, 2017. http://edition.cnn.com/2016/10/26/politics/un-resolution-cuba-embargo-us-abstains/index.html.

Rusin, Sylvia, Jie Zong, and Jeanne Batalova. 2015. Cuban Immigrants in the United States. *Migration Information Source*, April 7, 2015. Migration Policy Institute. Accessed January 2, 2019. https://www.migrationpolicy.org/article/cuban-immigrants-united-states.

Sagebien, Julia, and Eric Leenson. 2016. Cuba's Chance to Get Back to the Future … in a Sustainable Way. In *Cuba-US Relations: Normalization and Its Challenges*, ed. Margaret E. Crahan and Soraya M. Castro Mariño, 259–282. New York: Institute of Latin American Studies, Columbia University.

Sato, Erika. 2016. Cuba's Tourism, the Embargo, and the Environment. *Council on Hemispheric Affairs*, June 7, 2016. Accessed June 9, 2017. http://www.coha.org/cubas-tourism-the-embargo-and-the-environment/.

Scott, Dylan. 2016. Obama Administration Signs Historic Health Agreement. *Huffington Post*, June 14, 2016. Accessed June 7, 2017. http://www.huffingtonpost.com/stat/obama-administration-signs-historic-health-agreement_b_10458026.html.

Sirius XM Holdings Inc. 2015. Sirius XM's Joe Madison the Black Eagle Airs Live from Cuba in Historic Broadcast. *PR Newswire*, June 11, 2015. Accessed June 5, 2017. http://www.prnewswire.com/news-releases/siriusxms-joe-madison-the-black-eagle-airs-live-from-cuba-in-historic-broadcast-300098020.html.

Thale, Geoff. 2016. U.S.-Cuba Security Cooperation After D17: Opportunities and Challenges. In *Cuba-US Relations: Normalization and Its Challenges*, ed. Margaret E. Crahan and Soraya M. Castro Mariño, 225–240. New York: Institute of Latin American Studies, Columbia University.

Thale, Geoff, and Marguerite Rose Jiménez. 2018. Why the U.S. Should Deepen Security Cooperation with Cuba. *WOLA*, April 13, 2018. Accessed November 24, 2018. https://www.wola.org/analysis/us-deepen-security-cooperation-cuba/.

The Cuba Consortium. 2016. The Opening to Cuba: Annual Report of the Cuba Consortium. October 3, 2016. Accessed June 3, 2017. http://files.thecubaconsortium.org/media/TheCubaConsortiumAnnualReport11.3.16.pdf.

The White House, n.d. Changing Course in Cuba: The Progress We've Made Since 2014. Accessed June 2, 2017. https://obamawhitehouse.archives.gov/issues/foreign-policy/cuba.

The White House Office of the Press Secretary. 2017. Statement by the President on Cuban Immigration Policy. January 12, 2017. Accessed June 2, 2017. https://obamawhitehouse.archives.gov/the-press-office/2017/01/12/statement-president-cuban-immigration-policy.

Trotta, Daniel, and Sarah Marsh. 2018. Cuban Deal with MLB Allows Players to Sign Without Defecting. *Reuters*, December 19, 2018. Accessed January 4, 2019. https://www.reuters.com/article/us-usa-cuba-baseball/cuban-deal-with-mlb-allows-players-to-sign-without-defecting-idUSKCN1OI2L5.

Tugend, Alina. 2016. Cuba in All Its Natural Glory at the American Museum of Natural History. *The New York Times*, October 24, 2016. Accessed June 4, 2017. https://www.nytimes.com/2016/10/30/arts/design/cuba-in-all-its-natural-glory-at-the-american-museum-of-natural-history.html.

Tvevad, Jesper. 2015. Cuba, the USA and the EU: Forging Closer Ties, Looking to the Future. European Union. Document DG EXPO/B/PolDep/Note/2015_287. Accessed June 3, 2017. http://www.europarl.europa.eu/RegData/etudes/IDAN/2015/549075/EXPO_IDA(2015)549075_EN.pdf.

U.S. Chamber of Commerce. 2016. U.S.-Cuba One Year Anniversary of Re-Established Diplomatic Relations. Accessed November 4, 2017. https://www.uschamber.com/issue-brief/us-cuba-one-year-anniversary-re-established-diplomatic-relations.

U.S. Department of Agriculture. 2017. U.S.-Cuba Animal and Plant Health Memorandum of Understanding. Accessed June 7, 2017. https://www.fas.usda.gov/sites/default/files/2017-02/signed_animal_plant_health_mou_english_spanish_01_2017.pdf.

U.S. Department of Homeland Security. 2016. Statement by Press Secretary Marsha Catron on Deputy Secretary Mayorkas' Upcoming Trip to Cuba. Accessed June 7, 2017. https://www.dhs.gov/news/2016/05/13/statement-press-secretary-marsha-catron-deputy-secretary-mayorkas-upcoming-trip-cuba.

U.S. Department of State. 2016. Counternarcotics Arrangement Signed During Third Counternarcotics Technical Exchange Between the United States and Cuba. Accessed January 3, 2019. https://2009-2017.state.gov/r/pa/prs/ps/2016/07/260396.htm.

———. 2017. United States and Cuba Sign Maritime Boundary Treaty. Accessed June 7, 2017. https://2009-2017.state.gov/r/pa/prs/ps/2017/01/267117.htm.

———. 2018. United States and Cuba Hold Biannual Migration Talks in Washington, DC. Accessed January 3, 2019. https://www.state.gov/r/pa/prs/ps/2018/07/284020.htm.

U.S. Department of the Treasury. 2015a. Fact Sheet: Treasury and Commerce Announce Regulatory Amendments to the Cuba Sanctions. Accessed June 2, 2017. https://www.treasury.gov/press-center/press-releases/Pages/jl9740.aspx.

———. 2015b. Treasury and Commerce Announce Further Amendments to the Cuba Sanctions Regulations. Accessed June 2, 2017. https://www.treasury.gov/press-center/press-releases/Pages/jl0169.aspx.

———. 2016a. Treasury and Commerce Announce Further Amendments to Cuba Sanctions Regulations. Accessed June 2, 2017. https://www.treasury.gov/press-center/press-releases/Pages/jl0328.aspx?mod=article_inline.

———. 2016b. Treasury and Commerce Announce Further Amendments to Cuba Sanctions Regulations. Accessed June 2, 2017. https://www.treasury.gov/press-center/press-releases/Pages/jl0581.aspx.

———. 2016c. Treasury and Commerce Announce Significant Amendments to the Cuba Sanctions Regulations Ahead of President Obama's Historic Trip to Cuba. Accessed June 2, 2017. https://www.treasury.gov/press-center/press-releases/Pages/jl0379.aspx.

———. 2017. Cuba Designations Removals. Accessed June 2, 2017. https://www.treasury.gov/resource-center/sanctions/OFAC-Enforcement/Pages/20170106.aspx.

U.S. Embassy in Cuba. 2016. Counternarcotics Arrangement Signed During Third Counternarcotics Technical Exchange Between the United States and Cuba. Accessed November 3, 2017. https://cu.usembassy.gov/counternarcotics-arrangement-signed-third-counternarcotics-technical-exchange-united-states-cuba/.

———. 2019. Decreasing B2 Visa Validity for Cuban Nationals. Accessed March 16, 2019. https://cu.usembassy.gov/decreasing-b2-visa-validity-for-cuban-nationals/.

U.S.-Cuba Trade and Economic Council, Inc. n.d. U.S. Companies with a Presence in Cuba Since 17 December 2014. Accessed January 18, 2019. https://static1.squarespace.com/static/563a4585e4b00d0211e8dd7e/t/5c2e41b370a6ad1b09a6dee4/1546535347973/USCompaniesAndCuba.pdf.

Western Union. 2016. Western Union Pioneers Digital Money Transfer to Cuba. June 7, 2016. Accessed June 7, 2017. http://ir.westernunion.com/news/archived-press-releases/press-release-details/2016/Western-Union-Pioneers-Digital-Money-Transfer-to-Cuba/default.aspx.

Whitefield, Mimi. 2017. Could 1 Million More Cubans Be Deemed Ineligible for Remittances? *Miami Herald*, June 23, 2017. Accessed December 29, 2018. https://www.miamiherald.com/news/nation-world/world/americas/cuba/article157721249.html.

———. 2018a. Has President Trump's Year-Old Cuba Policy Helped the Cuban People? *Miami Herald*, June 14, 2018. Accessed December 28, 2018. https://www.miamiherald.com/news/nation-world/world/americas/cuba/article212497419.html.

———. 2018b. After a Wave of Enthusiasm, American Companies' Interest in Cuba As a Business Partner Cools. *Miami Herald*, October 31, 2018. Accessed January 18, 2019. https://www.miamiherald.com/news/nation-world/world/americas/cuba/article220335990.html.

WSVN. 2016. TV Series Shoots in Havana Amid Growing Demand for Filming in Cuba. January 23, 2016. Accessed June 4, 2017. http://wsvn.com/news/tv-series-shoots-in-havana-amid-growing-demand-for-filming-in-cuba/.

CHAPTER 6

Limits on the Cuba-U.S. Relationship

In light of the advances made since December 17, 2014 (17D), in the diplomatic relationship between the United States and Cuba, as outlined so far, this chapter examines more closely the obstacles—both those that have remained and those that are new—which hinder the advancement of the bilateral relationship. Most of the areas discussed below relate to challenges in the immediate post-17D environment. At the same time, any such discussion must also analyze the role of policy adjustments under President Donald Trump and how these pose limits to the evolving Cuba-U.S. relationship. This chapter also discusses expectations unmet and the difficulties surrounding the implementation of the measures announced by the United States, particularly in the economic sphere.

Difficulties for Bilateral Trade

Several factors hinder bilateral trade relations between the two countries. One of these is the fact that U.S. products that can be sold to Cuba are very limited. The list of U.S. exports that can be sent to Cuba, in compliance with the new measures put in place since 17D without the authorization of the U.S. Department of Commerce, is limited to "only telecommunications products and services, construction materials and equipment and tools for use in the non-State sector of the economy" (Republic of Cuba 2016, 7). The sale of other U.S. products and services is prohibited—unless authorized by the U.S. Department of Commerce,

© The Author(s) 2020
J. Laguardia Martinez et al., *Changing Cuba-U.S. Relations*,
https://doi.org/10.1007/978-3-030-20366-5_6

through specific approved permits which expire after a stipulated period of time (Republic of Cuba 2016).

U.S. agricultural exports are possible due to the 2000 Trade Sanctions Reform and Export Enhancement Act (TSRA). In November 2001, the United States exported food to Cuba in more than 40 years following a request from the Cuban government after Hurricane Michelle hit the island. From 2003 to 2012, the United States was the leading exporter of agricultural goods to Cuba, becoming second in 2013 and third in 2014 behind the EU and Brazil. Between 2012 and 2014, U.S. agricultural exports to Cuba totaled USD 365 million per year, with chicken meat, corn, soybean meal, and soybeans representing 84 percent of the total value (Zahniser and Cooke 2015). Exports from Alabama, in particular, increased to over USD 126 million in 2004. Cuba accounted for a quarter of Alabama's agricultural export revenue in 2006 (Copeland et al. 2011). Cuba is a net food importer; the island imports around 70 percent of the food it consumes (Muñoz Puente 2016). Figure 6.1 shows recent figures of U.S. exports to Cuba. Piccone (in Anderson and Piccone 2017) has indicated that U.S. exports of food to Cuba will continue to decline because of U.S. law: under U.S. law, Cuba cannot receive credit and

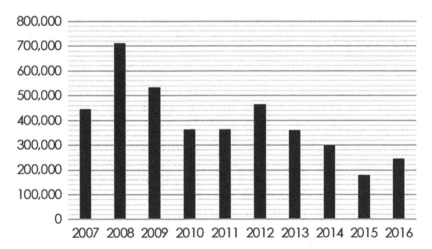

Fig. 6.1 U.S. exports to Cuba, 2007–2016 (in USD thousands). Source: U.S. Census Bureau (n.d.)

therefore must purchase in cash upfront from the United States. Given that Havana can make purchases on credit from neighboring countries like Mexico, Argentina, and Brazil, this makes purchasing from the United States a less attractive option (ibid.).

A second obstacle to bilateral trade relations is that U.S. imports of Cuban goods are practically zero (Kotschwar and Cimino 2015). Authorizations to import are given for Cuban goods and services produced by the non-state sector. This excludes tobacco, nickel, rum, and biotechnological products, as well as medical and educational services. Even if these goods and services were permitted entry into the United States, the tariffs imposed on them would be among the highest in the U.S. Harmonized Tariffs Schedule because Cuba has been placed in the most restrictive category of importation tariffs in the schedule and also because the country does not benefit from most favored nation treatment (Republic of Cuba 2016).

In May 2016, the U.S. Department of State announced that coffee was among the products that Cuba could export to the United States. In that same month, Cuba's National Association of Small Farmers denounced this, pointing out that it had been impossible for them to export Cuban coffee to the United States due to high tariffs; the practical impossibility of using U.S. dollars in international transactions; and the ban that still exists on U.S. companies engaging in any kind of business transactions involving foreign trade with Cuban state-owned enterprises (ANAP 2016). Still today Cuban state enterprises cannot export to the U.S. market and U.S. affiliated firms in third countries cannot maintain economic relations with Cuban entities (Romero 2016).

Changes to maritime transportation norms to allow ships participating in "humanitarian trade and commerce" with Cuba to enter U.S. ports prior to 180 days after having touched Cuban ports are not in force. According to Cuba's 2016 report on United Nations (UN) General Assembly Resolution 70/5, on the necessity of ending the U.S. embargo against it: "it is also quite improbable that ships moving commercial cargos to Cuba would limit themselves to transporting foods, medicines, medical equipment or the other U.S.-authorized exports" since "shipping contracts are not restricted to the transport of one single type of product" (Republic of Cuba 2016, 7).

Using gravity model analysis, Hufbauer and Kotschwar (2014) estimate that under normalized relations, U.S. exports of goods and services to Cuba could reach USD 6 billion per year, while Cuban exports to the

United States could reach USD 7 billion. There is no record of bilateral trade in services, and consequently, the estimated gains would start from a low baseline: USD 2 billion in U.S. service exports to Cuba, and USD 1 billion in Cuban service exports to the United States. With full normalization, Cuba could attract USD 2 billion of foreign direct investment (FDI) from the United States (Kotschwar and Cimino 2015). Cuba needs imports to support investment and for consumption (food, consumer goods, consumer durables), and U.S. exporters are best positioned to address these needs (Engage Cuba 2017). The U.S. Department of Agriculture projects that once restrictions placed on exports are fully removed, U.S. agricultural sales could reach USD 1 billion (Kotschwar and Cimino 2015). It must be noted that business competitors from countries like China, Russia, and Brazil, among others, which are already established in Cuba, are poised to expand if U.S. companies are kept out (Engage Cuba 2017).

Difficulties for Financial Relations

One of the main obstacles preventing smoother financial relations between Cuba and the United States is the fact that the Helms-Burton Act is still in force—the ban on financial operations remains in place in spite of the measures taken by the Obama administration (Kotschwar and Cimino 2015). The Cuban government has confirmed that the authorization to use U.S. dollars in Cuba's international transactions has not materialized, since Cuban institutions have not been able to use U.S. dollars for international transactions; nor has the possibility materialized for U.S. banks to provide loans to Cuban importers of authorized U.S. products. Cuban banks are forbidden to open corresponding accounts in U.S. banks (Republic of Cuba 2016; Ramírez Cañedo 2017). Cuba's 2016 report on UN General Assembly Resolution 70/5 indicates that:

> this restriction prevents establishing direct banking relations between the two countries and makes Cuba's commercial operations with that country more expensive due to the necessity of triangulating them and paying commissions to intermediaries. The negative repercussions of strengthening the financial persecution of Cuban transactions and their marked extraterritorial nature during the last seven years continues to manifest in the continued refusal by banks in the United States and other countries to make transfers with Cuba, even in other currencies other than the U.S. dollar. (Republic of Cuba 2016, 8)

In addition, even though the use of debit and credit cards in Cuba was allowed by the Obama administration, only one bank—the Stonegate Bank—has been authorized to offer Mastercards for use in Cuba. Many legal and financial obstacles impede the implementation of this measure; most of them related to limitations established by the embargo (Weissenstein 2016).

The U.S. government has not issued any official statement or legal document that would clarify the framework of the revised financial relations, neither has explained to banks that business with Cuba is legitimate and that sanctions will not be levied against them (Vidal 2016). Adding to the misperception is the fact that the United States has continued to enforce penalties on banks and foreign financial entities that engage in business with Cuba (Romero 2016). Since the announcements of 17D, the U.S. government has fined 11 entities—seven U.S. companies and four foreign entities—to the tune of USD 2.9 billion in total. Until mid-January 2017, there had been 52 accounted fines imposed during the Obama administration for violations of sanctions against Cuba and other countries. The accumulated value of the penalties amounts to USD 14.4 billion (Cubadebate 2017a). Some of the companies fined after 17D are WATG Holdings Inc., PayPal Inc., CGG Services, and Halliburton (Ensign 2015).

These sanctions result in a feeling of intimidation among U.S. and international banks. Foreign financial institutions have refused to process Cuban banking transactions, including the World Bank's International Financial Corporation; Bank of the Bahamas; Royal Bank of Canada; Mitsui Sumitomo of Japan; and Spanish banks, Santander and Caixa Bank (Cubadebate 2017b).

Difficulties for U.S. Investments in Cuba

Except in the case of telecommunications, U.S. investments in Cuba are not authorized under general licenses. In November 2016, Cuba denied approval to the proposal of the Cleber Company to build small, low-cost tractors in the Mariel Special Development Zone (*Zona Especial de Desarrollo Mariel*, simply called ZED Mariel). Among the reasons given by Cuban officials for this move was that they were looking for more high-tech ventures for the zone. Cuba says Cleber can still pursue a factory outside ZED Mariel, but the company would lose all the duty and ownership benefits that it could benefit from if it were operating within the zone (Padgett 2016).

In 2014, Cuba passed a new foreign investment law to attract capital to key economic sectors such as tourism, mining, and other industries. However, investors have complained about the slow pace of, and bureaucracy involved in, project evaluation and approval. In December 2016, President Raúl Castro criticized the excessive delays of the negotiating process and urged overcoming the obsolete mentality, one full of prejudice, against foreign investment (Castro Morales 2017).

The Trump Administration's Cuba Policy[1]

During his campaign, presidential candidate Donald Trump indicated several times that creating an avenue that leads to the opening up of Cuba is logical, but he believed that President Barack Obama had not negotiated well enough to the advantage of the United States. He also suggested that he would close the U.S. embassy in Havana until a better deal was forthcoming from the Cuban side (The Cuba Consortium 2016; Wootson 2016). Conversely, as a candidate, Trump came under scrutiny following allegations that he had violated the U.S. embargo against Cuba in the 1990s. A *Newsweek* story said that Trump had spent USD 68,000 to send business consultants to Cuba (Eichenwald 2016).

As President-elect, Trump weighed in twice on the death of former Cuban leader, Fidel Castro. First, he offered up a four-word tweet shortly after 8 a.m. on November 25, 2016, saying simply: "Fidel Castro is dead!" He followed that up a few hours later with a lengthier statement, in which he called Castro a "brutal dictator" and said that "our administration will do all it can to ensure the Cuban people can finally begin their journey toward prosperity and liberty" (Wootson 2016). In May 2017, President Trump insisted on the idea that "[t]he Cuban people deserve a government that peacefully upholds democratic values, economic liberties, religious freedoms, and human rights, and [his] Administration is committed to achieving that vision" (The White House Office of the Press Secretary 2017).

In February 2017, the White House announced that a comprehensive review of U.S. policy on Cuba was being carried out, under the direction of the National Security Council, and that human rights on the island—a

---

[1] The authors wish to recognize the contribution of Miss Marissa Diaz, Research Assistant at The University of the West Indies (UWI) Institute of International Relations in the preparation of this section.

major point of contention between the two countries—would be a key aspect of any future strategies concerning Cuba (Spetalnick 2017).

Once the review was completed, President Trump revealed a revised U.S. policy toward Cuba on June 16, 2017. The White House (2017) outlined the four main objectives of the president's new policy:

1. Focusing on compliance with U.S. law, specifically the embargo and a ban on self-organized people-to-people trips
2. Holding the Cuban government accountable for oppression and human rights abuses
3. Advancing the national security and foreign policy interests of the United States and those of the citizens of Cuba
4. Empowering the Cuban people to develop their economic and political freedom

To implement President Trump's policy changes, the U.S. Departments of the Treasury and Commerce amended the Cuban Assets Control Regulations (CACR) and Export Administration Regulations (EAR) in November 2017. The new regulations require people-to-people travel to be under the auspices of an organization specializing in such trips and forbid financial transactions with organizations controlled by the Cuban military. The U.S. Department of State took complementary action by publishing a list of 180 such entities, including "2 ministries, 5 holding companies and 34 of their sub-entities—including the Mariel ZED – 84 hotels, 2 tourist agencies, 5 marinas, 10 stores in Old Havana, and 38 entities serving the defense and security sectors" (U.S. Department of State 2017; In Focus 2018). On March 2019, new entities were added to the list, four of them hotels, to the list of firms "controlled by military services". The first expansion to the list was registered on November 2018, when 26 entities (16 of them hotels) were added (Cubadebate 2019).

The ban on self-organized people-to-people trips is essentially a reversal of policy under the Obama administration and goes back to the previous policy which prohibited individual visits, and authorized visits only as part of groups licensed by the Department of the Treasury and accompanied by a group representative (DeYoung 2017). This ban has had an adverse impact on U.S. visitor flows because it discourages visitors and it is very difficult to ensure that tourist dollars do not flow to companies associated with the Cuban military or party hierarchy (Betancourt 2017).

During the first three months of 2018, Cuba recorded a 7 percent decline in overall tourism due partly to the sharp drop in U.S. travel to Cuba. U.S. visitor travel to Cuba is only 56.6 percent of what it was in 2017. This decrease in U.S. "tourism" is a result of President Trump's stricter travel restrictions; U.S. and Canadian governments advisoried against travel to Cuba following alleged health attacks (discussed below) and the effects of Hurricane Irma and tropical storm Alberto (Sesin 2018). In 2018, over 4,750,000 international visitors arrived in Cuba (Luis Castro and Besada Basabe 2018).

Piccone (2018) contends that President Trump's election pledge to "cancel" former President Obama's normalization policy is likely to see Cuba-U.S. relations go from "bad to worse", a situation that can adversely impact security cooperation. Signs of an impending reversal by the Trump administration to the previous stance are already visible. Travel warnings have again become part of the toolbox used by the U.S. Department of State because of the health incidents that occurred at the U.S. embassy in Havana.

Precisely a key episode that has further deteriorated the bilateral relationship under the Trump administration is the claim, made by the U.S. Department of State, that 26 members of its embassy community in Havana had suffered hearing loss and cognitive issues. The related incidents were reported to have occurred from November 2016 to August 2017, with two further incidents occurring in May 2018. The Department of State maintains that the U.S. investigation has not reached any definitive conclusion regarding the cause or source of the incidents, or any kind of technologies that may have been used in them. The Federal Bureau of Investigation (FBI), however, revealed that their investigations had not uncovered any kind of acoustic attack. The resulting reduction in staff at the U.S. embassy in Havana has affected consular operations and has made bilateral engagement more difficult. Furthermore, in January 2019, the results of research done by scientists[2] indicate that the sounds heard by the U.S. diplomats may have been coming from a cricket species found in the Caribbean (Brueck 2019).

To deepen the setback on the U.S.-Cuba policy, in April 2019, the White House announced that the United States will no longer suspend Title III of the Helms–Burton Act. Since President Clinton, Title III has been periodically suspended to avoid conflicts with foreign investors in

---

[2] The scientists are Alexander Stubbs of the University of California, Berkeley, in the United States and Fernando Montealegre-Zapata of the University of Lincoln in the UK (AP and Tidey 2019).

Cuba, mostly from Europe and Canada. The current situation allows U.S. courts to penalize third-party companies since they are allegedly "trafficking" in property formerly owned by U.S. citizens and by Cubans who have become U.S. citizens but nationalized after 1959 (Cohen and Hansler 2019). Under the Trump administration, efforts continue to overthrow the Cuban government. The U.S. Congress has provided funding for democracy assistance and for sponsoring broadcasting to Cuba. For the 2017 financial year, Congress appropriated USD 20 million in funds for democracy promotion in Cuba and USD 28.1 million for broadcasting to the island. For 2018, Congress appropriated the same amount for democracy programs and USD 28.9 million for broadcasting. For 2019, the administration requested USD 10 million for democracy assistance to Cuba and USD 13.7 million for broadcasting. The House Appropriations Committee's State Department and Foreign Operations Bill, H.R. 6385, was expected to approve USD 30 million for democracy programs, while the Senate committee's version, S. 3108, was expected to approve USD 15 million in 2019. Both bills were expected to provide USD 29 million for broadcasting (In Focus 2018).

The antagonistic freeze in the Cuba-U.S. relationship has impacted negatively not only on the tone of the bilateral dialogue but also on the possibility of short and medium-term progress. Due to the significant asymmetries between the two countries, the freeze and partial step back have had acute adverse impacts on Cuba. The effects have turned out to be quite negative for that part of the Cuban private sector heavily dependent on tourism and for bilateral cooperation on issues like migration, and academic, scientific, and cultural exchanges, among others. Also, it has discouraged foreign investors and partners from participating in joint economic projects with Cuba, for fear of financial penalties under U.S. sanctions against Cuba.

The Trump administration's partial reversal of Obama-era policies toward Cuba may have serious repercussions for the United States as well. According to a study released by Engage Cuba (2017), the policy reversal would cost the U.S. economy USD 6.6 billion and affect 12,295 American jobs during President Trump's first term in office. The addition of restrictions on travel to, and trade with, Cuba is most damaging to those communities that are highly dependent on the agricultural, manufacturing, and shipping industries. The new regulations concerning agriculture-related exports to Cuba could cost the United States a further USD 1.5 billion and affect 2205 more U.S. jobs. This assessment does not include agricultural and medical exports as allowances were made in 2001, by the U.S.

Congress for limited exports in these sectors (before the changes instituted by the Obama administration). Enforcing these regulations against Cuba would principally threaten the creation of jobs and the growth of the economy in the Gulf states, which include Alabama, Florida, Georgia, Louisiana, Mississippi, and Texas—all states that supported President Trump in the 2016 election. Box 6.1 summarizes some of the consequences that the United States could face by reversing Obama-era adjustments.

> **Box 6.1 Cost Summary for the United States, According to Engage Cuba Report**
>
> Travel: U.S. travel to Cuba was liberalized through expanding legal travel in 12 categories, self-authorization, and allowing both airlines and cruise lines to offer passenger service to the island. Rolling back expanded travel could cost airlines and cruise lines USD 3.5 million and affect 10,154 jobs in those industries.
>
> Manufacturing: manufacturing companies in the energy, chemical, and technology industries are finalizing commercial contracts that will create USD 929 million worth of exports from the United States to Cuba up to 2020. Revoking authorization for manufacturing exports would deal a blow of nearly USD 1 million to American businesses and could cost up to 1359 jobs.
>
> Remittances: over four years, cutting the remittance flow could cost American money transfer companies USD 1.2 million and affect 782 jobs. Additionally, the increased flow of remittances has significantly helped Cuba's growing private sector.
>
> Immigration: in January 2017, the Obama administration and Cuba reached a deal to end the wet foot, dry foot policy, which granted permanent residency to Cuban immigrants who arrived in the United States by land. Because the policy granted refugees access to federal social and health care entitlements, reinstating it would cost U.S. taxpayers USD 953 million.
>
> Notes: All estimates represent an accumulated cost over the four years of President Donald Trump's first term in office. Estimates do not include agricultural exports, which would bring the totals to USD 8.1 million and 14,500 jobs.
>
> Source: Engage Cuba (2017)

President Trump's policy on Cuba seeks to reaffirm the embargo and opposes calls at the UN and other international fora for its termination. In 2017 at the United Nations General Assembly calling for the United States to lift its embargo against Cuba, the U.S. outright opposed, action that was a clear indication of a reversal to the old posture of confrontation, different from the 2016 U.S. vote on the resolution (UN News Centre 2017). The same decision was taken in 2018. The approach of the U.S. Congress to Cuba after 2017 is also a significant area deserving of attention. As positions on the embargo cross party lines, it is difficult to anticipate the final position of Congress on this issue.

Even more worrying are the labeling of Cuba, Nicaragua, and Venezuela—all with leftist-leaning governments—as a "troika of tyranny" by U.S. National Security Adviser John Bolton in November 2018 and the imposition of new sanctions on Cuba and Venezuela, with the promise of similar actions against Nicaragua (MercoPress 2018). This hard-line policy position against countries deemed socialist by the Trump administration has triggered renewed fears that the United States will miss out on real opportunities to secure peace, prosperity, and stability in its "backyard".

In response to Bolton's troika of tyranny labeling and the imposition of sanctions by the U.S. government, Cuban President Miguel Díaz-Canel met with the Russian President, Vladimir Putin, and signed several agreements, bolstering Cuban-Russian relations. These included agreements in the sectors of energy, transportation, metallurgy, and biotechnology, among others, to address Cuba's energy security, and railway infrastructure development on the island (Puig Meneses 2018). This may be a sign of another phase in Cuba-Russia engagement, with Cuba having once again become a prime national security interest for both Russia and China, and with Moscow as well as Beijing each seeking to woo the new Díaz-Canel administration and establish a firm military and commercial presence in Cuba. One example to reinforce this idea comes from 2017, when 16 retired U.S. military flag officers sent a letter with their concerns to General H.R. McMaster, then the National Security Adviser in the Trump administration. In the letter, the officers advocated for continuing a policy of bilateral engagement with Cuba, based on the growing threat posed by Russian and Chinese expansion and the security risks of allowing current Cuba-U.S. collaboration to disintegrate (Jorgensen 2018, 7).

While Russia's defense minister announced, in 2016, the possibility of reopening military bases in Cuba, China has become Cuba's largest trading partner and holder of Cuban government debt (Eaton and Mcginnis

2017). Chinese telecommunications giant Huawei is now in direct competition with Google to provide Internet access throughout Cuba (Eaton and Mcginnis 2017). The significance of both Russia and China vying for influence in Cuba, which is situated less than 100 miles from the United States, cannot be overstated. At a time when the Trump administration is being "bullish" on its policies toward Cuba, and Latin America in general, its "America First" rhetoric may ring hollow if Russia and China succeed in establishing a firm presence in Cuba.

In addition to these policies toward Cuba, other Trump administration foreign policy priorities must also be taken into consideration. There are five foreign policy concerns so far that have been recognized as being central to the early Trump era, and seem critical to track: the U.S.-Mexico border, Russia, the defense budget, trade, and the Islamic State of Iraq and Syria (ISIS) (Beauchamp et al. 2017). The commercial confrontation with China has added as another key issue as well. In other words, Latin America and the Caribbean—Cuba included—seem not to be key concerns for the Trump administration except for the Venezuelan crisis that demands the U.S. attention intermittently. With Cuba, the interest seems to be driven by the will of dismantling Obama's legacy and winning Republican sympathies toward the 2020 electoral campaign.

Concluding Reflections

There is room to keep advancing in the normalization process between Cuba and the United States, if it is the will of the U.S. president. In 2009, a report by the Brookings Institution recognized that despite having to depend on Congress to legislate policy change on Cuba, past events have demonstrated that U.S. presidents retain the authority to adopt measures that either reinforce or weaken the embargo according to their discretion. For example, a U.S. president could essentially lift the current trade embargo, by using the licensing authority to permit U.S. exports of specified goods and services, as well as reciprocal trade encompassing a broad range of different goods and services, and to allow an extensive range of categories of travel (Brookings Institution 2009, 6). Furthermore, the U.S. president has the constitutional authority to override specific limits imposed by Congress—such as the tourist travel ban—and to waive certain restrictions that in his consideration are contrary to U.S. foreign policy interests.

It means that the process of removing more U.S. sanctions against Cuba was stalled with the election of Donald Trump as President. This is unfortunate, since the entire embargo can be virtually undone with bold executive action (Heifetz and Jeydel 2016). Since the U.S. Congress has specifically prohibited only a handful of activities related to Cuba, this leaves open a broad range of potential activities that can yet receive authorization. The Secretary of the Treasury, for example, could allow U.S. manufacturing and energy companies to commence operations in Cuba.

Even though the Trump administration has taken several steps back from the Obama administration's Cuba policy, it remains unclear as to the exact policy toward Cuba that the current administration will fully commit to: "We do not know if Trump's next tweet will reflect the man obsessed with reversing everything Obama did, or the one who dreams of a Trump Tower in Havana" (Reid, cited in Sosin 2017). There are three main possible alternatives, in relation to President Obama's legacy: (1) continuity; (2) reversion; and (3) freezing. Let us consider that a main feature of Trump presidency has been its apparent unpredictably.

According to Grabendorff (2017), the shift in Trump's policy toward Cuba can be best characterized as a half-measure, to satisfy both the Cuban American politicians who wish to reverse President Obama's policies, on the one side, and U.S. business interests in Cuba, on the other.

The actions taken by the current U.S. government indicate a clear stalling, and potential reversal, of what had already been done. Deep divisions remain on critical issues, including the embargo, Guantánamo Bay Naval Base, and human rights, among others. However, Cuba's economic reforms and international engagements will almost certainly continue to expand (Bach et al. 2017).

Very few countries have been as dependent for their economic development on external actors as Cuba has been. Since the triumph of the Cuban Revolution in 1959, the country has suffered from the impact of international politics related to ideological, economic, and geopolitical factors (Grabendorff 2017). Being a Caribbean small island developing state, this dependence on external actors and its related dynamics will continue in the future. The role of the United States, a superpower located less than 100 miles from the island, must be taken into consideration in Cuba's foreign policy and international relations.

As Cuba undergoes significant political and economic changes, at the same time that Russia and China are extending their influence into the Western Hemisphere, the United States should recognize that its national security interests are at risk and take steps to engage with the new government of Cuba led by President Díaz-Canel. A logical first step would be to fully re-staff the U.S. embassy in Havana (Jorgensen 2018).

References

Anderson, Ric, and Ted Piccone. 2017. The Direction of U.S.-Cuba Relations Under Trump: An Interview with Ted Piccone. *Brookings*, April 17, 2017. Accessed June 9, 2017. https://www.brookings.edu/blog/order-from-chaos/2017/04/17/the-direction-of-u-s-cuba-relations-under-trump-an-interview-with-ted-piccone/.

Asociación Nacional de Agricultores Pequeños (ANAP). 2016. No es posible exportar café cubano a EEUU: declaración de la ANAP. *Cubadebate*, May 5, 2016. Accessed June 4, 2017. http://www.cubadebate.cu/noticias/2016/05/05/no-es-posible-exportar-cafe-cubano-a-eeuu-declaracion-de-la-.

Associated Press (AP) and Alice Tidey. 2019. Crickets Behind 'Sonic Attack' on US Staff in Cuba, Scientists Say. *EURONEWS*, January 8, 2019. Accessed February 6, 2019. https://www.euronews.com/2019/01/08/crickets-behind-sonic-attack-on-us-staff-in-cuba-scientists-say.

Bach, Robert, Ralph Espach, and William Rosenau. 2017. *From Threat to Partner? A Regional Security Framework for Engaging Cuba*. CNA Occasional Paper series. Accessed December 27, 2018. https://www.cna.org/cna_files/pdf/COP-2016-U-014218-1Rev.pdf.

Beauchamp, Zack, Yochi Dreazen, Zeeshan Aleem, and Sarah Wildman. 2017. President Trump's Speech to Congress: 5 Foreign Policy Issues to Watch For. *Vox*, February 28, 2017. Accessed June 9, 2017. https://www.vox.com/world/2017/2/28/14761182/president-trump-speech-congress-2017-foreign-policy.

Betancourt, Roger. 2017. *Cuba's Normalization Policy in a Trump Administration: Political Economy Perspectives*. 2017 Annual Proceedings: The Association for the Study of the Cuban Economy 27. Accessed December 30, 2018. https://www.ascecuba.org/c/wp-content/uploads/2018/01/v27-betancourt.pdf.

Brookings Institution. 2009. *Cuba: A New Policy of Critical and Constructive Engagement*. Report of the Brookings Project on U.S. Policy Toward a Cuba in Transition. Accessed June 2, 2017. http://www2.fiu.edu/~ipor/cuba-t/BrookingsCubaReport-English.pdf.

Brueck, Hilary. 2019. Mysterious 'Sonic Attacks' on US Diplomats in Cuba May Just Have Been Loud Caribbean Crickets. *Business Insider*, January 7, 2019. Accessed February 9, 2019. https://www.businessinsider.com/sonic-attacks-on-us-diplomats-in-cuba-crickets-2019-1.

Castro Morales, Yudy. 2017. Sacudirle las demoras a la inversión extranjera. *Granma*, December 21, 2017. Accessed January 26, 2019. http://www.granma.cu/cuba/2017-12-21/sacudirle-las-demoras-a-la-inversion-extranjera-21-12-2017-00-12-02.

Cohen, Zachary, and Jennifer Hansler. 2019. Trump Expected to Become First President to Target Cuba with this Controversial Policy. *CNN*. April 17, 2019. Accessed 04 28, 2019. https://edition.cnn.com/2019/04/16/politics/us-cuba-title-iii-venezuela/index.html.

Copeland, Cassandra, Curtis Jolly, and Henry Thompson. 2011. The History and Potential of Trade Between Cuba and the US. *Journal of Economics and Business*. Fox School of Business, Temple University, Philadelphia, PI, United States. Accessed April 13, 2017. http://www.auburn.edu/~thomph1/cuba-history.pdf.

Cubadebate. 2017a. *Impone Departamento del Tesoro nuevas multas por violaciones del bloqueo a Cuba*. January 16, 2017. Accessed June 2, 2017. http://www.cubadebate.cu/noticias/2017/01/16/impone-el-departamento-del-tesoro-nuevas-multas-por-violaciones-del-bloqueo-a-cuba/#.WTHWQ-vhDIU.

———. 2017b. *Washington retira de su lista de sanciones a 28 empresas e individuos que comercian con Cuba*. January 8, 2017. Accessed June 2, 2017. http://www.cubadebate.cu/noticias/2017/01/08/washington-retira-de-su-lista-de-sanciones-a-28-empresas-e-individuos-que-comercian-con-cuba/#.WTHWvevhDIU.

———. 2019. EEUU agrega cinco entidades cubanas a su "lista negra". March 11, 2019. Accessed March 12, 2019. http://www.cubadebate.cu/noticias/2019/03/11/eeuu-agrega-cinco-entidades-cubanas-a-su-lista-negra/#.XI2GeiJKjIU.

DeYoung, Karen. 2017. White House Implements New Cuba Policy Restricting Travel and Trade. *The Washington Post*, November 8, 2017. Accessed February 3, 2019. https://www.washingtonpost.com/world/national-security/white-house-implements-new-cuba-policy-restricting-travel-and-trade/2017/11/08/a5597dee-c49b-11e7-aae0-cb18a8c29c65_story.html?utm_term=.af7202d89a35.

Eaton, Paul D., and David L. Mcginnis. 2017. Trump's Critical Cuba Policy. *Politico*, May 17, 2017. Accessed February 3, 2019. https://www.politico.com/agenda/story/2017/05/17/trump-cuba-policy-threat-national-security-000442.

Eichenwald, Kurt. 2016. How Donald Trump's Company Violated the United States Embargo Against Cuba. *Newsweek*, September 29, 2016. Accessed June 4, 2017. http://www.newsweek.com/2016/10/14/donald-trump-cuban-embargo-castro-violated-florida-504059.html.

Engage Cuba. 2017. *The Economic Impact of Tightening U.S. Regulations on Cuba*. May 31, 2017. Accessed June 2, 2017. https://static1.squarespace.com/static/55806c54e4b0651373f7968a/t/592f36dbdb29d6c96a19e3ea/1496266459829/Economic+Impact+of+Tightening+U.S.+Regs+on+Cuba.pdf.

Ensign, Rachel Louise. 2015. PayPal to Pay $7.7 Million to U.S. Over Alleged Sanctions Violations. *The Wall Street Journal*, March 25, 2015. Accessed June 4, 2017. https://www.wsj.com/articles/paypal-to-pay-7-7-million-to-u-s-over-alleged-sanctions-violations-1427312161.

Grabendorff, Wolf. 2017. Cuba: The Challenges of Change. *Cuba y el proceso de actualización en la era de Trump in Pensamiento Propio* 45: 33–56.

Heifetz, Stephen, and Peter Jeydel. 2016. Time to Finally End the Cuba Embargo. *The Hill*, October 27, 2016. Accessed May 31, 2018. https://thehill.com/blogs/congress-blog/foreign-policy/303098-time-to-finally-end-the-cuba-embargo.

Hufbauer, Gary Clyde, and Barbara Kotschwar. 2014. *Economic Normalization with Cuba: A Roadmap for US Policymakers*. Washington, DC: Peterson Institute for International Economics.

In Focus. 2018. *Cuba: U.S. Policy Overview*. Congressional Research Service. Updated October 26, 2018. Accessed December 27, 2018. https://fas.org/sgp/crs/row/IF10045.pdf.

Jorgensen, Gabrielle. 2018. The Dangers of U.S. Withdrawal from a Post-Castro Cuba. *Engage Cuba*, April 16, 2018. Accessed December 27, 2018. https://static1.squarespace.com/static/55806c54e4b0651373f7968a/t/5adbf66803ce64e6836f0c25/1524364904467/The+Dangers+of+US+Withdrawal+from+a+Post-Castro+Cuba.pdf.

Kotschwar, Barbara, and Cathleen Cimino. 2015. *Towards Economic Normalization with Cuba: A Roadmap for US Policymakers*. Statement for United States International Trade Commission hearing on no. 332–552, "Overview of Cuban Imports of Goods and Services and Effects of US Restriction". June 2, 2015. Accessed May 27, 2017. https://usitc.gov/press_room/documents/testimony/332_552_012.pdf.

Luis Castro, Haroldo Miguel, and Alejandro Besada Basabe. 2018. ¿Cómo le fue al turismo en Cuba en 2018? *Cubahora*, December 28, 2018. Accessed December 30, 2018. http://www.cubahora.cu/economia/como-le-fue-el-turismo-en-cuba-en-2018-infografia.

MercoPress. 2018. More US Sanctions on the 'Troika of Tyranny' and Its Three Dictator 'Stooges'. November 2, 2018. Accessed December 30, 2018. http://en.mercopress.com/2018/11/02/more-us-sanctions-on-the-troika-of-tyranny-and-its-three-dictator-stooges.

Muñoz Puente, Carmen. 2016. El sector agroalimentario, el más atractivo para invertir en Cuba. *El País*, August 17, 2016. Accessed June 9, 2017. https://cincodias.elpais.com/cincodias/2016/08/17/empresas/1471458056_178440.html.

Padgett, Tim. 2016. Cuba Rejects Ballyhooed Plan for a U.S. Factory on the Island. *WRLN*, November 4, 2016. Accessed June 9, 2017. http://wlrn.org/post/cuba-rejects-ballyhooed-plan-us-factory-island.

Piccone, Ted. 2018. U.S.-Cuban Relations Are About to Get Worse. *Brookings*, April 16, 2018. Accessed January 3, 2019. https://www.brookings.edu/blog/order-from-chaos/2018/04/16/u-s-cuban-relations-are-about-to-get-worse/.

Puig Meneses, Yaima. 2018. Notes from an Important Visit. *Granma*, November 7, 2018. Accessed February 3, 2019. http://en.granma.cu/mundo/2018-11-07/notes-from-an-important-visit.

Ramírez Cañedo, Elier. 2017. Logros y frustraciones a tres años del 17D. *Juventud Rebelde*, December 16, 2017. Accessed February 3, 2019. http://www.juventudrebelde.cu/internacionales/2017-12-16/logros-y-frustraciones-a-tres-anos-del-17d.
Republic of Cuba. 2016. *Cuba's Report on Resolution 70/5 of the United Nations General Assembly: Necessity of Ending the Economic, Commercial and Financial Blockade Imposed by the United States of America Against Cuba*. June. Accessed June 3, 2017. http://www.cubavsbloqueo.cu/sites/default/files/Informe Bloqueo2016EN.pdf.
Romero, Antonio. 2016. *Re-Establishing Diplomatic Relations Between Cuba and USA: Economic Implications for Caribbean*. Paper presented at the Tenth International Conference on Caribbean Studies, Havana, Cuba, December 7, 2016.
Sesin, Carmen. 2018. Sharp Decline in US Travel to Cuba Spurs Overall Drop in Tourism for the Island. *NBC News*, April 25, 2018. Accessed December 10, 2018. https://www.nbcnews.com/news/latino/sharp-decline-u-s-travel-cuba-spurs-overall-drop-tourism-n868856.
Sosin, Eileen. 2017. La normalización con los Estados Unidos: ¿hacia dónde? *Revista Temas*, June 1, 2017. Accessed June 3, 2017. http://www.temas.cult.cu/catalejo/la-normalizaci-n-con-los-estados-unidos-hacia-d-nde.
Spetalnick, Matt. 2017. Trump Administration Nearing Completion of Cuba Policy Review: Sources. *Reuters*, May 30, 2017. Accessed June 5, 2017. http://www.reuters.com/article/us-cuba-usa-trump-idUSKBN18Q09D.
The Cuba Consortium. 2016. *The Opening to Cuba: Annual Report of the Cuba Consortium*. October 3, 2016. Accessed June 3, 2017. http://files.thecubaconsortium.org/media/TheCubaConsortiumAnnualReport11.3.16.pdf.
The White House. 2017. *Fact Sheet on Cuba Policy*. Accessed November 11, 2017. https://www.whitehouse.gov/blog/2017/06/16/fact-sheet-cuba-policy.
The White House Office of the Press Secretary. 2017. Statement from President Donald J. Trump on Cuban Independence Day. May 20, 2017. Accessed June 2, 2017. https://www.whitehouse.gov/the-press-office/2017/05/21/statement-president-donald-j-trump-cuban-independence-day.
U.S. Census Bureau. n.d. U.S. Exports to Cuba by 5-Digit End-Use Code: 2007–2016. Accessed June 3, 2017. https://www.census.gov/foreign-trade/statistics/product/enduse/exports/c2390.html.
U.S. Department of State. 2017. United States and Cuba Sign Maritime Boundary Treaty. Accessed June 7, 2017. https://2009-2017.state.gov/r/pa/prs/ps/2017/01/267117.htm.
United Nations (UN) News Centre. 2017. *UN General Assembly Again Calls for Lifting US Embargo Against Cuba*. November 1, 2017. Accessed January 5, 2018. http://www.un.org/apps/news/story.asp?NewsID=58011#.WlBGTlWnHMU.

Vidal, Josefina. 2016. The Blockade Is an Outdated Policy and Must End. Interviewed by Sergio Alejandro Gómez. *Granma*, July 20, 2016. Accessed June 3, 2017. http://en.granma.cu/cuba/2016-07-20/the-blockade-is-an-outdated-policy-and-must-end.

Weissenstein, Michael. 2016. Florida Bank Issues First US Credit Card for Use in Cuba. *AP News*, June 14, 2016. Accessed June 4, 2017. https://apnews.com/b325b8b31f8640bb9e0e350df43c8e5e/florida-bank-issues-first-us-credit-card-use-cuba.

Wootson, Cleve R., Jr. 2016. How Donald Trump Responded to the Death of Fidel Castro, 'a Brutal Dictator'. *The Washington Post*, November 26, 2016. Accessed June 4, 2017. https://www.washingtonpost.com/news/the-fix/wp/2016/11/26/here-is-donald-trumps-reaction-to-fidel-castros-death/?utm_term=.138bed4b9a40.

Zahniser, Steven, and Bryce Cooke. 2015. U.S.-Cuba Agricultural Trade: Past, Present, and Possible Future. *USDA, Economic Research Service*, August 3, 2015. Accessed March 4, 2017. https://www.ers.usda.gov/amber-waves/2015/august/us-cuba-agricultural-trade-past-present-and-possible-future/.

CHAPTER 7

Factors and Actors Impacting Cuba-U.S. Relations

This chapter summarizes the factors and actors that are either driving or obstructing positive shifts in Cuba-U.S. relations. For this chapter, the input provided by the experts interviewed proved to be fundamental. Among the identified factors which drove 17D, were U.S. fear of diplomatic isolation in the Hemisphere, Obama's push for a more stable global system and Washington's desire to undermine progressive regional integration, expanding economic opportunities in Cuba, shared Cuba-U.S. security concerns, and existing transcultural ties between populations on both sides. Factors posing obstacles include divergent views on what normalization means, economic and political asymmetries, persistent ideological differences and unresolved issues surrounding sovereignty and territorial integrity. Actors impacting on the new era of Cuba-U.S. relations include states (Canada, Latin America and the Caribbean countries), the younger generation of Cuban diplomats, Pope Francis and the Catholic Church, civil society groups, academics, think tanks, and segments of the U.S. business community.

FACTORS PROMOTING POSITIVE CHANGE IN CUBA-U.S. RELATIONS

A major factor that promoted change in Cuba-U.S. relations, based on the responses of interviewees, was recognition on the part of the United States that its old policy toward Cuba had failed to accomplish its intended goal and that a new strategy—one centered on "smart power" and diplomacy—could be more effective. President Barack Obama was left with the conviction that the then U.S. policy toward Cuba was a failed policy. This became evident in his statement on changes to U.S.-Cuba policy on December 17, 2014 (17D), in which he highlighted that not only did the old policy *not* work, but it had only served to isolate the United States from other countries and from the Cuban people:

> we will end an outdated approach that, for decades, has failed to advance our interests, and instead we will begin to normalize relations between our two countries ... these 50 years have shown that isolation has not worked. It's time for a new approach ... I am convinced that through a policy of engagement, we can more effectively stand up for our values and help the Cuban people help themselves as they move into the 21st century ... I do not believe we can keep doing the same thing for over five decades and expect a different result. (Obama 2014)

Former U.S. Deputy Secretary of State, Antony J. Blinken, recognized that the embargo had good intentions, at least from a U.S. political perspective, but that it has not been effective; therefore, it made sense to try something different. According to Deputy Secretary Blinken, opening up the relationship is the best way to achieve the objectives of those who supported the embargo since it would allow the Cuban people to have more contact with the world and with the United States (Rizzi 2015). The measures taken intended to strengthen the Cuban middle class and private sector and were seen as the best instrument to achieve a "free, prosperous and democratic Cuba" (ibid.).

Another factor that contributed positively to the opening up of relations was President Obama's foreign policy goal of dismantling leftist trends in Latin America and the Caribbean. The policy toward Cuba is compatible with a framework of hemispheric relations in which political heterogeneity is perhaps its most distinctive feature. The change in Cuba--U.S. relations should have an impact on intra-hemispheric relations, especially in terms of better using Cuba's capacity to contribute to regional cooperation. This includes potential partnership schemes with the United States, especially considering, for example, the success of their cooperation in the fight against Ebola in West Africa (Monreal González 2015).

According to Ramírez Cañedo (2017), by promoting a rapprochement with Cuba, the United States also aimed to:

1. promote confusion and division among governments, social movements, and leftist sectors who might believe that the Cuban Revolution had given way by engaging in diplomatic relations with the United States;
2. diminish the influence of key global actors such as Russia and China;
3. undermine regional integration and cooperation initiatives such as the Community of Latin American and Caribbean States (CELAC), the Bolivarian Alliance for the Peoples of Our America – Peoples' Trade Treaty (ALBA-TCP), and PetroCaribe; and
4. reduce the symbolic reference that Cuba represents for the region and the world—a small island asserting its sovereignty against a hegemonic power.

For Latin American and Caribbean left-wing forces, the Cuba-U.S. conflict has been part of the imaginary of resistance for more than half a century. Changes in the bilateral relationship represent an important challenge for popular movements and revolutionary forces on the continent (Alzugaray Treto 2015; Feinberg 2015a).

The impact of Cuba's engagement with Latin America and the Caribbean, therefore, cannot be underestimated. As Latin American and Caribbean integration intensified in the early 2000s, Cuba increasingly assumed a role as an equal partner. Latin American and Caribbean political cooperation facilitated the reintegration of Cuba into the hemispheric community. Although political and ideological diversity exists in the region, as reflected in the Pacific and Atlantic axes, as well as positions regarding Venezuela, it has not served as a major impediment to Cuba's insertion in hemispheric affairs. Cuba shares to a fair extent the Latin American and Caribbean positions on a region-wide political, socio-economic, and security agenda. Priority items include poverty and inequality reduction, and the promotion of sustainable development, effective educational and public health systems, food security, and disaster risk reduction. There is regional consensus about the need for changes in the international financial architecture; about the need for cooperation in combatting terrorism, human and drug trafficking, and transnational criminal cartels; and on the importance of national and regional sovereignty, all of which have helped solidify Cuba's incorporation into the regional context and increase pressure for a change in U.S. policy (Marín Suárez 2016; Leogrande 2015a; Romero 2015; Serbin 2016; Lopez-Levy 2015).

In June 2009, the 39th General Assembly of the Organization of American States (OAS), held in San Pedro Sula, Honduras, unanimously decided to cancel the 1962 resolution excluding Cuba from the organization, thereby confirming that most Latin American and Caribbean governments agreed on Cuba's returning into the regional organization (Serbin 2016). In 2014, at the Summit of the Americas held in Santiago, Chile, the United States stood alone on two points: its policy toward Cuba and the war on drugs (Chomsky in Muñiz and Pardo 2016).

Cuba's interactions at the international level are also significant, especially its dialogue with the European Union (EU). In 2014, before 17D, Cuba and the EU opened negotiations on a bilateral Political Dialogue and Cooperation Agreement (PDCA). These negotiations were completed after seven rounds in March 2016, and then in December 2016, the PDCA was signed. This agreement represented a first of its kind between the EU and Cuba, established a revised legal framework for EU-Cuba relations, and anticipated improved political discourse, enhanced mutual collaboration, and the advancement of cooperative action in multilateral arenas (European Council 2016).

Another factor that has contributed to positively developing Cuba-U.S. relations relates to the potential economic opportunities (trade, investment, finance) Cuba could offer to the U.S. business community. Cuba has mineral deposits of chromite, cobalt, copper, iron, nickel, manganese, tungsten, and zinc, as well as unexplored petroleum potential. The major agriculture exports from Cuba are cigars, citrus, coffee, fish, and sugar. These crops complement U.S. cotton, feed grains, meat, poultry, rice, soybeans, and wheat; and U.S. investment could revive Cuban livestock (Copeland et al. 2011).

Cuba is recognized as a potential market of 11 million consumers with a highly educated and healthy labor force, low crime rates, and countless unexploited opportunities to start businesses in almost every sector. Cuba is interested in having the United States as an economic and trading partner, and as a source of tourists and foreign direct investment (FDI) (Alzugaray Treto 2017a).

Currently, and depending on if the exports will be beneficial to the citizens of Cuba, the U.S. Department of the Treasury offers licenses for U.S. exports to Cuban state businesses, with each case being considered individually. This policy, along with the manner in which it is assessed, could be expanded to U.S. investments in Cuba, including those in joint enterprises with Cuban firms. As it now stands, the list of goods and services coming from Cuban private enterprises that are allowed to be exported to the United States has the potential to be more encompassing, including, for instance, Cuban-produced pharmaceuticals (the Cuba Consortium 2016; Leogrande 2016).

As alluded to earlier, Cuba is also continuing to make progress in the implementation of its "Lineamientos de la Política Económica y Social del Partido y la Revolución" (Economic and Social Policy Guidelines of the Party and the Revolution). The guidelines target attraction of investment to increase Cuban productive capacity (Republic of Cuba 2011). Cuba does not have the capacity to largely export manufactured goods, but this would develop with foreign investment. Investment is needed in telecommunications, agriculture, construction, housing, pharmaceuticals and biotechnology, energy and tourism.

Facilities in the sphere of tourism development have also experienced an increase. At the end of 2015, the number of rooms in the tourism sector totaled 63,657. Most of them were distributed across 372 facilities of the five main Cuban hotel companies: Gaviota (24,497); Cubanacán (15,463); Gran Caribe (12,169); Islazul (9925); and Habaguanex (598) (Perelló Cabrera 2017, 69).

Cuban private entrepreneurship has expanded on the island, fueled by increased travel and remittances from the United States (Engage Cuba 2016). The Cuban government could facilitate the process toward normalization by easing import and export licenses for non-state sector Cuban businesses, as well as by reducing the bureaucratic requirements for U.S. businesses interested in trade and investments with the island, with the result that proposals receive more timely responses. Also, foreign businesses could be allowed to hire their workforce directly, rather than having to go through a state employment agency.

As indicated by some of the interviewees (CARICOM 04; Cuba 03, 08), the opening of the Cuban economy would help the country achieve its socio-economic goals in a sustainable manner, and even more so if the blockade is removed. Furthermore, the influence that the United States exerts on the global market makes positive engagement between the two countries a more attractive prospect for Cuba. While commercial advantages are to be achieved by the United States vis-à-vis investing in Cuba, this also reinforces to the international community that Cuba is a safe place for investment. These new opportunities will not impact solely on the Cuban economy, but also extend to bearing positive impact at regional and international levels. At the same time, the Cuban government needs to continue to improve basic infrastructure, including energy, transportation, and communications—especially the Internet—and to move ahead with the promised currency unification, so exchange rates are clear and businesses can accurately assess their costs (Leogrande 2016; The Cuba Consortium 2016). Cuba is interested in normalizing its participation in the international financial system, and normal relations with the United States are fundamental for achieving this goal.

As discussed in Chap. 5, shared security concerns have also propelled the Cuba-U.S. relationship forward. Both countries have a mutual interest in collaborating to deal with transnational criminal cartels, border controls, and financial crimes, including money laundering and cybercrime; and to combat human trafficking (Alzugaray Treto 2010).

The strong transcultural ties between the two countries also contribute to the advances made. Contact between Cubans and U.S. people has been occurring systematically since the nineteenth century (Pérez 2008). There is extensive knowledge in Cuba about the United States, and U.S. cultural production is highly consumed—similar to what happens in the rest of Latin America and the world—and contacts between artists, intellectuals, scientists, and military officials have developed despite political differences and the bilateral conflict (Alzugaray Treto 2017a; Leogrande 2015b; Bustamante 2015; Domínguez 2010; Hernández Trejo 2007; Fernández Pérez 2007). There is a large Cuban diaspora in the United States, mainly in Florida. More relations between the peoples of both countries can only help in building mutual trust (Monreal González 2015; Hernández Martínez 2015).

Factors Impacting Negatively on Cuba-U.S. Relations

One of the fundamental issues to consider here is "normalization" does not mean the same for the United States and Cuba. Normalization of diplomatic relations means that acting on equal terms and on the basis of reciprocity, both countries will develop relations founded on respect based on the principles of the UN Charter and international law (Valdés Paz 2015). Given the conflicted history of Cuba and the United States, their asymmetries, and their proximity, this kind of relationship might be difficult to establish since relations between them have never been "normal": the two countries cannot restore something that has never existed (Salinas Figueredo 2017; Vidal 2016; Pertierra 2015; Hernández 2010; Alonso 2015). This is supported by the views of the experts interviewed. The collective view is that what has been taking place cannot be considered normalization once certain elements remain in place and present obstacles to substantial changes in the current relationship. This section highlights some of these obstacles.

The normalization process is complex and often contradictory since it does not mean the same for all actors included in the negotiation. Both the Cuban and U.S. negotiators have admitted that the process is difficult and progress in introducing new regulations and directives has been slow and arduous (Salinas Figueredo 2017; Vidal 2015, 2016; Feinberg 2015a). Among the challenges is developing a common vocabulary regarding issues of sovereignty, democracy, and human rights, for instance.

One of the more obvious challenges to normalization rests in the fact that there exist fundamental ideological differences between the U.S. and Cuba. The United States' understanding of democracy, political and civil liberties, and social and economic rights is remarkably different from Cuba's vision (Lage Dávila 2016; Hernández 2016; The Cuba Consortium 2016; Alonso 2015). Liberal representative democracy, rooted in a political party's system, as well as checks and balances between the three branches of government, has served as a basis for the U.S. concept of national sovereignty. In Cuba, the Spanish legacy has inclined the country toward a stronger executive branch and weaker system of checks and balances by the legislative and judicial branches (Miller and Piccone 2016), reinforced by the socialist system built upon participatory democracy that does not recognize political parties—the Communist Party of Cuba (PCC) is not a political party as the concept is understood by Western democracies. At the same time, the renewed relations do not change the fact that the foreign policies of both countries continue to be determined by interests of different types that are not just dissimilar, but also antagonistic. The core of the issue at hand here is that the cessation of open hostility does not mean the end of discrepancies (Monreal González 2015; Hernández Martínez 2015). According to Cuba's top negotiator, Josefina Vidal (2015):

> It cannot be expected that in order to improve relations with the United States, or to advance in this long, complex process toward normalization which we have before us, that Cuba is going to negotiate questions of an internal nature, in exchange for a policy change on the part of the United States, when

they themselves recognize that it has failed. Nor are we going to negotiate questions of an internal nature, of Cuban sovereignty, in exchange for the lifting of the blockade. Beyond this, during the negotiation process, anything which does not compromise state sovereignty, everything else can be part of the negotiation process ... We were able to identify, on the basis of absolute respect for sovereign equality and the independence of our countries, very important questions in which we share common interests and which we could resolve.

There is also tension that results from acknowledging that there can be no complete normalization until the following issues are addressed: the embargo, Guantánamo Bay Naval Base, U.S. financing to groups and individuals promoting a regime change in Cuba, and the mutual claims for reparation (Vidal 2015, 2016; Vidal in Elizalde 2015). One of the key ideas raised by the interviewees centered on the idea that a continuation of the blockade does not encourage or help to promote the spirit of 17D: "normalization" cannot occur if there does not exist a mutual recognition of equality between the two countries and if the United States continues to use the blockade as leverage to coerce Cuba into doing what it wants.

Concern also stems from having to reaffirm Havana's independence in its foreign policy. Cuba's government will continue to conduct an independent foreign policy, which implies an anti-hegemonic stance against the United States trying to impose their decisions on the rest of the world, particularly on Latin America and the Caribbean. Therefore, the attempt at engaging in a different way with the United States does not imply that Cuba is renouncing its foreign policy principles; rather, the country remains committed to the protection of peoples' right to self-determination, and support for other countries on cooperation initiatives on health care and education mostly (Vidal 2016; Alzugaray Treto 2017b).

In order to avoid U.S. interventionism in Cuba's domestic affairs, in the context of their long history of conflict and significant asymmetries (Lopez-Levy 2015), Cuba continues to carefully evaluate its next steps and did not rush the normalization process under the Obama presidency. Because of the unevenness in their relationship, exacerbated by years of political hostility, it is difficult for Cuba to adopt anything other than a reactionary response to actions stemming from the United States. This does not imply that Cuba is helpless as a global actor: its interaction in the wider Caribbean region with CARICOM, its status as a symbol of imperial resistance within Latin America and the world, and the assistance it offers and relations it pursues, and maintains, with major actors outside of the region all demonstrate the capacity that Cuba has to maneuver in the global system and affirm its place within it.

The persistence on the part of the United States to promote regime change in Cuba must also be considered an obstacle to normalization. Cuba is the only country whose domestic political regime the United States is "still committed by law and policy to replace, albeit by peaceful means" (Domínguez 1997). Since 1995, the United States Agency for International Development (USAID) and the U.S. Department of State have been conducting programs that are intended to peacefully promote a shift to democracy in Cuba which Cuba considers as illegal interference in its affairs. Because of this, the Cuban government often mistrusts U.S. approaches, arguing that U.S. support to nongovernmental organizations and private groups in Cuba is supportive of efforts to destabilize their social and political institutions. For instance, the USAID has been directly involved in a series of "democracy promotion programs" that the Cuban government understands as explicit actions to overthrow the Revolution. Cuba has criminalized involvement with these programs. Notwithstanding the changes instituted during his presidency, the Obama administration maintained the support to these programs, and as it currently stands, they are not subject to negotiation (The Cuba Consortium 2016; Leogrande 2015a). This stance is being further reinforced by the Trump administration that recognizes that any future potential improvements in the Cuba-U.S. relationship remain largely dependent on "the Cuban government's willingness to improve the lives of the Cuban people by promoting rule of law and taking concrete steps toward greater political and economic freedoms" (The White House 2017).

In January 2016, the U.S. State Department's Bureau of Democracy, Human Rights, and Labor distributed a request for proposals to spend USD 5.6 million on "Programs Fostering Civil, Political, and Labor Rights in Cuba". The National Endowment for Democracy (NED) continues to be a major recipient of funds from USAID. Its 2017 programs to promote democracy in Cuba were allocated USD 3.8 million. Among the several grants were included: USD 220,000 to the *Asociación Diario de Cuba* for the promotion of freedom of expression; USD 99,997 to the *Instituto Político para la Libertad Perú*, which aimed to encourage a pro-democracy mindset among young Cuban political activists; USD 127,974 to the *Observatorio Cubano de Derechos Humanos*, which sought to highlight human rights violations in Cuba at the international level; and USD 110,000 to the Center for a Free Cuba for humanitarian and logistical support for human rights activists (NED n.d.). Miami-based Radio and TV Martí, established in 1984 on the model of Radio Free Europe, are still in operation and are considered central to the democratic transition in Cuba, as well as a powerful instrument the United States has in place to help shape the regime change (Johnson and Wimbush 2015). Cuba regards all this as interference in its internal affairs and as violating international broadcasting standards.

Bilateral relations have not erased the contradiction between the U.S. desire to intervene in the island's domestic issues and Cuba's determination to be independent (Vidal 2016; Toledo Sande 2015; Leogrande 2015b). Some of the interviewees for this research indicated that, from the Cuban perspective, it is important to note that the new nature of their engagement with the United States has not masked the nature of their engagements in the past (Cuba 02, 04, 07). President Obama's visit to Cuba helped to create a more positive image of the U.S. presidency and promoted the idea that friendly relations are possible, but this cannot wipe off all that has transpired in the past, especially—as one interviewee (Cuba 02) reminded us—the loss of lives on Cubana de Aviación Flight 455 in 1976, and the lack of recourse taken against Posada Carriles in the United States.

On the occasion of President Obama's visit in 2016, Fidel Castro published a commentary in Cuba's main newspaper *Granma* which was accompanied by critical comments from others, indicating that distrust of U.S. motives remains among Cuban leaders and intellectuals (F. Castro 2016a; Pérez Benítez 2016; Ramírez Cañedo 2016a; August 2016; Sánchez 2016; Ubieta 2016; Machado Rodríguez 2016; González 2016; Rodríguez Rivera 2016; Hernández 2016). In the Central Report to the Seventh Congress of the PCC, presented in April 2016, President Raúl Castro warned Cubans about U.S. imperial intentions: "Relations with the United States have historically represented a challenge for Cuba, given their permanent pretension of exercising domination over our nation, and the determination of Cubans to be free and independent" (R. Castro 2016b). For many Cubans, the United States is an imperialist power that has historically been opposed to Cuba's independence, and therefore everything that comes from the northern neighbor must be viewed with suspicion; while for many U.S. Americans, the Cuban government or "los Castro" is a horrible communist tyrannical regime that constitutes a latent danger for the United States. These stereotypes generate distrust and may change as bilateral contacts and relations increase (Alzugaray Treto 2015; Romero 2015).

This mistrust was linked to the view of some interviewees (CARICOM 02; Cuba 01, 02, 04; U.S. 01, 03) that the Obama-era strategy would be ineffective because of what they considered as the underlying motivating factor for this "soft power" approach. Generally, this approach was seen as an extension of the subversive tactics traditionally employed by the United States toward Cuba. These interviewees were conscious of the fact that the United States has the power to influence the domestic affairs of Cuba, and consequently, Cuba needed to remain aware that the change in U.S. strategy did not imply a change in the U.S. objective of subverting the Cuban model. While Cuba recognizes that there are elements of its system that can be improved, the United States must recognize Cuba's sovereignty and not try to interfere in its affairs.

Some interviewees (CARICOM 03, 04, 05; Cuba 03, 05, 06, 07, 08; U.S. 02) had predicted that the Obama-era strategy would be a more effective approach than the more aggressive one of the past, and that the change in strategy and methods, coupled with constant dialogue, is a better approach—although it would not completely guarantee a fulfillment of U.S. objectives. Cuba is willing to keep communication between the two countries open, once the United States stops making threats to its sovereignty: in response to Trump policy, Cuban President Miguel Díaz-Canel acquiesces that the relationship between the two countries is in decline, but insists that Cuba will "maintain channels of dialogue" and does not "reject the possibility of dialogue at any time, but it must be between equals" (*Eyewitness News* 2018).

Furthermore, the slow advance of the normalization process and the persistence of the embargo inhibit any kind of significant progress forward. In the current political context, expectations have ceded to skepticism. In the United States, agricultural producers have seen imports from Cuba decline after 17D as compared to figures from 2008. In Cuba, mainly small businesses in the form of private restaurants and rental houses, and tourism-orientated service providers were the ones benefitting from the 17D. Under the Trump restrictions on business interactions with Cuba, the island's private sector is expected to be most negatively affected as "some 60 percent to 70 percent of [private sector] spending goes to Cuban workers for wages, to local suppliers, and maintenance and utility expenditures largely unaffiliated with the military" (Leogrande and Newfarmer in Bandow 2018).

Because of the embargo, most transactions between the United States, or persons subject to U.S. jurisdiction, and Cuba are prohibited, and the Treasury Department's Office of Foreign Assets Control (OFAC) continues to enforce the prohibitions of the Cuban Assets Control Regulations (CACR) diligently. President Raúl Castro called the embargo "the most important obstacle to the economic development and the well-being of the Cuban people" (The Cuba Consortium 2016, 18). President Obama encouraged Congress to revoke the embargo, and he licensed exceptions to the embargo with the hope of opening up of travel and commercial ties that support Cuban small businesses (The Cuba Consortium 2016).

President Obama's appeal to the U.S. Congress resulted from the fact that there are four aspects of the embargo on which the president of the United States cannot act (Laguardia Martinez 2016; The Cuba Consortium 2016; Vidal in Elizalde 2015):

1. The prohibition on U.S. subsidiaries in third countries from trading products with Cuba (1992 Cuban Democracy Act [CDA])
2. The prohibition on carrying out transactions with U.S. properties that were nationalized in Cuba (Helms-Burton Act of 1996)
3. The obligation to pay in cash and in advance for purchases of agricultural products by Cuba in the United States (2000 Trade Sanctions Reform and Export Enhancement Act [TSRA]) and
4. The prohibition of American citizens to travel to Cuba as tourists (2000 TSRA)

It stands to reason that ending the embargo requires new legislation. The decision to remove this major obstacle to normal relations rests with the U.S. Congress, not the executive. Lifting the sanctions would require changing the CACR of July 1963; the 1992 CDA, which prohibits trade with Cuba via subsidiaries of U.S. corporations abroad; the Helms-Burton Act of 1996, which strengthened the embargo; and the 2000 TSRA, which prohibited financing for agricultural exports and banned tourism.

The U.S. International Trade Commission conservatively estimates that the embargo costs the United States USD 1.2 billion annually in lost export revenue. While this may not represent a huge amount, it is focused on specific industries and regions (Kotschwar and Cimino 2015) and affects the southeastern states in particular (Copeland et al. 2011).

According to Morales Domínguez and Ramírez Cañedo (2015), the Obama administration never intended to seriously push for an end to the embargo. The more sophisticated Obama policy preferred to use the embargo as a key token of a policy that followed two different tracks at the same time. On the one hand, there was a relaxation in the U.S. provisions that directly affect Cuban common citizens—those related to ending restrictions on visiting relatives in Cuba or receiving remittances—while, on the other hand, there was the application of sanctions to banks and enterprises from third countries engaged in business with Cuba (Morales Domínguez and Ramírez Cañedo 2015).

A clear statement on that perspective is that, despite the scenario of 17D, President Obama renewed the existing sanctions against Cuba under the 1917 Trading with the Enemy Act (TWEA)—an Act which constitutes the foundation for the laws and regulations that make up the embargo—citing foreign policy interests as the motivation for doing so. As a result, some of the interviewees (Cuba 01, Cuba 04, Cuba 07) considered U.S. moves as possessing a lack of intention to demonstrate that it wanted to carve out a new kind of relationship, that is, one not rooted in ideas of hegemony and superpower dominance. President Trump has maintained sanctions under the TWEA.

The feedback received from the experts interviewed was quite similar to what has been presented here. For the most part, the persons interviewed were not optimistic about any significant changes taking place in the short term with regard to the blockade. Many were of the view that the Congress in the United States plays a major role in determining the future of the embargo, but because of the structure of the U.S. political system, this is problematic for those within that system who want to see changes made to the policy concerning it. This is exacerbated by the existence of, and active lobbying against the removal of the blockade by,[1] members of the Cuban American community, who occupy an important place in the U.S. political arena, and whom President Trump seeks to appease in determining his policies toward Cuba.

In terms of making advances toward ending the blockade, some of the interviewees (Cuba 02, 04, 06), saw the support of the international community, and specific sectors from within that community, along with pressure from Cuba, Latin America, and the Caribbean as a means to ensuring that the strides made so far do not suffer setbacks and do continue to advance.

---

[1] In the book, the term "blockade" has been used on occasions instead of "embargo". It will depend mostly on the sources referred due to the fact that most Cuban sources employed the term "blockade". In Cuba, it is considered that the U.S. embargo has surpassed the effects associated with a bilateral embargo and it produces the impacts usually associated to a larger economic blockade exerted from different actors in the international system.

One interviewee (Cuba 05), however, was of the view that the blockade could eventually represent just a formal policy rather than one that is actually practiced, if the kinds of exchanges that had already been taking place (e.g. travel to Cuba) were to continue. When considering the reversion by President Trump to pre-Obama travel regulations, however, this idea perhaps becomes more hopeful than possible. The policy changes contained within the Trump administration's National Security Presidential Memorandum reinforce the earlier statutory ban on U.S. tourism to Cuba. The self-directed, individual travel permitted by the Obama administration has been barred, while travel for non-academic educational purposes will, once again, be limited to group travel. Criticism of President Trump's directive came from representatives of business interests such as the U.S. Chamber of Commerce, which argued that the directives will hurt U.S. businesses. Although the directive makes individual and personal travel to Cuba more difficult for U.S. citizens, direct flights and cruise lines between the two countries would be protected, resulting from an exception to the prohibition on transactions with military-controlled entities (Whitford 2017). As a consequence of the Trump regulations, airlines are beginning to drop Cuban destinations off their routes, as previously mentioned.

Apart from the embargo, there are other economic factors to consider which affect Cuba-U.S. relations; among these is the process by which the U.S. government, acting on behalf of U.S. firms and citizens, is seeking compensation for nationalized properties in Cuba. The Foreign Claims Settlement Commission (FCSC), a quasi-independent entity positioned within the U.S. Department of Justice, has gone through the applications of U.S. citizen and corporate claimants, and has verified almost 6000 claims as being legitimate. Estimates by the FCSC place the value of these claims at USD 1.9 billion (this figure excludes the accumulated simple interest of 6 percent per annum typically awarded by the Commission). This situation is unique in different ways, but specifically because of the distinctly higher U.S. dollar value of the claims and the long period of time that has passed since the properties changed hands (Feinberg 2015b). Cuba has stated that it is prepared to compensate U.S. property owners for their losses, while the United States has recognized the island's sovereign right to expropriate in accordance with international legal standards and with compensation. Difficulties also arise when dealing with claims that go beyond property losses resulting from expropriation and, in some cases, involve judgments by U.S. courts (Coll 2016). Table 7.1 summarizes some of these claims.

The Cuban government has also forwarded claims for damages inflicted by U.S. aggressions and for compensation for the human and economic

Table 7.1 Top 12 U.S. claims on confiscated property by Cuba (over USD 50 million)

Name of claimant	Amount of loss certified (USD)
Cuban Electric Company	267,568,414
North American Sugar Industries, Inc.	97,373,415
MOA Bay Mining Company	88,349,000
United Fruit Sugar Company	85,100,147
West Indies Sugar Corp.	84,880,958
American Sugar Company	81,011,240
ITT as Trustee	80,002,794
Exxon Corporation	71,611,003
The Francisco Sugar Company	52,643,438
Starwood Hotels & Resorts Worldwide, Inc.	51,128,927
International Telephone and Telegraph Co.	50,676,964
Texaco, Inc.	50,081,110

Source: Feinberg (2015b, 42)

damage caused by the blockade and other U.S. sanctions against the island (Tvevad 2015). The economic impacts experienced by Cubans as a result of the blockade, even while considering the depreciation of the U.S. dollar in relation to the price of gold on the international market, amount to USD 753.7 billion. Damages at current prices are over USD 125.9 billion (Republic of Cuba 2016).

Additionally, Cuba's economic model is based on state-owned enterprises and a centrally planned economy. The Cuban model poses several difficulties for foreign firms that wish to gain access to its domestic market. To invest in Cuba, multinational companies must nearly always form joint ventures with state-run enterprises, hire Cubans who have been assessed by the government, and consent to being subject to price controls and other state interventions (Kotschwar and Cimino 2015).

Non-economic factors also inhibit normalization between the two countries. One of these is the U.S. military base in Guantánamo, which is a hindrance to the advances under way, a view supported by some of the interviewees (CARICOM 04; Cuba 02, 04). Cuba considers that the territory of the naval base under U.S. control as a consequence of a bilateral treaty is today illegally occupied, and its return to Cuban jurisdiction is fundamental for the full normalization of relations (Tvevad 2015). Cuba "demands that the United States return the base to Cuban control. The United States recognizes Cuban sovereignty over the territory but insists on the validity of the 1934 treaty leasing it permanently to the United States. Arguing that the base still has operational value, the Obama Administration was not willing to discuss its return" (The Cuba Consortium 2016, 18). This is one area where there seems to be bipartisan agreement in the United States: in January 2018, President Trump issued an executive order which "authorized the U.S. military and intelligence community to 'transport additional detainees to U.S. Naval Station Guantánamo Bay when lawful and necessary to protect the Nation'" (Thiessen 2018).

Finally, it must be noted that the changes in U.S. policy toward Cuba are slow, new, and untested. Companies approach business opportunities in Cuba with caution, mindful of the "fine print". The Obama administration's measures, their partial reversal under the Trump administration, together with the persistence of the embargo architecture, has resulted in a mess of rules and regulations. Businesses are often deterred from pursuing what ought to be lawful opportunities because their lawyers can rarely give them the green light in view of the complexities and uncertainties (Heifetz and Jeydel 2016). The slow pace of change may discourage companies who see opportunities for profit on the island.

Apart from these factors, there have been several actors working toward the goal of "normalization" between Cuba and the United States as will be discussed in the following section.

Actors Supporting the Changing Relationship

Political actors have been instrumental in effecting change in the nature of the Cuba-U.S. relations being witnessed today. The interviewees were not reserved in their praise for the leadership of Presidents Raúl Castro and Barack Obama in opening the way for these changing relations, and specific mention was made of the legitimacy with which President Castro's role as president and leader of the Cuban Revolution was viewed on the island (CARICOM 02), as well as of the political will demonstrated by President Obama (Cuba 04).

President Obama achieved progress by returning to President Jimmy Carter's approach toward Cuba, and he advanced this vision by using a soft power strategy as part of the broader smart power doctrine. President Obama maintained the foreign policy goal of recomposing bilateral and multilateral relations for two key reasons. First, given the substantial realignments taking place in international relations, the United States was seeking to construct new relations with countries and regional groups by employing a combination of soft and smart power, to create a more stable and sustainable international system that ultimately benefits U.S. interests. From the perspective of a great power and in terms of realpolitik, the objective was clear: it was the reincorporation of Cuba into a set of subordinated countries and its insertion into the U.S. sphere of influence (Salinas Figueredo 2017; Domínguez López 2016; Alzugaray Treto 2015). Second, the United States risked becoming isolated in the hemisphere because of its stubbornness toward Cuba (Alonso 2015; Smith 2015; Monreal González 2015; Hernández 2010; Hernández Martínez 2015). It is this solidarity at the international level with Cuba, but more so at the regional level, which led the United States to re-examine its stance toward Cuba. This idea was also supported by several of the interviewees. Washington realized that it was alone in its policy toward Cuba, and the pressure that it felt from Latin America and the Caribbean reinforced the possibility that it would be alone in its stance as it concerned Cuba.

The Obama strategy of demonstrating a willingness to engage in open and respectful dialogue with Cuba, while expressing opposition to the embargo,[2] is a good example of how diplomacy still works in today's global system once both sides are open to the process. As a result, Presidents Barack Obama and Raúl Castro were able to meet as equals at multilateral meetings such as the Summit of the Americas held in Panama, and address thorny issues such as human rights, claims for nationalized U.S. properties, and Cuban demands for economic damages at a dialogue table. President Obama also issued a Presidential Policy Directive on United States-Cuba Normalization (PPD-43),[3] and the voting pattern of the United States at the United Nations (UN) regarding the embargo changed during the last part of the Obama administration when the United States abstained instead of voting against the Cuban resolution condemning the U.S. embargo on the island.

Besides Presidents Obama and Raúl Castro, other actors that have had significant impact on the changing Cuba-U.S. relationship have been governments in the international community, especially those from Latin America and Caribbean countries. The Latin America and Caribbean region's political and economic integration since the 1990s facilitated the

---

[2] Presidents Jimmy Carter and Bill Clinton did the same, but only after leaving the White House.

[3] President Jimmy Carter had done this previously, but kept it a secret.

repositioning of Cuba within the region, reducing Cuban isolation within the hemisphere. Latin American and Caribbean nations made it clear in 2009 that the exclusion of Cuba from the inter-American community, and specifically from the Summit of the Americas meetings, would no longer be accepted (Leogrande 2015a; Romero 2015). Cuba has continually been invited to attend regional summits and high-level meetings and now participates regularly in many important regional political events. In addition, Cuba and different countries and regional organizations in Latin America have signed several treaties and agreements. Cuba was one of the founders of CELAC and the ACS. Cuba also exercised a key diplomatic role in its facilitation of dialogues between the Colombian government and the *Fuerzas Armadas Revolucionarias de Colombia* (FARC) and *Ejército de Liberación Nacional* (ELN) guerrillas in 2012 (Serbin 2016).

Public opinion on President Obama's opening to Cuba had been favorable and grew more positive as relations evolved. At the time, more than 25 public opinion polls showed consistent majority support from both Americans and Cubans in favor of the new Cuba policies for trade and travel (Engage Cuba 2016). A *New York Times*/CBS News poll taken just before the president's visit to Cuba found that 58 percent of the public supported restoring diplomatic relations and 52 percent supported the end of the embargo (The Cuba Consortium 2016, 4). A 2016 survey by the Pew Research Center revealed that 73 percent of the U.S. population are in favor of ending the embargo against Cuba and three-quarters of U.S. citizens (75 percent) say that they approve of the United States renewing ties with Cuba (Tyson 2016). A similar median of 77 percent across Argentina, Brazil, Chile, Mexico, and Venezuela approve of this action—this includes 79 percent of Chileans, 78 percent of Argentines, and 77 percent of Venezuelans. About three-quarters in the United States (72 percent) and in Latin America (a median of 76 percent) favor lifting the embargo (Poushter 2015). Important U.S. newspapers have published several editorials calling for changes in the Cuba policy (*The New York Times* 2014a, 2014b, 2014c, 2014d, 2014e, 2014f, 2014g, 2014h, 2015, 2016; *Los Angeles Times* 2015).

The experts interviewed (Cuba 03, Cuba 06) also made mention of the key role played by the Canadian government, as part of the international community, in facilitating the negotiations between the United States and Cuba, as well as the role played by various international non-state actors, especially progressive civil society groups in Latin America.

The emergence of an increasing, favorable trend toward the normalization of relations with Cuba has not only reached the political class but also the opinions of the Cuban community and Cuban Americans living in the United States, and this trend keeps growing. These changes are linked to demographic changes. Cuban exiles who arrived in the United States in the 1960s and 1970s were motivated to make this move mainly by their opposition to the Revolution. Those who arrived during and after the Mariel exodus in 1980, however, were more likely to have taken this decision because of economic reasons. It is these more recent arrivals, particularly those who came in the post-Cold War period, who are more likely to have maintained ties with their relatives in Cuba and who are more likely to support policies that remove obstacles to maintaining family connections (Leogrande 2015a). In September 2016, Florida International University (FIU) released a poll of Miami Cubans showing strong support for a U.S. policy of normalization with Cuba. The poll shows almost two-thirds of Miami-Dade's Cuban cohort support normalization, 69 percent support the re-establishment of diplomatic relations and 63 percent oppose the embargo - the highest level of support for lifting the embargo since the FIU poll began in 1997 (Engage Cuba 2016).

Various academics, think tanks, and lobbies have systematically promoted a change in U.S. policy toward Cuba. Exchanges between government officials and academics and think tank experts became particularly common as the Obama administration entered its second term. Comparable exchanges occurred in Cuba between scholars and policymakers (Crahan 2016; Martínez Reinosa 2011; Lutjens 2010).

One cannot overlook the diplomatic role played by the Catholic Church in the changing relationship, an idea supported by interviewees (Cuba 03). Pope Francis and high-ranking Catholic priests played a key positive role during the 18-month secret negotiations between Washington and Havana. For a long time, the Vatican has voiced its opposition to the economic blockade. Pope Francis wrote letters to the Cuban and U.S. presidents to encourage a change in their relations and facilitated secret talks between officials of the two countries, building on the work of his predecessors (Squires 2015; Diario de Cuba 2017).

The U.S. business community also has a significant place in the developments that have come about. Since 17D, important U.S. companies such as Caterpillar, Cargill, Marriot International, Hilton, Four Seasons, Hyatt, Radisson, Jackson Health System, Google, Wheels Up, Eagle Lake Ventures, Colgate Palmolive, General Electric, General Motors, Johnson

& Johnson, Dell, Microsoft, Pizza Hut, Taco Bell, American Airlines, McDonald, Stanley Morgan, Home Depot, Boeing, and Heinz Kraft have visited Cuba to explore business possibilities (Pérez Villanueva 2015). These possibilities would be profitable for both Cuba and the United States: apart from the economic benefits to be derived, U.S. businesses operating in Cuba would help to mitigate the effects of the U.S. embargo on Cuba and therefore remove this as a talking point as it concerns the discordant relations between the two countries.

Another actor to consider is the U.S. political class: in the 1980s, a group of wealthy Cuban Americans in Miami decided to mobilize the influence of the Cuban community by employing votes and campaign contributions. The political and economic power of conservative Cuban Americans, led by the Cuban American National Foundation (CANF), gave the Cuban diaspora in the United States a great amount of influence over U.S. policy from 1981 to 2008. The CANF won a series of political victories, including the creation of Radio and TV Martí, the 1992 CDA, and the Helms-Burton Act of 1996 (Leogrande 2015a, 476). Cuban American conservative influence, which was at its peak during the Ronald Reagan administration, declined substantially during the Obama administration, and pro-normalization lobbies emerged (Barberia 2010). In December 2015, ten bipartisan members of the U.S. House of Representatives came together to form the bipartisan Cuba Working Group (Politico) with the purpose of voicing their support for ending the embargo. The members of Congress who have joined the working group represent a wide array of industries, including agriculture, manufacturing, and tourism (Engage Cuba 2016). Around 40 legal initiatives regarding Cuba were presented in Congress. The purpose of some of these, though, was to reinforce several fundamental aspects related to the implementation of the embargo and prevent the approval of new executive measures by the president, as well as the implementation of those which have already been adopted. Although the differing opinions on the shift in U.S. policy toward Cuba can generally be considered as following the Democrat-Republican demarcation, it is not completely straightforward, as evidenced by the cross-party support in Congress for legal initiatives aimed at both stopping and continuing the embargo (Tvevad 2015).

Several of the experts interviewed maintained that some of the key actors influencing the changes in the Cuba-U.S. relationship come from economic actors in the United States, specifically the agriculture and fishing sectors, who wish to have a greater presence in the Cuban market. The business sector has shown an interest in the economic changes taking place in Cuba, and in addition to recognizing the opportunities that could be open to them, also recognizes the risk of being excluded from a market that holds many possibilities for expansion.

Some respondents also highlighted the important role played by the younger generation in Cuba, who comprised the Cuban negotiating team, and who are considered to be determined to create a more economically prosperous society (Cuba 01, 05; U.S. 02). However, it was also underscored (Cuba 06) that they should *not* be considered as actors who influenced the changing relations, as they are only now assuming more responsibility and held a secondary role in the decision-making process. As Alzugaray Treto (in Luxner 2017) pointed out, Cuba is "going to have a generational change in power [and] new leaders will introduce economic reforms toward the creation of a mixed economy". How Cuba-U.S. relations progress will rest in large part, then, on the younger generation of leaders.

Actors Opposing the Changing Relationship

While there are actors in favor of the moves being made in Cuba-U.S. relations, there are likewise those who oppose such moves. There is, first of all, among Cuban Americans, firm opposition to U.S. normalization of relations with Cuba especially among those who reside in Florida and among those who are Republicans (CaPRI 2016). Rogue actions taken by individuals who oppose normalization, given the number of former terrorists still at large in the Cuban diaspora, may be expected. Groups such as Alpha 66, Comandos F4, Acción Cubana, and Brigade 2506 are still able to train, acquire weapons, and plan acts of sabotage with relative impunity, according to a 2008 profile of their activities (Brenner and Scribner 2016). Additionally, there is some influence coming from the U.S. political class. A hard-line sector, headed by Senator Marco Rubio and vertically opposed to normalizing relations with Cuba, has some support in Congress and in the executive (Alzugaray Treto 2017b). On the other side, there are political actors in Cuba, mostly from the "generación histórica", that distrust the United States and do not share optimism or hopes on improving the bilateral relation with Washington.

Concluding Reflections

Despite the advancements made in improving relations, challenges remain and continue to resurface because the basic conflict between Cuba and the United States continues. The new U.S. policy has not abandoned the intent of intervening in Cuban social, political, and economic affairs (Castro Mariño 2016; Ramírez Cañedo 2016b; Lechuga Hevia 2016; Ubieta 2016; Sánchez 2016; González 2016; Rodríguez Rivera 2016; Lage Dávila 2016; Hernández 2016; Alzugaray Treto 2015; Muse 2014). Most of the measures favor the growth of the private sector within society, while observing a trend that discriminates against the state sector of the Cuban economy (Ramírez Cañedo 2017; Alzugaray Treto 2017b), which further puts Cubans dependent on state jobs for their livelihood at a severe economic disadvantage.

The Obama Presidential Policy Directive was a significant step in the process toward lifting the blockade and ameliorating relations between the two countries since it recognized, in theory, the independence, sovereignty, and self-determination of Cuba. However, the directive did not hide the purpose of promoting changes in Cuba, neither did it hide the intention to continue developing interventionist programs that respond to the interests of the United States by involving sectors of Cuban society (Vidal, in Elizalde 2015; Valdés 2016; Ramírez in Penín 2016).

The normalization process is a delicate one. Unfortunately, the dialogue is not being continued by those who started it—and while there may be continuity on Cuba's part and its commitment to the process, the same cannot be said of the United States and its current administration's perspective. Even though the Cuban government and the Obama administration endeavored to make the advances irreversible so that following administrations or events do not return to a relationship characterized by implacable hostility (Brenner and Scribner 2016), few changes were effectively institutionalized. Such circumstances expose normalization to different spoilers (Rappeport 2015), as has already been seen in the Trump presidency. According to Domínguez (2015), the utility of reaching agreements on "discrete matters" resulted in measures of rapid application that generate a multilevel process of chain negotiation that created new levels of trust, strengthened bilateral credibility, and allowed for more agreements that led to fundamental changes. It is evident that the partial reversal of policies made under Obama's administration and the old rhetoric that once characterized the Cuba-U.S. relationship do not help to promote the trust that is needed to facilitate any of these changes and advancements.

Nevertheless, these "agreements on discrete matters" do not add up well—they developed isolated from each other, and their very limitation in scope implies precariousness. In addition, major impediments, such as the

U.S. embargo and legal claims by both parties, for instance, and changes in the international and regional levels—characterized at present by economic and political instability—impact negatively on the normalization. The state of the region itself with the rise of protectionism and anti-regionalism trends, together with an upsurge of anti-globalization and ideological extremism, the persistence of poverty, and the intensification of inequality (UN ECLAC 2016), impacts on the process of normalization. The difficult situation in Venezuela has increased regional tensions and polarization and has further widened the gap between U.S. and Cuban positions.

The normalization process affects Cuba's internal dynamics both positively and negatively. In terms of positive impact, the island's economic reform could benefit from more commercial, financial, and investments links with U.S. companies; Cuban entrepreneurs who need financing, technologies, and know-how can receive these from U.S. institutions and individuals; and tourism, infrastructure, and job creation on the island can develop through increased contacts with the United States (Monreal González 2015; Feinberg 2015a), if these are allowed to be made and maintained. In addition, Cuba's mistrust and besieged fortress mentality, developed through its conflicted historical relations with the United States, seemed to relax in an environment of respectful relations with the United States, which allowed more room for political debate without necessarily changing the socialist orientation of the Cuban model (Leogrande 2015a).

However, the impact of the normalization process can also include negative outcomes. Social inequality could be reinforced, and an eventual "Tijuanization"[4] of the Cuban labor market may occur. Entrusting the regulation of the process of normalization to market forces could prove disastrous for Cuban society (Monreal González 2015; Feinberg 2015a).

REFERENCES

Alonso, Aurelio. 2015. Cuba y Estados Unidos: los dilemas del cambio. *Cubaposible*, cuaderno 4. Accessed June 11, 2017. https://cubaposible.com/cuaderno/cuba-estados-unidos-los-dilemas-del-cambio/.
Alzugaray Treto, Carlos. 2010. La seguridad nacional de Cuba frente a los Estados Unidos: conflicto y ¿cooperación? *Revista Temas*, 62–63 (April–September), 43–53.

---

[4]An informal binational economic arrangement in which one country—in this case, Cuba—is dependent on another—in this case, the United States (Varela Pérez 2010).

———. 2015. El 17D: secuencias y consecuencias (primera entrega). *Catalejo: el blog de Temas*, January 5, 2015. Accessed March 4, 2019. https://dialogardialogar.wordpress.com/2015/01/07/el-17d-secuencias-y-consecuencias/.

———. 2017a. *Perspectives for Normalization of Cuban-US relations in 2017: From No Drama Obama to All Trauma Trump*. Paper presented at the forum *Cuba's Economy and Foreign Policy After the Re-Establishment of Diplomatic Relations with the United States*, Diplomatic Academy and Institute of International Relations, the University of the West Indies, Saint Augustine, Trinidad and Tobago, March 15, 2017.

———. 2017b. Esperando por el señor Trump en la Habana. *Revista Temas*, June 1, 2017. Accessed June 4, 2017. http://www.temas.cult.cu/catalejo/esperando-por-el-se-or-trump-en-la-habana.

August, Arnold. 2016. Obama in Cuba: Will the Visit Advance the US Cultural War Against Cubans? *Global Research*, March 13, 2016. Accessed June 3, 2017. http://www.globalresearch.ca/obama-in-cuba-will-the-visit-advance-the-us-cultural-war-against-cubans/5513854.

Bandow, Doug. 2018. It's Time for a Policy Change on Cuba. *The National Interest*, December 6, 2018. Accessed December 28, 2018. https://nationalinterest.org/feature/its-time-policy-change-cuba-37992.

Barberia, Lorena G. 2010. Cuba, su emigración y las relaciones con los Estados Unidos. *Revista Temas*, 62–63 (April–September), 103–112.

Brenner, Philip, and Colleen Scribner. 2016. Spoiling the Spoilers: Evading the Legacy of Failed Attempts to Normalize U.S.-Cuba Relations. In *Cuba-US Relations: Normalization and Its Challenges*, ed. Margaret E. Crahan and Soraya M. Castro Mariño, 385–419. New York: Institute of Latin American Studies, Columbia University.

Bustamante, Michael. 2015. Cuba y Estados Unidos: los dilemas del cambio. *Cubaposible*, cuaderno 4. Accessed June 11, 2017. https://cubaposible.com/cuaderno/cuba-estados-unidos-los-dilemas-del-cambio/.

Caribbean Policy Research Institute (CaPRI). 2016. The Opening Up of Cuba: Implications for Jamaica of United States Policy Changes Towards Cuba. October. Accessed June 3, 2017. http://www.capricaribbean.com/sites/default/files/public/documents/report/the_opening_up_of_cuba.pdf.

Castro, Fidel. 2016a. Brother Obama. *Granma*, March 28, 2016. Accessed June 3, 2017. http://en.granma.cu/cuba/2016-03-28/brother-obama.

Castro, Raúl. 2016b. The Development of the National Economy, Along with the Struggle for Peace, and Our Ideological Resolve, Constitute the Party's Principal Missions. Council of State transcript. Translated by Granma International. *Granma*, April 18, 2016. Accessed April 9, 2017. http://en.granma.cu/cuba/2016-04-18/the-development-of-the-national-economy-along-with-the-struggle-for-peace-and-our-ideological-resolve-constitute-the-partys-principal-missions.

Castro Mariño, Soraya M. 2016. The New Era of Cuba-U.S. Relations: Breaking Down Axioms and Establishing Lasting Legacies? In *Cuba-US Relations: Normalization and Its Challenges*, ed. Margaret E. Crahan and Soraya M. Castro Mariño, 49–82. New York: Institute of Latin American Studies, Columbia University.

Coll, Alberto. 2016. U.S.-Cuba Property Claims: The Way Forward. In *Cuba-US Relations: Normalization and Its Challenges*, ed. Margaret E. Crahan and Soraya M. Castro Mariño, 201–224. New York: Institute of Latin American Studies, Columbia University.

Copeland, Cassandra, Curtis Jolly, and Henry Thompson. 2011. The History and Potential of Trade Between Cuba and the US. *Journal of Economics and Business*. Fox School of Business, Temple University, Philadelphia, PI, United States. Accessed April 13, 2017. http://www.auburn.edu/~thomph1/cuba-history.pdf.

Crahan, Margaret E. 2016. Academics and Think Tanks: Have They Influenced Normalization of U.S. Relations with Cuba? In *Cuba-US Relations: Normalization and Its Challenges*, ed. Margaret E. Crahan and Soraya M. Castro Mariño, 169–184. New York: Institute of Latin American Studies, Columbia University.

Diario de Cuba. 2017. Jaime Ortega publica un libro sobre las negociaciones entre Washington y La Habana. April 28, 2017. Accessed June 9, 2017. http://www.diariodecuba.com/cuba/1493381300_30719.html.

Domínguez, Jorge I. 1997. U.S.-Cuban Relations: From the Cold War to the Colder War. *Journal of Interamerican Studies and World Affairs* 39 (3) (Fall): 49–75. Accessed April 11, 2017. http://www.jstor.org/stable/166485.

———. 2010. Reconfiguración de las relaciones de los Estados Unidos y Cuba. *Revista Temas*, 62–63 (April–September), 4–15.

———. 2015. El 17D: secuencias y consecuencias (primera entrega).*Catalejo: el blog de Temas*, January 5, 2015. Accessed March 3, 2019. https://dialogardialogar.wordpress.com/2015/01/07/el-17d-secuencias-y-consecuencias/.

Domínguez López, Ernesto. 2016. Factors Determining Dialogue: Cuba in the U.S. Strategic Plan for the 21st Century. In *Cuba-US Relations: Normalization and Its Challenges*, ed. Margaret E. Crahan and Soraya M. Castro Mariño, 83–104. New York: Institute of Latin American Studies, Columbia University.

Elizalde, Rosa Miriam. 2015. Josefina Vidal: se han registrado progresos importantes entre Cuba y EEUU. *Cubadebate*, December 16, 2015. Accessed June 9, 2017. http://www.cubadebate.cu/noticias/2015/12/16/josefina-vidal-se-han-registrado-progresos-importantes-entre-cuba-y-eeuu/#.WTTB0-vhDIU.

Engage Cuba. 2016. A Timeline of the U.S.-Cuba Relationship Since the Thaw December 17, 2014–Present. December 19, 2016. Accessed June 2, 2017. https://cubacentral.files.wordpress.com/2017/01/0badf-2016-12-19-timelinesincethethaw.pdf.

European Council. 2016. EU-Cuba: Council Opens New Chapter in Relations. Press Release. December 6, 2016. Accessed June 3, 2017. http://www.consilium.europa.eu/en/press/press-releases/2016/12/06-eu-cuba-relations/.
Eyewitness News. 2018. US-Cuba Relations 'In Decline,' President Says. September 16, 2018. Accessed January 3, 2019. https://ewn.co.za/2018/09/17/us-cuba-relations-in-decline-president-says.
Feinberg, Richard E. 2015a. El 17D: secuencias y consecuencias (tercera entrega). *Catalejo: el blog de Temas*, January 19, 2015. Accessed March 3, 2019. http://cubaadiario.blogspot.com/2015/01/el-17d-secuencias-y-consecuencias_19.html.
———. 2015b. *Reconciling U.S. Property Claims in Cuba: Transforming Trauma into Opportunity*. Washington, DC: Latin America Initiative at Brookings. Accessed June 3, 2017. https://www.brookings.edu/wp-content/uploads/2016/07/Reconciling-US-Property-Claims-in-Cuba-Feinberg.pdf.
Fernández Pérez, Pablo Armando. 2007. *Cuba y los Estados Unidos: ¿nada cambia*. Discussion panel at the Centro Cultural Cinematográfico (ICAIC), Havana, Cuba, January 25, 2007.
González, Omar. 2016. Esperábamos un discurso más serio. *Cubadebate*, March 23, 2016. Accessed June 4, 2017. http://www.cubadebate.cu/opinion/2016/03/23/esperabamos-un-discurso-mas-serio/#.WTR-uevhDIU.
Heifetz, Stephen, and Peter Jeydel. 2016. Time to Finally End the Cuba Embargo. *The Hill*, October 10, 2016. Accessed May 31, 2017. http://thehill.com/blogs/congress-blog/foreign-policy/303098-time-to-finally-end-the-cuba-embargo.
Hernández, Rafael. 2010. Enemigos íntimos: paradojas en el conflicto Estados Unidos-Cuba. *Revista Temas*, 62–63 (April–September), 16–29.
———. 2016. Sobre las lecciones de Obama ante la sociedad civil cubana. *Cubadebate*, March 25, 2016. Accessed June 4, 2017. http://www.cubadebate.cu/opinion/2016/03/25/sobre-las-lecciones-de-obama-ante-la-sociedad-civil-cubana/#.WTR-l-vhDIU.
Hernández Martínez, Jorge. 2015. El 17D: secuencias y consecuencias (tercera entrega). *Catalejo: el blog de Temas*, January 19, 2015. Accessed March 3, 2019. http://cubaadiario.blogspot.com/2015/01/el-17d-secuencias-y-consecuencias_19.html.
Hernández Trejo, Helmo. 2007. *Cuba y los Estados Unidos: ¿nada cambia?* Discussion panel at the Centro Cultural Cinematográfico, Havana, Cuba, January 25, 2007.
Johnson, A. Ross, and S. Enders Wimbush. 2015. Radio and TV Marti Cuba Have Roles to Play As Cuba Enters a New Era. *The Washington Post*, January 9, 2015. Accessed June 9, 2017. https://www.washingtonpost.com/opinions/radio-and-tv-marti-have-roles-to-play-as-cuba-enters-a-new-era/2015/01/09/ebf4bd48-97ff-11e4-aabd-d0b93ff613d5_story.html?utm_term=.a99a11993a34.

Kotschwar, Barbara, and Cathleen Cimino. 2015. Towards Economic Normalization with Cuba: A Roadmap for US Policymakers. Statement for United States International Trade Commission hearing on no. 332–552 "Overview of Cuban Imports of Goods and Services and Effects of US Restriction." June 2, 2015. Accessed May 27, 2017. https://usitc.gov/press_room/documents/testimony/332_552_012.pdf.
Lage Dávila, Agustín. 2016. Obama y la economía cubana: entender lo que no se dijo. *Cubadebate*, March 23, 2016. Accessed June 4, 2017. http://www.cubadebate.cu/opinion/2016/03/23/obama-y-la-economia-cubana-entender-lo-que-no-se-dijo/#.WTR-sOvhDIU.
Laguardia Martinez, Jacqueline. 2016. CARICOM and Cuba in a Changing Hemispheric Environment: A Balance Since 17D. Henricus Heidweiller Memorial Lecture, Anton de Kom University, Paramaribo, Suriname, May 18, 2016.
Lechuga Hevia, Carlos. 2016. Carlos Lechuga y su historia no contada de las relaciones Cuba-EEUU. *Cubadebate*, November 5, 2016. Accessed June 4, 2017. http://www.cubadebate.cu/especiales/2016/11/05/carlos-lechuga-y-su-historia-no-contada-de-las-relaciones-cuba-eeuu/#.WTQ-qOvhDIU.
Leogrande, William M. 2015a. El 17D: secuencias y consecuencias (primera entrega). *Catalejo: el blog de Temas*, January 5, 2015. Accessed March 3, 2019. https://dialogardialogar.wordpress.com/2015/01/07/el-17d-secuencias-y-consecuencias/.
———. 2015b. Normalizing US-Cuba Relations: Escaping the Shackles of the Past. *International Affairs* 91 (3): 473–488.
———. 2016. Chipping Away at the Embargo: President Obama and the U.S. Economic Sanctions Against Cuba. In *Cuba-US Relations: Normalization and Its Challenges*, ed. Margaret E. Crahan and Soraya M. Castro Mariño, 187–200. New York: Institute of Latin American Studies, Columbia University.
Lopez-Levy, Arturo. 2015. Cuba-EE.UU.: el 17 de diciembre en la lógica de las relaciones asimétricas. In *Implications of Normalization: Scholarly Perspectives on U.S.-Cuban Relations*. Washington, DC: American University, April. Accessed June 11, 2017. https://www.american.edu/centers/latin-american-latino-studies/upload/2015-AU-SSRC-Lopez-Levy-El-17-de-Diciembre-en-la-l%C3%B3gica-de-las-relaciones-asim%C3%A9tricas.pdf.
Los Angeles Times. 2015. Another Outdated U.S. Policy Toward Cuba: Immigration. February 10, 2015. Accessed June 5, 2017. http://www.latimes.com/nation/la-ed-cuba-immigration-20150211-story.html.
Lutjens, Sheryl. 2010. Corrientes académicas y culturales Cuba-Estados Unidos: temas y actores. *Revista Temas*, 62–63 (April–September), 124–135.
Luxner, Larry. 2017. Interview: Carlos Alzugaray, Cuba's Former Ambassador to the European Union. *Cuba Trade*, October 23, 2017. Accessed December 9, 2017. http://www.cubatrademagazine.com/interview-carlos-alzugaray-cuba-former-ambassador/.

Machado Rodríguez, Darío. 2016. ¿Obama 'el bueno'? *Cubadebate*, March 23, 2016. Accessed June 4, 2017. http://www.cubadebate.cu/opinion/2016/03/23/obama-el-bueno/#.WTR-wOvhDIU.

Marín Suárez, Claudia. 2016. Latin American and Caribbean Regional Integration in the Context of Re-Establishing U.S.-Cuba Diplomatic Relations. In *Cuba-US Relations: Normalization and Its Challenges*, ed. Margaret E. Crahan and Soraya M. Castro Mariño, 105–128. New York: Institute of Latin American Studies, Columbia University.

Martínez Reinosa, Milagros. 2011. Cuba y Estados Unidos: entre la oportunidad y los desafíos de la diplomacia académica. *Pensamiento Propio* 34 (July–December). Accessed April 14, 2017. http://www.cries.org/wp-content/uploads/2012/01/34.pdf.

Miller, Ashley, and Ted Piccone. 2016. Toward a Common Vocabulary? Cuba, the U.S. and the Concept of Sovereignty. In *Cuba-US Relations: Normalization and Its Challenges*, ed. Margaret E. Crahan and Soraya M. Castro Mariño, 307–323. New York: Institute of Latin American Studies, Columbia University.

Monreal González, Pedro. 2015. El 17D: secuencias y consecuencias (primera entrega). *Catalejo: el blog de Temas*, January 5, 2015. Accessed March 3, 2019.

Morales Domínguez, Esteban, and Elier Ramírez Cañedo. 2015. *Aproximaciones al conflicto Cuba-Estados Unidos*. Havana: Editora Política.

Muñiz, Manuel, and Pablo Pardo. 2016. Noam Chomsky: 'No es extraño que a la gente no le entusiasme la democracia'. *El Mundo*, April 18, 2016. Accessed June 4, 2017. http://www.elmundo.es/cronica/2016/04/18/57122930ca474118338b45f0.html.

Muse, Robert. 2014. Endnotes: U.S. Presidential Action on Cuba: The New Normalization? *Americas Quarterly* (Fall 2014). Accessed June 4, 2017. http://americasquarterly.org/charticles/the-new-normalization/.

National Endowment for Democracy (NED). n.d. Cuba 2018. Accessed March 9, 2019. https://www.ned.org/region/latin-america-and-caribbean/cuba-2018/

Obama, Barack. 2014. Statement by the President on Cuba Policy Changes. The White House, Office of the Press Secretary, December 17, 2014. Accessed March 3, 2019. https://obamawhitehouse.archives.gov/the-press-office/2014/12/17/statement-president-cuba-policy-changes.

Penín Matos, Lisbet. 2016. Elier Ramírez: por ser transparente no deja de ser injerencia. *Cubadebate*, November 1, 2016. Accessed June 4, 2017. http://razonesdecuba.cubadebate.cu/articulos/elier-ramirez-por-ser-transparente-no-deja-de-ser-injerencia/.

Perelló Cabrera, José Luis. 2017. El turismo internacional en Cuba y sus implicaciones en el Caribe ante un escenario de relaciones diplomáticas con los Estados Unidos. In *Cuba en sus relaciones con el resto del Caribe: continuidades y rupturas tras el restablecimiento de las relaciones diplomáticas entre Cuba y los Estados Unidos*, ed. Jacqueline Laguardia Martinez, 63–77. Buenos Aires: El Consejo Latinoamericano de Ciencias Sociales (CLACSO).

Pérez, Louis A. 2008. *Cuba in the American Imagination: Metaphor and the Imperial Ethos*. Chapel Hill, NC: University of North Carolina Press.
Pérez Benítez, Santiago. 2016. ¿Gato por liebre? Notas sobre la visita de Obama a Cuba. *Cubadebate*, March 24, 2016. Accessed June 3, 2017. http://www.cubadebate.cu/opinion/2016/03/24/gato-por-liebre-notas-sobre-la-visita-de-obama-a-cuba/#.WTMQruvhDIU.
Pérez Villanueva, Omar Everleny. 2015. La inversión extranjera directa en Cuba: sus implicaciones para la región. Paper presented at the workshop *Understanding Changing Cuba-US Relations: Political, Economic and Institutional Dimensions and Implications*, Institute of International Relations, the University of the West Indies, St Augustine, Trinidad and Tobago, November 4.
Pertierra, José. 2015. Relación Cuba-EEUU: ¿Normal? *Cubadebate*, July 8, 2015. Accessed June 9, 2017. http://www.cubadebate.cu/opinion/2015/07/08/relacion-cuba-eeuu-normal/#.WTTHOuvhDIU.
Poushter, Jacob. 2015. People in U.S., Latin America Approve of Renewing U.S. Ties with Cuba. *Pew Research*, August 14, 2015. Accessed June 5, 2017. http://www.pewresearch.org/fact-tank/2015/08/14/people-in-u-s-latin-america-approve-of-renewing-u-s-ties-with-cuba/.
Ramírez Cañedo, Elier. 2016a. Una breve opinión sobre la visita de Obama a Cuba. *Cubadebate*, March 19, 2016. Accessed June 3, 2017. http://www.cubadebate.cu/especiales/2016/03/19/una-breve-opinion-sobre-la-visita-de-obama-a-cuba/#.WTMQvuvhDIU.
———. 2016b. ¿Qué entender por una normalización de las relaciones entre Cuba y EEUU? *Cubadebate*, November 2, 2016. Accessed June 4, 2017. http://www.cubadebate.cu/opinion/2016/11/02/que-entender-por-una-normalizacion-de-las-relaciones-entre-cuba-y-eeuu-2/#.WTQ-revhDIU.
———. 2017. El legado de Obama en la política hacia Cuba. *Cubadebate*, November 21, 2017. Accessed June 2, 2018. http://www.cubadebate.cu/opinion/2016/11/21/el-legado-de-obama-en-la-politica-hacia-cuba/#.WTHXtOvhDIU.
Rappeport, Alan. 2015. First Draft: Jeb Bush Assails Obama on Removing Cuba from Terror List. *The New York Times*, May 29, 2015. Accessed April 9, 2017. https://www.nytimes.com/politics/first-draft/2015/05/29/jeb-bush-assails-obama-on-removing-cuba-from-terror-list/?emc=edit_tnt_20150604&nlid=1293235&tntemail0=y.
Republic of Cuba. 2011. Lineamientos de la política económica y social del partido y la revolución. Accessed July 18, 2017. http://www.cubadebate.cu/wp-content/uploads/2011/05/folleto-lineamientos-vi-cong.pdf.
———. 2016. *Cuba's Report on Resolution 70/5 of the United Nations General Assembly: Necessity of Ending the Economic, Commercial and Financial Blockade Imposed by the United States of America Against Cuba*. Accessed June 3, 2017. http://www.cubavsbloqueo.cu/sites/default/files/InformeBloqueo2016EN.pdf.

Rizzi, Andrea. 2015. El deshielo reforzará a la clase media de Cuba. *El País*, July 27, 2015. Accessed June 2, 2017. http://internacional.elpais.com/internacional/2015/07/27/actualidad/1438021772_833235.html.

Rodríguez Rivera, Guillermo. 2016. El progreso de Cuba y su sector privado. *Cubadebate*, March 23, 2016. Accessed June 4, 2017. http://www.cubadebate.cu/opinion/2016/03/23/el-progreso-de-cuba-y-su-sector-privado/#.WTR-sevhDIU.

Romero, Antonio. 2015. El 17D: secuencias y consecuencias (tercera entrega). *Catalejo: el blog de Temas*, January 19, 2015. Accessed March 9, 2019. http://cubaadiario.blogspot.com/2015/01/el-17d-secuencias-y-consecuencias_19.html.

Salinas Figueredo, Darío. 2017. América Latina, el Caribe y los Estados Unidos: grietas en la hegemonía y reconfiguración del mapa político regional. *Cuadernos de Nuestra América* 26 (49) (January–June). Accessed June 9, 2017. http://www.cipi.cu/sites/default/files/2017-04/CNA_49.pdf.

Sánchez, Iroel. 2016. ¿Obama en el gran teatro o el gran teatro de Obama en la Habana? *Cubadebate*, March 23, 2016. Accessed June 4, 2017. http://www.cubadebate.cu/opinion/2016/03/23/obama-en-el-gran-teatro-o-el-gran-teatro-de-obama-en-la-habana/#.WTR-0OvhDIU.

Serbin, Andrés. 2016. Onstage or Backstage? Latin America and U.S.-Cuban Relations. In *A New Chapter in US-Cuba Relations, Studies of the Americas*, ed. E. Hershberg and W.M. LeoGrande, 179–189. Cham: Palgrave Macmillan.

Smith, Wayne. 2015. El diplomático que vio bajar y verá subir la bandera de EE. UU. en Cuba. *Agencia EFE*, August 14, 2015. Accessed June 5, 2017. http://www.efe.com/efe/america/entrevistas/el-diplomatico-que-vio-bajar-y-vera-subir-la-bandera-de-ee-uu-en-cuba/50000489-2688287.

Squires, Nick. 2015. How the Pope Played a Crucial Role in US-Cuba Deal. *The Telegraph*, September 18, 2015. Accessed June 9, 2017. http://www.telegraph.co.uk/news/worldnews/centralamericaandthecaribbean/cuba/11873213/How-the-Pope-played-a-crucial-role-in-US-Cuba-deal.html.

The Cuba Consortium. 2016. *The Opening to Cuba*. Annual Report of the Cuba Consortium. October 3, 2016. Accessed June 3, 2017. http://files.thecubaconsortium.org/media/TheCubaConsortiumAnnualReport11.3.16.pdf.

The New York Times. 2014a. Obama Should End the Embargo on Cuba. October 11, 2014. Accessed June 5, 2017. https://www.nytimes.com/2014/10/12/opinion/sunday/end-the-us-embargo-on-cuba.html.

———. 2014b. Cuba's Impressive Role on Ebola. October 19, 2014. Accessed June 5, 2017. https://www.nytimes.com/2014/10/20/opinion/cubas-impressive-role-on-ebola.html.

———. 2014c. The Shifting Politics of Cuba Policy. October 25, 2014. Accessed June 5, 2017. https://www.nytimes.com/2014/10/26/opinion/sunday/the-shifting-politics-of-cuba-policy.html.

———. 2014d. A Prisoner Swap with Cuba. November 2, 2014. Accessed June 5, 2017. https://www.nytimes.com/2014/11/03/opinion/a-prisoner-swap-with-cuba.htm.
———. 2014e. In Cuba, Misadventures in Regime Change. November 9, 2014. Accessed June 5, 2017. https://www.nytimes.com/2014/11/10/opinion/in-cuba-misadventures-in-regime-change.html?mtrref=www.google.tt&gwh=0B8C6A0E14FAECE6913499C6BE4DA7FD&gwt=pay&assetType=opinion.
———. 2014f. A Cuban Brain Drain, Courtesy of the U.S. November 16, 2014. Accessed June 5, 2017. https://www.nytimes.com/2014/11/17/opinion/a-cuban-brain-drain-courtesy-of-us.html?mtrref=www.google.tt&gwh=C090B4371D685B29469662EB346AA9CC&gwt=pay&assetType=opinion.
———. 2014g. Cuba's Economy at a Crossroads. December 14, 2014. Accessed June 5, 2017. https://www.nytimes.com/2014/12/15/opinion/cubas-economy-at-a-crossroads.html?mtrref=www.google.tt&gwh=A1A452BDDADEAB44002A74D0D5B33E69&gwt=pay&assetType=opinion.
———. 2014h. Mr. Obama's Historic Move on Cuba. December 17, 2014. Accessed June 5, 2017. https://www.nytimes.com/2014/12/18/opinion/a-new-beginning-with-cuba.html?mtrref=www.google.tt&gwh=44AF0BF79C9E61C676D4A5BEE14154AB&gwt=pay&assetType=opinion.
———. 2015. Growing Momentum to Repeal the Embargo. August 3, 2015. Accessed June 5, 2017. https://www.nytimes.com/2015/08/03/opinion/growing-momentum-to-repeal-cuban-embargo.html?ref=opinion&mtrref=www.cubadebate.cu&gwh=33BBC517C52F9CB7D26398850780B679&gwt=pay&assetType=opinion.
———. 2016. Neighbors Question Cuba Migration Policy. August 31, 2016. Accessed June 5, 2017. https://www.nytimes.com/2016/08/31/opinion/neighbors-question-cuba-migration-policy.html?mtrref=www.google.tt&gwh=D19C3BB0FE41C46A6C194954F165AB3F&gwt=pay&assetType=opinion.
The White House. 2017. Fact Sheet on Cuba Policy. Accessed November 11, 2017. https://www.whitehouse.gov/blog/2017/06/16/fact-sheet-cuba-policy.
Thiessen, Marc A. 2018. Send Islamic State Fighters Held in Syria to Guantanamo Bay. *The Washington Post*, December 27, 2018. Accessed January 4, 2019. https://www.washingtonpost.com/opinions/send-islamic-state-fighters-held-in-syria-to-guantanamo-bay/2018/12/27/081d7ef6-09ee-11e9-88e3-989a3e456820_story.html?utm_term=.ecc5c55d16c3.
Toledo Sande, Luis. 2015. Cuba y los Estados Unidos: ¿normalidad posible? *Cubadebate*, July 8, 2015. Accessed June 9, 2017. http://www.cubadebate.cu/opinion/2015/07/08/cuba-y-los-estados-unidos-normalidad-posible/#.WTTHN-vhDIU.
Tvevad, Jesper. 2015. *Cuba, the USA and the EU: Forging Closer Ties, Looking to the Future*. European Union. Document DG EXPO/B/PolDep/Note/2015_287. Accessed June 3, 2017. http://www.europarl.europa.eu/RegData/etudes/IDAN/2015/549075/EXPO_IDA(2015)549075_EN.pdf.

Tyson, Alec. 2016. Americans Still Favor Ties with Cuba After Castro's Death, U.S. Election. *Pew Research Center*, December 13, 2016. Accessed March 2, 2019. http://www.pewresearch.org/fact-tank/2016/12/13/americans-still-favor-ties-with-cuba-after-castros-death-u-s-election/.

Ubieta, Enrique. 2016. Lo que dice y no dice Obama. *Cubadebate*, March 23, 2016. Accessed June 4, 2017. http://www.cubadebate.cu/opinion/2016/03/23/lo-que-dice-y-no-dice-obama/#.WTR-w-vhDIU.

United Nations Economic Commission for Latin America and the Caribbean (UN ECLAC). 2016. *Horizontes 2030: la igualdad en el centro del desarrollo sostenible*. Document LC/G.2660/Rev.1. Accessed July 18, 2017. http://repositorio.cepal.org/bitstream/handle/11362/40159/4/S1600653_es.pdf.

Valdés, Nelson P. 2016. Una lectura entre líneas de la directiva presidencial de política de Obama. *Cubadebate*, October 21, 2016. Accessed June 4, 2017. http://www.cubadebate.cu/opinion/2016/10/21/una-lectura-entre-lineas-de-la-directiva-presidencial-de-politica-de-obama/#.WTRAOevhDIU.

Valdés Paz, Juan. 2015. Cuba y Estados Unidos: los dilemas del cambio. *Cubaposible*, cuaderno 4. Accessed June 11, 2017. https://cubaposible.com/cuaderno/cuba-estados-unidos-los-dilemas-del-cambio/.

Varela Pérez, Jesús. 2010. *The Nostalgia of Change: A History of Mexican Return Migration to Acámbaro, Guanajuato, 1930–2006*. PhD thesis. University of California, San Diego, CA, United States. Accessed February 4, 2019. https://escholarship.org/uc/item/9xm7h7cc.

Vidal, Josefina. 2015. The Blockade Has Not Ended. *Wisconsin Coalition to Normalize Relations with Cuba*, March 16, 2015. Accessed June 3, 2017. https://wicuba.wordpress.com/2015/03/16/the-blockade-has-not-ended-interview-with-josefina-vidal-cubas-top-negotiator-foreign-ministry-head-for-u-s-affairs/.

———. 2016. The Blockade Is an Outdated Policy and Must End. Interviewed by Sergio Alejandro Gómez. *Granma*, July 20, 2016. Accessed June 3, 2017. http://en.granma.cu/cuba/2016-07-20/the-blockade-is-an-outdated-policy-and-must-end.

Whitford, David. 2017. Trump's Cuba Moves 'An Epic Disaster' for Entrepreneurs. Inc., June 20, 2017. Accessed February 5, 2019. https://www.inc.com/david-whitford/appraising-trumps-cuba-deal.html.

CHAPTER 8

Background: U.S. Impact on the Cuba-CARICOM Relationship

This chapter highlights the main aspects of the relationship between Cuba and its Caribbean Community (CARICOM) neighbors, with an emphasis on the developments after independence in the Anglophone Caribbean. The chapter explores some of the underlying factors that have created challenges in Cuba-CARICOM relations. Reference is made to the evolution of the relationship since the establishment of diplomatic relations between Cuba and Barbados, Jamaica, Guyana, and Trinidad and Tobago in December 1972, and in the period following the end of the Cold War. The analysis is made in light of how U.S.-Caribbean relations have impacted the Cuba-CARICOM relationship.

CARICOM Approaches Toward Cuba Before and After 17D: Key Notes

CARICOM countries have, from the outset, clearly and consistently stated their position on U.S. policy to isolate Cuba and opposed U.S. efforts to dictate Cuban internal affairs while insisting that Cuban sovereignty should be preserved (González Núñez and Verba 1997). Most notably, in 1972, four future CARICOM member countries[1]—Jamaica, Trinidad and Tobago, Barbados, and Guyana—established diplomatic ties with Cuba in

---

[1] The Caribbean Community was established in 1973 by the Treaty of Chaguaramas (see Chap. 3).

a clear breach from U.S. foreign policy toward the island and the regional approach, backed by the Organization of American States (OAS), to segregate Cuba from the hemispheric community. CARICOM's persistent support, to date, for ending the U.S. embargo against Cuba is an indication of its defiance of the United States. This behavior illustrates CARICOM's respect for Cuba's political and economic diversity, autonomy, and sovereignty, despite the concerns about the spread of communism in the region.

In the period of the post-Cold War, once the communist threat disappeared, Latin America and the Caribbean advanced their relations with Cuba. The 1990s saw CARICOM making an effort to increase its engagement with the island. At the 11th CARICOM Summit, held in August 1990, discussions were launched on the possibility of greater economic cooperation with Cuba. Progress was initially hindered by CARICOM's disapproval of Havana's ruptured relations with Grenada following the end of the Grenada Revolution in 1983, but then in 1994, the two island countries resumed diplomatic relations. Since then, Cuba has offered assistance to Grenada in the areas of health, education, and sport, among others; and in a show of appreciation, in 2017, Grenada unveiled a monument commemorating the 24 Cuban workers who were killed during the U.S.-led invasion in 1983. The resumption of diplomatic relations between Cuba and Grenada opened the door to greater CARICOM engagement with Havana in various ways, including through the expansion of diplomatic relations and approval of Cuban membership in the Caribbean Tourism Organization (CTO).

While CARICOM countries have resisted U.S. efforts to isolate Cuba and, by extension, encouraged initiatives for regional cooperation, they "have not pushed for an expeditious rapprochement" (González Núñez and Verba 1997, 89). For instance, when the Cuba-U.S. conflict escalated with the tightening of the embargo in 1992, CARICOM countries

> situate[d] themselves equidistant from the two. Attempting to maintain a delicate balance between the two nations in conflict, they [...] adopted a strategy of cautious rapprochement with Cuba deploying tactics that, on the one hand, [would] not damage the process or the general interests of Cuba and, on the other hand, [would] not be interpreted by the United States as threatening to its interests in the region. (ibid., 90)

The CARICOM voting behavior at the United Nations, at the end of 1992, on a Cuban resolution advocating "the sovereign equality of States, non-intervention and non-interference in their internal affairs and freedom of trade and international navigation" (United Nations 1992) is similarly illustrative. The Caribbean countries cast their votes as follows: three in favor and eight abstentions, with four absences.[2] One can infer that this behavior was intended to avoid directly opposing the 1992 Cuban Democracy Act (CDA), which had strengthened the U.S. embargo and to which Cuba was responding through this resolution. Caribbean countries demonstrated their holding of the middle ground through their vote on the subsequent U.S. resolution "condemning alleged human rights violations in Cuba" (González Núñez and Verba 1997, 90), with one voting in favor while nine abstained, with five absences (ibid., 90).[3]

Another example of this Caribbean position is to be found in CARICOM's denial, on the one hand, of the Cuban request for official observer status at the regional organization, but its willingness, on the other, to instead form a CARICOM-Cuba Joint Commission (González Núñez and Verba 1997). This joint commission was set up to foster greater cooperation in trade, tourism, culture, biotechnology, human resource development, and the environment, among other areas. A similar approach was evidenced in the behavior of the Dominican Republic—a non-CARICOM member country—during the early 1990s, when the government in Santo Domingo, while being open to cooperation, did not support forging diplomatic relations with Cuba. Cuba and the Dominican Republic resumed diplomatic relations in 1998. Cuba and Dominican Republic, together with the rest of CARICOM member states, are members of CARIFORUM due to their relations with the EU as part of the African, Caribbean, and Pacific (ACP) group.

However, as González Núñez and Verba (1997, 90) highlight, "this political strategy of gradualism and equilibrium" was not the same across all Caribbean countries; and, as Erisman (1994, 11) writes, "[b]y November 1993 [CARICOM's voting at the UN] had radically changed; ten of the twelve CARICOM members of the UN ... censured Washington's position ... Only Grenada and Antigua-Barbuda chose once again to remain on the sidelines".

---

[2] In favor: Barbados, Haiti, Jamaica. Abstaining: Antigua and Barbuda, the Bahamas, Belize, Guyana, St. Lucia, St. Vincent and the Grenadines, Suriname, Trinidad and Tobago (United Nations 1993, 234).
[3] In favor: Dominica. Abstaining: Antigua and Barbuda, the Bahamas, Barbados, Belize, Guyana, Jamaica, St. Kitts and Nevis, St. Lucia, St. Vincent and the Grenadines, Suriname, Trinidad and Tobago (United Nations 1993, 803).

Despite the disquiet felt by some Caribbean countries, the view that there is value in fostering closer relations with Cuba has been widely held. This view was reflected in CARICOM's consideration of the Cuban request for observer status in the 1990s. Although this request was eventually not approved—as just noted above—the CARICOM-Cuba Joint Commission was established in 1993 arguably as an initial step toward Cuban membership of CARICOM in the future (Erisman 1994). Despite CARICOM's caution, it is noteworthy that "CARICOM ... had not bowed [completely] to U.S. pressure, but instead remained committed to developing a closer, more cooperative relationship with Havana" (ibid., 10).

Caribbean private sector actors, too, explored commercial and business opportunities in Cuba in the 1990s, but these attempts were not sufficient to exploit and expand the potential which existed in Cuba, and the obstacles to commercial interactions remained (González Núñez and Verba 1997).

> In 1998, five years after the Joint Commission was established, the region saw that expectations within the CARIFORUM [Forum of the Caribbean Group of ACP States] business communities regarding the sourcing of goods and services, the exchange of trade and investment information, the harmonization of trade rules and regulations and the establishment of reciprocal payment and credit systems had not been met. Contact among Chambers of Commerce was minimal and the work of Caribbean Export and other Trade Promotion Organizations (TPOs) in promoting exports to Cuba was only just beginning to produce tangible results. (Trade Wins 2000)

A key step taken by CARICOM toward closer relations with Cuba was the signing of the Trade and Economic Cooperation Agreement (TECA) in 2000. The signatories to the agreement are Cuba and CARICOM member countries, all except the Bahamas and Haiti. Its objective is to strengthen commercial and economic relations between Cuba and CARICOM through trade in goods; financial arrangements to facilitate trade; promotion of market access; joint ventures; and information exchange. The CARICOM-Cuba Joint Commission has the responsibility to oversee the implementation, evaluation, review, and amendment of the agreement, as well as the settlement of disputes relating to it. TECA is a reciprocal, partial scope agreement (goods only). It also envisages the signing of further agreements on double taxation, intellectual property rights, and the protection and promotion of investment; and provides for the setting up of a CARICOM-Cuba Business Council for exploring business opportunities, providing information, and promoting trade (CARICOM and Republic of Cuba 2001). (For more on TECA, see Chap. 10.) By 2000, with the TECA in place and the opening of the Caribbean Export office in Havana, the situation became more favorable for greater trade and investment links between Cuba and other Caribbean countries. However, the private sector remained largely ignorant of potential business opportunities.

At the Eighth CARICOM-Cuba Joint Commission Meeting (at the level of senior officials), in 2014, the parties:

1. agreed to focus on three priority areas for implementation: trade financing, tourism and transportation (air and maritime);
2. planned to establish expert working groups to develop these work programs;
3. agreed to the exchange of export services portfolios;
4. examined market access difficulties experienced (related to currency controls, registration, regulations, information asymmetries, lack of transparency, complicated bureaucracy, high transportation and marketing costs, planned purchases, and insufficient support structures for exporters in Cuba);
5. gave consideration to the provisions on administrative cooperation and on the rules of procedure for the Joint Commission;
6. exchanged views on the reactivation of the CARICOM-Cuba Business Council, which last met in 2008, in order to resuscitate trade;
7. agreed that CARICOM should identify an interlocutor to replace the Caribbean Association of Industry and Commerce (CAIC);
8. agreed to CARICOM submitting a draft text on product-specific rules of origin by the end of March 2015;
9. requested the expansion of preferential access by Cuba and CARICOM; and
10. agreed that once these further negotiations were completed, a protocol would be prepared for adoption by the parties reflecting all the agreed amendments to the TECA.

The process of revising the TECA—started in 2006—became urgent following 17D: "after eight years without any work being done, CARICOM was forced to revive talks in 2014 after signals that the Cuban market could be more open with the normalization of relationships with the United States" (Johnson 2016). The process was further delayed as CARICOM expressed the need to translate the proposed revisions of the agreement into English and as both sides deliberated and conducted consultations on whether the offers made were in their best interest (ibid.).

At the Fifth Meeting of the Ministers of Foreign Affairs of CARICOM and Cuba, on March 11, 2017, ministers pledged to, among other things, address the challenges of sustainable development, particularly in the economic and environmental spheres; to work toward justice and equity for their peoples; and to "continue to strengthen the CARICOM-Cuba mechanism" (CARICOM 2017). At this meeting, Cuba and CARICOM agreed to an extension of the TECA through a Second Protocol to the agreement. The Second Protocol was signed in November 2017 during the 45th Meeting of the Council for Trade and Economic Development (COTED) celebrated in Georgetown, Guyana, and provides access to hundreds of CARICOM products to the Cuban market and further facilitates Cuba-CARICOM trade (CARICOM Press Releases 2017).

Among the several initiatives in which CARICOM has engaged to foster friendly relations with Cuba is the commemoration of CARICOM-Cuba day on December 8. The date marks the establishment of Cuba-CARICOM relations. This annual recognition "was inaugurated in 2002 at the time of the signing of the Havana Declaration" (CARICOM 2004). It happened in the context of the First Cuba-CARICOM Summit. CARICOM countries and Cuba share membership in various organizations. Cuba is a founding member of the Association of Caribbean States (ACS) in 1994. It is also a member of the Latin American and Caribbean Economic System (SELA) and the Latin American Integration Association (LAIA), and participates in the Ibero-American Summits (Martínez Reinosa 2015).

U.S. Impact on Cuba-CARICOM Relationship

Historically, Cuba-Caribbean relations have been affected by Cuba-U.S. political tensions. Relations between Cuba and CARICOM stem from U.S. security interests in the Caribbean region. According to González Núñez and Verba 1997, 82), "geopolitical considerations derived from U.S. security interests in the region have consistently frustrated the development of conventional relations between Cuba and the Caribbean nations" (see also Erisman 1994). The Caribbean specifically has traditionally been concerned about the withdrawal of U.S. aid and technical assistance through the application of the Helms-Burton Act of 1996 by the United States against it.

8 BACKGROUND: U.S. IMPACT ON THE CUBA-CARICOM RELATIONSHIP   149

Due to the Caribbean's dependence on the U.S. economy, the region's foreign policy has, for the most part, been shaped by Cuba-U.S. relations:

> Attempts [by the Caribbean] to establish any type of relationship with Cuba have consequently been perceived as incompatible with U.S. interests and made the object of coercive measures aimed at discouraging them. The extreme dependency of the Caribbean nations on the United States makes them very vulnerable to U.S. pressure tactics. This has forced them to take U.S. sentiment toward Cuba as a reference point in developing their own views on the subject. We can infer from all this that the Cuba-U.S. conflict is the most important factor in a Caribbean nation's decision whether or not to develop stronger ties with Cuba. (González Núñez and Verba 1997, 83)

The United States has not always explicitly dissuaded the Caribbean's engagement with Cuba or suppressed any potential socialist orientation. However, it has used manipulative tactics to dictate Caribbean foreign policy:

> An example of this can be seen in [the U.S.] signing of the Marco Accord with the CARICOM, one of the agreed-upon steps for implementing the Initiative of the Americas, in which it forgave Jamaica a portion of its debt. Jamaica has actively advocated expanded relations with Cuba, and had the United States believed it in its best interest it would certainly have tried to use the Jamaican foreign debt as a tool of coercion, for this is precisely what it did in the 1970s when the very same Jamaican party was in power. (ibid., 84)

During the Cold War, the fear that Cuba's socialist philosophy would spread to the rest of the Caribbean was a real issue in the Cuba-Caribbean relationship:

> In the 1970s, Cuba's policy of prioritizing its relations with Norman Manley's Jamaica, Guyana, and Grenada—countries with left-leaning governments in the 1970s—was widely perceived as ideologically-driven, which served to bolster the widely held opinion that Cuba was not interested in balanced bilateral relations between states for the purpose of mutual benefit. (ibid., 88; see also Erisman 1994)

As it later became known, the U.S.-led invasion of Grenada in October 1983 was carried out with the acquiescence and active support of the Organization of Eastern Caribbean States (OECS). OECS member countries provided a letter requesting military assistance from the United States to address the upheaval in Grenada at the time and deployed troops to lend support to the U.S. military effort. Cuban assistance to Grenada was met with disapproval, and there were concerns that Cuba's agenda was to incite revolution and replace the existing socio-economic systems of the English-speaking Caribbean with socialist ideologies and systems (González Núñez and Verba 1997). Moreover, some thought that Cuba was merely an avenue for promoting Soviet interests in the region. Interestingly, this negative view of Cuba, held primarily by the Anglophone Caribbean, served to recognize the Cuban Revolution as a political reality and helped to legitimize Cuba's position in the region (González Núñez 2002). This view was not helped by the fact that in the 1980s, Cuba's external projection prioritized Central America and other parts of the global South over the Caribbean (González Núñez and Verba 1997).

The close trade relationship between the United States and the rest of the Caribbean has produced adverse impacts on the level and quality of the Caribbean's commercial relations with Cuba, resulting in a mutual unfamiliarity between the Cuban and other Caribbean markets (González Núñez and Verba 1997). This has been compounded by the extraterritorial application of the U.S. economic embargo, which allows the United States to impose sanctions on third countries' citizens, institutions, and companies conducting business with Cuba and poses a significant problem. The possibility of sanctions makes it difficult for the Caribbean to conduct trade and financial transactions or to transact in U.S. currency with Cuba. The reality of this situation is illustrated by the examples provided by former Cuban ambassador to Trinidad and Tobago, Humberto Rivero: if a Caribbean vessel goes to Cuba, it has to wait six months before it is allowed to land in the United States; Caribbean subsidiaries of U.S. companies are prohibited from undertaking business transactions with Cuba; and companies are unable to export products or equipment that contain more than 10 percent of U.S. parts to Cuba and cannot sell products to the United States that contain inputs from Cuba (Lall 2012).

Changes in the global political economy in the 1990s—the end of the Cold War, in particular—lowered the geopolitical significance of the Caribbean to the United States. This in turn placed relations with Cuba higher on the Caribbean's agenda. Unlike the 1970s, when only four newly independent Caribbean countries established ties with Cuba, under the new dispensation, a "regional consensus" existed for the first time about "the importance of incorporating Cuba into the region" (González Núñez and Verba 1997, 87; Erisman 1994). As the USSR disintegrated and Soviet assistance to Cuba eroded, Havana also sought to rejuvenate and increase its efforts toward forging ties with the independent Caribbean (Erisman 1994).

Cuba-CARICOM relations have further been maintained through Cuba-CARICOM summits and other bilateral initiatives. Since the 1990s, Cuba has increased the number of scholarships to Caribbean nationals wishing to study in Cuba; skilled Cuban professionals such as teachers, doctors, and other healthcare professionals have been deployed to the Caribbean; and Cuban medical professionals were sent to Haiti before and after the earthquake of 2010 (Byron 2014; Girvan 2012).

Laguardia Martinez and Martínez Reinosa (2019)[4] have proposed an outline of Cuba-CARICOM relations consisting of six phases. The current phase, which started in 2004, is considered in terms of an adjustment and re-energizing of the regional projection of the relations as they progress contemporarily. Cuba-CARICOM summits have been one of the key elements of this phase of the relationship. The summits provide an avenue for coordinating actions that promote national development, as well as for making progress on common interests in the context of initiatives toward deeper integration and cooperation.[5] These meetings and initiatives, combined with existing cooperation arrangements in the areas of education and health, among others, point to continued positive relations between Cuba and CARICOM.

The Sixth CARICOM-Cuba Summit was held in December 2017. The interactions at the summits continue to be significant for both sides for two reasons. First, they demonstrate a commitment on the part of the countries involved to sustain their relationship—2019 marked 47 years of Cuba-CARICOM diplomatic relations—and second, they illustrate the resolve of the countries involved to confront and address global issues, particularly as they affect the Caribbean, based on the recognition that individual action is not sufficient and that regional cooperation on these issues is necessary for the well-being of the region and its people (see Chap. 3).

---

[4] For more information on the six stages of Cuba-Caribbean relations after the triumph of the Cuban Revolution, consult the chapter 'The Foreign Policy of the Cuban Revolution: Half a Century of Cuba-Caribbean Relations' in *Selected Essays on Contemporary Caribbean Issues Vol. II*, edited book by Dr. Mark Kirton, November 2019 (estimated date of publication).

[5] Translated from the original: "se han convertido en un foro óptimo para coordinar acciones conjuntas relativas a los esfuerzos de desarrollo nacional, así como para lograr el avance de los intereses comunes dentro del contexto de procesos de integración y cooperación más amplios" (Martínez Reinosa 2015, 223).

Challenges on the Cuba-CARICOM Relations: The Caribbean Perspective

Besides U.S. pressures and role in the Caribbean, several factors have traditionally affected the Cuba-CARICOM relationship. These include: insufficient transportation links; linguistic barriers; insensitivity toward the business climate and economic systems on both sides; the inadequate number of institutions to facilitate trade or investment; CARICOM's lack of proactivity and relative inaction with regard to relations with Cuba; and continued Cuban foreign exchange constraints (see Chap. 11 for recommendations on addressing these challenges).

The preference of both parties to engage in deeper relationships with different external actors, based on their respective histories, has also acted as a distancing factor despite their close geographic proximity. Cuba and the rest of the Caribbean countries have, for the most part, tended to relate to countries with which they have had links in the past. Historically, independent Cuba had forged ties primarily with Latin American countries and the United States, and with the USSR (later Russia) after the Revolution. After the Cold War, more involvement has occurred with the EU member countries, especially with Spain, as well as with Canadá and China. CARICOM states, meanwhile, have emphasized intra-CARICOM relations and have fostered relations with the United Kingdom (UK) and the European Community (now the EU) via the Lomé framework and with the United States via the Caribbean Basin Initiative (Erisman 1994).

Despite the consensus on the need for establishing closer links between Cuba and the rest of the Caribbean and regardless of the new developments since December 17, 2014 (17D), the perceived challenges of forging links with Cuba are linked to Cuba's conflict with the United States. The obstacles to commercial relations posed by the U.S. embargo and by fear of U.S. retaliation remain as a significant dissuasive factor for advancing trade, investments, and financial relations with Cuba. After 17D, new concerns related to Cuba encompass fears and perceived threats of a potential increase in competition for tourists and foreign direct investment (FDI), brought about by the possible transformation of the Cuban economy; and the inertia of the CARICOM private sector toward availing itself of the favorable prospects in Cuba.

This argument is partially supported by the information gathered from the interviews conducted for this research. Among the challenges identified for the Caribbean, as a result of Cuba's opening up to diplomatic relations with the United States, is competition for tourism, and trade and investments. Tourism, in particular, has been one of the major points of discussion around the new regional relations. As the experts interviewed noted (CARICOM 02; Cuba 05, 06), it is inevitable that there will be some movement in the sphere of tourism away from traditional Caribbean locations toward Cuba. The newness of Cuba as a tourist destination, especially for those coming from the United States, will drive this movement. This issue was discussed in some detail in Chap. 5. One interviewee (CARICOM 05) pointed out, however, that Cuba is relatively new to the tourist industry and will have to develop the services it offers to visitors if it is to keep tourist interest in the island.

The changes occurring in Cuba are a result not only of 17D but also of internal dynamics brought about by the processes of adapting to a younger leadership and of undertaking constitutional and economic reforms. These domestic political changes are important for Cuba-CARICOM relations. There is apprehension that future developments in Cuba could place the region in a disadvantageous position and destabilize Caribbean economies.

In April 2018, Cuba's National Assembly of People's Power voted First Vice President Miguel Mario Díaz-Canel Bermúdez as the new President of the Council of States and the Council of Ministers, while Raúl Castro continues to head the Communist Party of Cuba (PCC) until 2021. President Díaz-Canel is 58 years old, and his election reflects the generational change in Cuban leadership. The new president faces significant challenges, the most pressing being to deepen the economic reform in response to demands for economic growth and welfare. Another inherited key problem is determining to what extent the Cuban model can be adapted to the changing conditions of a globalized world, which seems extremely difficult and risky to count on resources coming from the diaspora or close allies (Grabendorff 2017).

It is important to note that President Díaz-Canel attended the 39th regular meeting of the Conference of Heads of Government (CHG) of CARICOM, held in Jamaica in July 2018. The visit confirmed the new Cuban government's commitment to CARICOM and to cooperation with the Caribbean. The Cuban president was one of the special guests at the meeting, along with Chilean President Sebastián Piñera (Sputnik 2018).

On December 24, 2018, the National Assembly of People's Power voted in favor of a new draft constitution, which was approved on a popular referendum on February 24, 2019. The approved text had been modified after a period of public consultation in the last months of 2018, with debates held in various public fora, parks, and working areas. The debates showed that Cuban citizens were informed and interested to talk about the new constitution and the future of the country. They also confirmed the extent to which debate and popular feedback exists and functions in the Cuban system.

It is important to note that most of the proposed constitutional changes are not fundamental reforms. The new constitution reaffirms Cuba's commitment to build a socialist state. However, important changes include: the restructuring of government with the creation of the post of prime minister and of the posts of local governors; the recognition of private property; and the possibility of authorizing gay marriage, a final decision which is to be made by a popular referendum in the coming years. Changes on the property regime may have an impact on Cuba's larger economic possibilities to engage with external partners as the ones in the Caribbean.

Concluding Reflections

Cuba and CARICOM have a long history of good relations upon which they can build, and which can help in further institutionalizing Cuba-CARICOM relations. For a long time, Cuba and the Caribbean have shown mutual interest in engagement (Byron 2014). In spite of the tensions resulting from the Cuba-U.S. conflict, they have both benefited from cooperation and diplomatic relations, and their relationship has blossomed in the post-Cold War era. CARICOM has not supported the U.S. blockade against Cuba and awarded the Order of the Caribbean Community to Fidel Castro, the first non-CARICOM citizen to be given this honor.

All scenarios considered, the strengthening of relations between Cuba and CARICOM in a post 17D reality could open the door to new and greater economic opportunities and increased functional cooperation, and indirectly build the capacity of CARICOM countries, laying a foundational step toward boosting cooperation and encouraging regional integration.

To achieve such goals, though, it seems necessary to go beyond maintaining diplomatic, economic, and cooperative relations—each party must also seek out the benefits of being in the relationship, and how this can foster its own development while simultaneously promoting the advancement and development of the region as a whole. The next chapter focuses on this aspect, by addressing the specific areas in which the Cuba-CARICOM relationship could be beneficial for both parties, even in a context where the normalization of Cuba-U.S. relations still is a work in progress.

REFERENCES

Byron, Jessica. 2014. Development Regionalism in Crisis? Rethinking CARICOM, Deepening Relations with Latin America. *Caribbean Journal of International Relations & Diplomacy* 2 (4): 23–50.

CARICOM. 2004. CARICOM and Cuba to Celebrate Thirty-Two Years of Relations. Press Release. December 6, 2004. Accessed February 7, 2019. http://caricom.org/media-center/communications/press-releases/caricom-and-cuba-to-celebrate-thirty-two-years-of-relations.

———. 2017. Final Declaration: Fifth Meeting of Ministers of Foreign Affairs of CARICOM and the Republic of Cuba 2017. Accessed February 3, 2019. http://caricom.cubaminrex.cu/article/final-declaration-fifth-meeting-ministers-foreign-affairs-caricom-and-republic-cuba.

CARICOM Press Releases. 2017. More Opportunities Provided for Private Sector as CARICOM, Cuba Expand Duty-Free Market Access. *CARICOM*, November 10. Accessed March 3, 2019. https://caricom.org/media-center/communications/press-releases/more-opportunities-provided-for-private-sector-as-caricom-cuba-expand-duty-free-market-access.

CARICOM and Republic of Cuba. 2001. Trade and Economic Co-Operation Agreement Between the Caribbean Community (CARICOM) and the Government of the Republic of Cuba. Accessed July 18, 2017. http://investmentpolicyhub.unctad.org/Download/TreatyFile/2498.

Erisman, Michael H. 1994. *Evolving Cuban-CARICOM Relations: A Comparative Cost/Benefit Analysis*. Presentation at the Annual Conference of the Caribbean Studies Association, Merida, Mexico, May 23–28.

Girvan, Norman. 2012. *The Caribbean and Cuba: Cuba and the Caribbean: A Reflection*. Panel Discussion at the Havana International Book Fair, Havana, Cuba, February 11, 2012.

González Núñez, Gerardo. 2002. *Cuba's Relations with the Caribbean: Trends and Future Prospects*. Executive Summary. FOCAL, September. Accessed February 3, 2019. http://www.focal.ca/pdf/cuba_Gonzalez_Cuban%20relations%20Caribbean%20trends%20prospects_September%202002_RFC-02-2.pdf.

González Núñez, Gerardo, and Ericka Kim Verba. 1997. International Relations Between Cuba and the Caribbean in the 1990s: Challenges and Perspectives. *Latin American Perspectives* 24 (5): 81–95.

Grabendorff, Wolf. 2017. Cuba: The Challenges of Change. *Cuba y el proceso de actualización en la era de Trump in Pensamiento Propio* 45: 33–56.

Johnson, Jovan. 2016. Further Delays for CARICOM-Cuba Revised Trade Agreement Signing. *The Gleaner*, July 6, 2016. Accessed February 7, 2019. http://jamaica-gleaner.com/article/news/20160706/further-delays-caricom-cuba-revised-trade-agreement-signing.

Lall, Raphael John. 2012. T&T Braves Embargo to Attend Cuba Trade Fair. *The Business Guardian*, November 15, 2012.

Martínez Reinosa, Milagros. 2015. Las relaciones de Cuba con la Comunidad del Caribe (CARICOM): contando la historia y pensando el futuro. In *El ALBA-TCP: origen y fruto del nuevo regionalismo latinoamericano y caribeño*, compiled by Maribel Aponte García and Gloria Amézquita Puntiel and edited by Pablo Gentili, 193–237. Buenos Aires: El Consejo Latinoamericano de Ciencias Sociale (CLACSO).

Sputnik. 2018. Presidente cubano llega a Jamaica para asistir a 39 Reunión de Caricom. July 5, 2018. Accessed March 3, 2019. https://mundo.sputniknews.com/america-latina/201807051080179324-diaz-canel-en-jamaica-cumbre-caricom/.

Trade Wins. 2000. Trade and Economic Cooperation Between CARIFORUM and Cuba. *Critical Issues for Business*. Accessed February 9, 2019. http://carib-export.com/login/wp-content/uploads/2010/01/Trade%20and%20Economic%20Cooperation%20between%20Cariforum%20and%20Cuba.pdf.

United Nations General Assembly. 1992. *Necessity of Ending the Economic, Commercial and Financial Embargo Imposed by the United States of America against Cuba*, a/RES/47/19, November 24, 1992. Accessed February 9, 2019. https://www.un.org/documents/ga/res/47/a47r019.htm.

———. 1993. *Yearbook of the United Nations 1992, Volume 46*. Dordrecht: Martinu Nijhoff Publishers. Accessed March 11, 2019. https://www.unmultimedia.org/searchers/yearbook/page.jsp?bookpage=1&volume=1992.

CHAPTER 9

Cuba-CARICOM Cooperation

This chapter outlines cooperation between Cuba and the Caribbean Community (CARICOM) in some key sectors such as health, education, disaster risk reduction, and cultural exchanges. Cuba recognizes cooperation with the global South as a key principle of its foreign policy and has strengthened cooperation initiatives with CARICOM countries through various government-led projects via Caribbean, bilateral agreements, regional projects, or triangular cooperation initiatives. These cooperation activities have been characterized by varying levels of successes and challenges for both sides.

Cuba's tradition of South-South cooperation is widely known. The Cuban policy of assisting fellow developing countries has become an axiomatic principle of its foreign policy. Since 1961, Cuba has provided development assistance to almost 160 countries, involving more than 400,000 collaborators. As of September 2017, more than 50,000 Cuban collaborators were working in 70 countries (Rooplall 2017).

As discussed in earlier chapters, the early 1970s saw significant developments in relations between Cuba and newly independent Caribbean countries. Caribbean governments and political forces of diverse ideological tendencies acknowledged that the Cuban process had much to contribute to the concerted search for solutions to underdevelopment. Since then, Cuba has expanded wide-ranging ties and contacts in the Caribbean,

© The Author(s) 2020
J. Laguardia Martinez et al., *Changing Cuba-U.S. Relations*,
https://doi.org/10.1007/978-3-030-20366-5_9

157

resulting in economic, scientific, and technical cooperation, and slowly increased trade with the region (González Núñez 2002).

Cuba has joined regional organizations such as the Latin American and Caribbean Economic System (SELA) and the Community of Latin American and Caribbean States (CELAC) and is a founding member of the Association of Caribbean States (ACS) and the Bolivarian Alliance for the Peoples of Our America – Peoples' Trade Treaty (ALBA-TCP). As a member of the African, Caribbean, and Pacific (ACP) group, Cuba is also part of the Forum of the Caribbean Group of ACP States (CARIFORUM). Cuba is not a member of CARICOM, but as one of the Caribbean small island developing states (SIDS), the island shares similar development challenges with most CARICOM member countries and, together with them, promotes common interests that lie at the core of steady cooperation—primarily in health and education, but also other sectors.

Cuba's cooperation initiatives with CARICOM countries have been institutionalized in agreements, with counterpart government institutions Caribbean whether through bilateral agreements or regional projects. One of the main characteristics of Cuba's cooperation, is that programs, projects, and actions have been oriented to development goals and have been implemented under institutional frameworks. Another key characteristic of Cuban cooperation is that the objectives and strategies of each project have been determined by both Cuba and recipient countries. Cuba has assumed the financial costs in cases where the poorest or most vulnerable countries have been unable to. For instance, in the CARICOM group, Haiti has been identified as a Caribbean country with particular development challenges and has received special treatment as a recipient of Cuban cooperation. In some cases, cooperation initiatives have been jointly funded by third parties as part of triangular cooperation schemes.

Cuba's cooperation in the Caribbean stretches across sectors and projects. According to figures from March 2017, more than 31,000 Cuban collaborators, most of them medical staff, have journeyed across the Caribbean and 3000 Caribbean students have been awarded scholarships to pursue studies in Cuba since the beginning of cooperation with Cuba (Gómez 2017).

At the end of 2016, the number of Cuban collaborators in Caribbean territories stood at 1572. Of these, 44 percent were based in Haiti, while about 12 percent were based in Jamaica and Guyana each. Table 9.1 gives more detail in this regard.

Table 9.1 Cuban collaborators working in Caribbean territories by country (December 31, 2016)

Caribbean territories	Cuban collaborators
Antigua and Barbuda	53
The Bahamas	87
Barbados	8
Belize	73
Curaçao	3
Dominica	30
Dominican Republic	30
Dutch Caribbean except Curaçao	1
Grenada	24
Guyana	193
Haiti	689
Jamaica	187
St. Kitts and Nevis	14
St. Lucia	27
St. Vincent and the Grenadines	5
Suriname	7
Trinidad and Tobago	141
Total	1572

Source: Based on MINCEX (2017)

By 2018, there were 1773 Cuban collaborators in the Caribbean (Concepción Pérez 2018).

Even when Cuba's economic situation has put a major stress on continuing cooperation initiatives under its traditional free-of-charge scheme, South-South cooperation has been maintained. The economic transformation that Cuba is currently undergoing, as part of the *Lineamientos*—the program ratified at the Sixth Congress of the Communist Party of Cuba (PCC) in 2011—emphasizes the importance of Cuba's relations with Latin America and the Caribbean region (PCC 2011).

However, some changes have been introduced to make cooperation actions financially sustainable. Changes to the cooperation model practiced by Cuba with the Caribbean were first discussed at the Third Cuba-CARICOM Summit in 2008. Cooperation actions were recognized as a central pillar of Cuba-CARICOM relations, but at the same time, the Cuban government indicated the inevitability of reformulating the cooperation model considering the difficult economic situation Cuba was facing. Havana retained the political will to continue the cooperation—especially the fully funded scholarship program to study at Cuban universities. However, modifications had to be introduced, such as transferring the implementation of some programs to recipient countries, as was the case with Operation Miracle (Martínez Reinosa 2015). Other changes announced included involving third parties in triangular cooperation engagements or asking recipient countries to contribute financial and material resources, based on a case-by-case approach. One example of third party involvement to partially fund cooperation projects was the case of Chile and Mexico participating with Cuba in a project to improve the use of geographic information in the Caribbean region, by offering a workshop, titled "Geographic Information Metadata", in March 2016 in Havana (Programa Iberoamericano para el Fortalecimiento de la Cooperación Sur-Sur 2016).

The rest of this chapter explores regional cooperation initiatives involving Cuba and CARICOM member states. Emphasis is placed on the areas in which cooperation actions have shown more dynamism over the years—namely health, education, environmental cooperation, and cultural cooperation—though initiatives in other areas are also included.

Health

Medical diplomacy, defined by Feinsilver (2010, 86) as "the collaboration between countries to simultaneously produce health benefits and improve relations", has been a cornerstone of Cuban foreign policy. It has helped Cuba garner symbolic capital and has contributed to making it a global player. What began as the implementation of a core value of the Cuban Revolution, namely health as a basic human right, has continued as both an idealistic and pragmatic pursuit (ibid.).

Providing medical aid has been a central element of Cuba's foreign relations. The country suffered from the loss of half of its doctors after 1959—when Cuban doctors decided to leave the country and establish themselves elsewhere, mostly in the United States—The brain drain guided the Cuban government's decision to reform the health care sector, modernize education in the field of medicine, and encourage growth in the number of trained doctors. It is these factors that have made the commitment to medical cooperation possible on such a massive scale. By the mid-1980s, Cuba was producing large numbers of doctors beyond the needs of its own health care system (ibid. 87).

Cuba's tradition of providing medical aid to the global South dates back to the early 1960s. The government provided emergency medical assistance to countries adversely affected by climatological events or armed conflicts, even when health professionals were truly required at home. Cuba's first medical mission arrived in Chile after the 1960 Valdivia earthquake of 9.5 magnitude. In 1962, Cuba sent 56 doctors to Algeria to support the newly independent country (Kirk 2016a; Feinsilver 2010).

During the 1970s and 1980s, Cuba implemented a larger civilian cooperation program—one disproportionate to its size—particularly in the medical sector, compared to its more developed partners: the USSR, Eastern European countries, and China. Cuban civilian collaborators constituted 19.4 percent of the total provided by these countries, although the island accounted for only 2.5 percent of their total population (Feinsilver 2010).

According to Feinsilver (2010), Cuba's medical cooperation actions can be divided into two categories: short-term and long-term initiatives. These are outlined in Table 9.2.

Up to 2014, Cuba had engaged in 595,482 medical missions in 158 countries with the participation of 325,710 medical collaborators, many of whom had been engaged in two or three missions, at times more (Juventud Rebelde 2014). As of March 2017, it was estimated that approximately 55,000 Cuban medical personnel were aiding in 67 countries (Kirk 2016a).

In 2014, 256 Cuban doctors out of 15,000 volunteers were selected to travel to Africa to respond to the Ebola epidemic in West Africa (Kirk 2016b). The initiative was supported by the World Health Organization (WHO) and allowed Cuban and U.S. medical staff to collaborate—together with doctors from other nationalities—in a joint health mission in Africa.

Cuba also sends medical personnel to wealthier countries that have a ability to pay, such as Saudi Arabia and Qatar (Kirk 2016a). It is reported that Cuba gains about USD 8 billion in revenues per year from professional services administered overseas by the island's medical personnel (doctors and nurses) as the government collects a portion of the incomes earned by its citizens working abroad. This program of international medical assistance has become one of Cuba's largest exports (Hurley 2017).

For the CARICOM Caribbean, Cuba's assistance in the medical sector has been fundamental. Cuban medical aid to the Caribbean began in the 1970s in Jamaica (MINREX 2017). At the Second Cuba-CARICOM

Table 9.2 Typology of Cuba's medical cooperation actions

Short-term initiatives	Long-term initiatives
Disaster relief	Direct provision of primary health care in beneficiaries countries, mostly in areas where local doctors are not willing to work
Epidemic control and epidemiological monitoring	Staffing of secondary and tertiary care hospitals in beneficiary countries
On-the-job training for health care professionals to improve their skills	Establishment of health care facilities as clinics, laboratories, hospitals in beneficiary countries
Direct provision of medical care in Cuba	Establishment of comprehensive health programs in beneficiary countries
Health system organizational, administrative, and planning advisory services	Establishment and/or staffing of medical schools in beneficiary countries and/or community clinic-based medical training combined with distance learning under Cuban monitoring in country
Donation of medicines, equipment, and medical supplies	Provision of full scholarships to study in Cuba for medical school and allied health professional students
Vaccination and health education campaigns	Scientific exchanges
Program for human resource development and for the provision of specific medical services	
Exchange of research findings and knowledge transfer through the sponsorship of conferences and publications in academic and scientific journals	

Source: Contents of the table drawn from Feinsilver (2010, 88–89)

Summit, held in Barbados in December 2005, it was recognized that at that time, 1142 Cubans were working in CARICOM countries and around 1000 of them were in the health sector (Kirk and Erisman 2009). By 2005, Cuban medical teams were implementing their model Comprehensive Health Program in CARICOM countries, specifically in Belize, Dominica, and Haiti. Two comprehensive diagnostic centers were established: one in Dominica, and one in Antigua and Barbuda. Both Jamaica and Suriname's health systems were bolstered by the presence of Cuban medical personnel implementing the Comprehensive Health Program (Feinsilver 2010).

By 2018, 1454 Cuban professionals worked in the health sector in the insular Caribbean (Concepción Pérez 2018). The island has sustained medical collaboration with all CARICOM states. Even with Barbados, where no medical personnel are based, there is academic and technical exchange (MINREX 2017).

One of the most relevant examples of triangular cooperation involving Cuba and CARICOM countries is Operation Miracle, aimed at providing free medical treatment for people with eye problems. It is integrated into the programs of ALBA-TCP. This program has provided free eye surgery to 3.9 million people in 34 countries, mainly in Latin America and the Caribbean (Kirk 2016b). At the Second Cuba-CARICOM Summit, it was documented that 11 Caribbean countries had benefited from Operation Miracle and in the almost five months that the program had been in place, over 33,000 citizens had received surgery in Cuba at no charge.

At the Third Cuba-CARICOM Summit in 2008, it was acknowledged that some 280,000 surgical procedures had been carried out by Cuban physicians on CARICOM citizens, 118,000 births had been attended by Cuban medical personnel, and 17 million medical consultations had been given. It was also confirmed that the number of patients treated under Operation Miracle had increased to 480,000 (Kirk and Erisman 2009).

Cuba has also responded to singular medical emergencies resulting from extreme climatological events. In February 2005, a 40-member medical team, together with six tons of medical supplies, was sent to Guyana to assist after severe flooding had affected the country. In September 2004, following floods in Gonaives in Haiti, Cuba donated 22 tons of food, medicines, and medical supplies and the Cuban brigade of over 400 professionals and technicians already working in Haiti was joined by 64 collaborators specializing in emergency situations. In response to the damage caused by Hurricane Ivan in September 2004 and Hurricane Emily in July 2005, Cuba sent two brigades of more than 30 electrical engineers and technicians to Grenada. Cuba donated more than 11 tons of food to Jamaica after Hurricane Ivan (MINREX 2007).

More recently, after Hurricane Maria devastated Dominica in September 2017, Cuba, though amid its own recovery efforts after Hurricane Irma, sent 300 tons of cargo to the island. The shipment included "cement, steel rods, water and food" (Martin 2017).

It is believed that Cuba's medical help to Haiti started after the 2010 earthquake. However, Cuba's support to Haiti on a large scale in the medical field started in 1998. More than 6000 Cuban medical professionals have worked in Haiti, while 1000 Haitians from poor families have pursued medical studies in Cuba at no cost (Kirk 2016a). Immediately after the earthquake, Cuba sent more doctors to reinforce the medical brigades already in the country (Kirk 2016a). Because the Cuban doctors were already working in all ten departments in Haiti and had been present in the country since 1998, they can be considered as the first foreigners to respond to the earthquake. After three weeks, the Cuban medical staff had assisted over 50,000 people, performed 3000 surgeries, delivered 280 babies, vaccinated 20,000 people against tetanus, established nine rehabilitation wards, and begun providing mental health care, particularly for children and youths (Feinsilver 2010). Between 1998 and 2012 in Haiti, Cuban health professionals conducted more than 20 million consultations free of charge, with a third of these carried out at the patients' houses. They performed more than 370,000 surgeries—140,191 of these were major surgeries—and helped deliver more than 150,000 births. Operation Miracle improved or restored the eyesight of approximately 60,000 Haitians. During the cholera epidemic, Cuban doctors assisted 76,897 patients (Kirk 2016b).

Education

Since 1961, some 50,000 students from 129 countries have graduated from Cuban universities (Jamaica Information Service 2009). The Cuban program of scholarships for foreign students has seen around 49,000 health professionals from 135 countries graduate (Rooplall 2017). CARICOM members, in particular, have benefited from Cuban cooperation in the area of education.

At the Second Cuba-CARICOM Summit, it was noted that 1957 students from 14 Caribbean countries had graduated from Cuban schools, while an additional 3118 were training in 33 graduate and technical specialties. By 2006, around 3000 students from the Caribbean were taking classes in Cuba, including 1145 Caribbean nationals studying medicine (Kirk and Erisman 2009). Table 9.3 adds to this picture of educational cooperation.

Cuba's Deputy Minister of Foreign Trade and Investment, Ileana Núñez, at the inauguration of the First ACS Cooperation Conference, on

Table 9.3 Caribbean university graduates in Cuba from 1961 to 2007–2008

Territories	Graduates
Antigua and Barbuda	100
The Bahamas	67
Barbados	42
Belize	134
Curaçao	2
Dominica	300
Grenada	211
Guadalupe	13
Guyana	232
Haiti	812
Jamaica	487
Montserrat	1
Martinique	4
Puerto Rico	23
Dominican Republic	307
St. Kitts and Nevis	62
St. Vincent and the Grenadines	149
St. Lucia	316
Suriname	43
Trinidad and Tobago	47
Total	3352

Source: Martínez Reinosa and García Lorenzo (2013, 352)

March 8, 2017, in Havana, stated that as part of cooperation efforts, over 20,000 students from ACS countries had graduated from Cuban universities, while over 3000 young people from ACS countries were studying on the island (Redacción Internacional 2017).

More than 800 Haitian doctors have pursued their studies in Cuba's medical schools (Kirk 2016b). As of December 2018, 6623 Caribbean nationals had graduated from Cuban institutions and 1094 young Caribbean nationals were studying in the country (Concepción Pérez 2018).

In medical education and training, the Latin American School of Medicine (ELAM) in Cuba—the world's largest medical school, educating socially committed physicians from low-income families—has played a major role. The school was inaugurated in 1999, as part of Cuba's humanitarian response to the devastation caused by Hurricane Mitch and Hurricane George. The first students arrived in February 1999. The six-year medical program is free for low-income students who commit to practice medicine in underserved communities in their own countries upon graduation (Feinsilver 2010). Through ELAM, 28,000 doctors from more than 80 countries have been trained (Rooplall 2017).

Cuba's cooperation in education within the Caribbean extends beyond providing tertiary education. The country systematically delivers technical and professional training in diverse areas. In 2009, more than 300 nursing students from the English-speaking Caribbean countries participated in the Cuba-CARICOM training program for the provision of services to HIV/AIDS patients (Feinsilver 2010).

Cuba has offered its expertise for the establishment of the Regional Centre for Stimulating the Development of Children and Young People with Special Educational Needs Associated with Disabilities, a facility located within the Cyril Potter College of Education compound in Guyana. The objective of the regional center is to train persons to manage individuals with disabilities. This training encompasses "language and occupational therapy, psychological treatment, evaluation and diagnosis, rehabilitation, and social integration services, using a psycho-pedagogical and socially-inclusive approach" (CARICOM 2016).

Another important contribution to the region in the area of education is related to the application of the "Yes I Can" (*Yo Sí Puedo*) literacy method that aims to provide free education to adults who cannot read or write. The method can teach in one to three months and uses pre-recorded lessons adapted for each country. Lessons are delivered by a local facilitator. "Yes I Can" has been most successful in Venezuela, where it was adopted in 2003. Just two years later, the United Nations Educational, Scientific, and Cultural Organization (UNESCO) declared Venezuela illiteracy free. Over 10 million people have learned to read and write through the program (Bagri 2017). This successful alphabetization method has also been applied in the Caribbean—specifically in the Dominican Republic, Grenada, and Haiti. The largest enrollment was in Haiti, where, by 2009, there were almost 160,000 newly literate citizens (Martínez Reinosa and García Lorenzo 2013). In 2006, Cuba was awarded the UNESCO King Sejong Literacy Prize for its work in advancing "individual and social potential through innovative teaching methods" globally (Bagri 2017).

In October 2016, Cuba hosted the Second Workshop on Approaches and Tools for Disaster Risk Management and Adaptation to Climate Change for Sustainable Development, with the participation of learners from 11 Caribbean small island developing states (SIDS): Antigua and Barbuda, the Bahamas, Dominica, Grenada, Guyana, Haiti, Jamaica, St. Lucia, St. Vincent and the Grenadines, Suriname, and Trinidad and Tobago. The workshop responded to a Cuban initiative launched at the Fifth Cuba-CARICOM Summit in 2014. The first of these training workshops took place in 2015. During the workshop, it was announced that during the subsequent three years, Cuban specialists would contribute to preparing and training CARICOM experts in disaster risk management (Prensa Latina 2016).

CLIMATE CHANGE AND DISASTER RISK REDUCTION

Caribbean insular territories face several negative impacts associated with climate change and other climatological events. These countries have, therefore, undertaken various cooperation actions aimed at promoting mitigation and adaptation strategies in response to climate change. While participating in multilateral initiatives on climate change as SIDS and members of the Alliance of Small Island States (AOSIS), the Caribbean has promoted the regional dimension of climate action cooperation.

Environmental cooperation, especially on adaptation to climate change has become a key area of Cuba's support to CARICOM and CARICOM countries. It mostly includes initiatives oriented toward designing, organizing, and delivering training courses and joint programs for weather modeling and forecasts.

Cuba has cooperated with the Caribbean Disaster Emergency Management Agency (CDEMA) and the Caribbean Community Climate Change Centre (CCCCC) (CCCCC 2012). In August 2015, at the Tenth Convention on Environment and Development—attended by 1000 delegates from 60 countries—Dr. Neville Trotz, a member of the CCCCC, praised Cuba's collaboration with CARICOM to tackle global warming. At the same meeting, the Director General of the Cuban Institute of Meteorology (INSMET), Dr. Celso Pazos, explained that Cuba carried out wide-ranging cooperation with several Caribbean countries through research projects, workshops, meetings, scientific exchanges, and training courses. In 2006, a memorandum of understanding (MoU) was signed between INSMET and the CCCCC to promote research on environmental issues and progress in climate modeling (Laguardia Martinez 2017, 58).

One interesting regional cooperation action involving INSMET and the CCCCC was the Caribbean Weather Impacts Group (CARIWIG) project implemented between 2012 and 2015, with funding from the

Climate Development Knowledge Network and with the participation of England's Newcastle University and The University of East Anglia, and The University of the West Indies (UWI). The objective was the development of a web service to provide weather data, build weather forecasts, and determine tropical cyclone trajectories, as well as tools for climate analysis (ibid.). This was another case of triangular cooperation involving Cuba and the rest of the Caribbean, with extra-regional actors in the role of donors.

It is important to note that based on the information received from the interviews conducted for this research, there is a general belief that changing Cuba-U.S. relations will encourage a greater degree of cooperation at the triangular level (United States-Cuba-CARICOM), which will serve to address some of the social development issues affecting the region, especially security issues related to health and the environment, and even more so, tackling natural disasters. Cuba's aim, according to one of the Cuban interviewees (Cuba 04), would be to contribute to the sustainable development of the smaller islands, especially.

Other examples of Cuba's environmental cooperation with CARICOM members include Cuba's support to St. Kitts and Nevis, and Haiti in the preparation of their first national communications for the Climate Change Convention; to St. Vincent and the Grenadines in the creation of its greenhouse gases inventory; and to Belize in assessing its coastal vulnerability (Opciones 2015).

In June 2015, the United Nations Development Programme (UNDP) published *Compartiendo experiencias: cooperación Sur-Sur para la reducción de riesgos de desastres en el Caribe*, which described the experience of Cuba's transfer of its national risk management model to Jamaica, Trinidad and Tobago, Dominican Republic, British Virgin Islands, and Guyana. Cuba provided the training and technical assistance, while each territory adapted the model to its institutional structures (PNUD 2015).

In 2007, Cuba, the Dominican Republic, and Haiti signed an agreement for the creation of the first biological corridor in the Caribbean to reduce the loss of biological diversity. This triangular cooperation initiative aims for the rehabilitation of the Artibonito River basin (Juventud Rebelde 2007). Based on this tripartite agreement, in 2010, with the support of the United Nations Environment Programme (UNEP), a new project was launched to establish biological connectivity between ecosystems and habitats for the long-term conservation of biodiversity. The first phase was completed in 2014, after which the European Union supported a transition phase between January 2015 and June 2016 focused on the Dominican Republic. A second phase is scheduled for 2017–2020 (PNUMA 2016).

OTHER INITIATIVES

Cuba sustains a dynamic cultural exchange programs and has developed various cooperation initiatives in culture and arts with the rest of the Caribbean, both under regional and bilateral agreements. In 2005, CARICOM and Cuba signed a Cultural Cooperation Agreement at the Second Cuba-CARICOM Summit, outlining the various ways in which CARICOM member states and Cuba can promote cultural exchange among themselves (CARICOM 2005).

Cuban musicians have offered concerts in all CARICOM countries, Cuban dance groups and theater troupes have performed all over the region, and Cuba has given technical support to Barbados for teaching classic ballet. Cuba participates in the Caribbean Festival of Creative Arts (CARIFESTA); as a guest country in book fairs held in Caribbean countries, mostly in the Dominican Republic and Haiti; and in fashion and music festivals such as Hot Couture in St. Lucia, and the Latin Festival in St. Kitts and Nevis. In 2012, the Cuba Book Fair was dedicated to Caribbean culture and peoples (CARICOM Secretariat 2006; Charles 2015; Hewlett 2016; UNESCO Havana 2012).

Among other significant cultural events that engage Caribbean culture, of which Cuba is a vibrant part, are the Festival of Fire, held annually in Santiago de Cuba, and the Caribbean Film Travelling Showcase, founded by the late Cuban filmmaker Rigoberto López. The latter project consists of selecting films from the Greater Caribbean to be shown in Caribbean countries, with subtitles in English, Spanish, French, and Creole. According to López, in the Caribbean, we do not see Caribbean cinema, so the project seeks to spread local cinema in the region. The showcase was created in 2006, with the support of the Cuban Institute for Cinema Arts and Industry (ICAIC) and the UNESCO regional office, after the celebration of the First Festival of Cuban Cinema in Jamaica. On this occasion, filmmakers and cultural officers from Cuba and Jamaica recognized the necessity of organizing a regional initiative to gather Caribbean film directors, producers, actors, and the public as a way to promote Caribbean culture and diversity using films created in the region (Telesur 2018; CARICOM 2007).

In terms of bilateral projects, it is worthwhile to highlight cultural cooperation between Cuba and Jamaica, two Caribbean cultural superpowers. Both countries have agreed on developing a Caribbean Regional School of Arts at the Edna Manley College of the Visual and Performing Arts in Kingston, for which Cuba would provide technical support. The CARICOM Secretariat has indicated that the regional organization, too, would engage with the Edna Manley school to explore avenues of support, since the project falls under a Cuba-CARICOM cooperation program agreed at the Cuba-CARICOM summit in 2014 (Hamilton 2017). In addition, Cuba and Jamaica signed a Cultural Cooperation and Exchange Agreement in 2013. Bilateral cooperation in education and culture between the two countries goes back to the time of Jamaican Prime Minister Michael Manley, a good friend of Cuban President Fidel Castro. That relationship allowed for the establishment of four schools—the José Martí High School, the Gravey Maceo High School, a college for Physical Education and Sports, and the Fidel Castro School—donated by Cuba to Jamaica, all of which are still operational and in good condition (Cabrera Domínguez 2016).

In September 2018, the Ministry of Culture of Cuba and the Organization of Eastern Caribbean States (OECS) signed a MoU, in Havana, to establish a cooperation framework for matters related to creative industries. According to the document, both parties will cooperate in the development of the creative industries, particularly the craft sector, and will promote cultural exchange among local artisans in Kalinago, Dominica, St. Vincent and the Grenadines, and other Caribbean territories. An OECS-Cuba handicraft fair would be organized to exhibit the art of the various artisan groupings, facilitate technical exchange, and provide economic opportunities for producers. Arrangements will remain in effect for a period of five years from October 2018 to September 2023 (Prensa Latina 2018).

Cuba has also contributed to infrastructure projects in the Caribbean. For instance, the island participated in the construction of the Argyle Airport in St. Vincent and the Grenadines, completed in 2017. Furthermore, Cuba has helped to create ophthalmological centers in Jamaica, Haiti, and St. Lucia; and has established 16 Comprehensive Diagnostic Centers in Antigua and Barbuda (1), Dominica (1), Guyana (4), and Haiti (10) (MINREX 2007). Projects under consideration included Cuba's technical support for the construction of a park for Caribbean heroes in Cuba and another park in Antigua and Barbuda to celebrate the emancipation of slaves and the end of slavery (MINREX 2017). In April 2019, the Caribbean Heroes Park was inaugurated in Havana as an expression of the unity of the Caribbean and to celebrate the bravery of the Caribbean peoples in their fights against colonialism (Márquez 2019).

Besides cultural cooperation and physical infrastructure development, Cuba and CARICOM countries have joint programs in the energy sector. With the exception of Trinidad and Tobago, the rest of the Caribbean insular territories are net importers of energy and have pushed for initiatives to develop renewable energy and energy conservation models. As part of this effort, Cuba has tied up with its Caribbean neighbors in energy-saving programs.

At the Fifth Cuba-CARICOM Summit, it was noted that a cooperation program to save energy was implemented in the Caribbean between 2006 and 2011 by Cuban experts in residential areas of Antigua and Barbuda, Dominica, Guyana, Haiti, Jamaica, St. Kitts and Nevis, St. Lucia, St. Vincent and the Grenadines, and Suriname. Eight million energy-saving bulbs were donated.

Finally, the geographic proximity of the countries of the Caribbean has also created avenues for security cooperation. For instance, in 2009, Cuba and Jamaica came to an agreement concerning the maritime boundary between the two islands, which allows for cooperation "in the development and the implementation of programs regarding the sea and navigation including preservation and protection of the marine environment" (InforMEA n.d.).

Regarding exchanges in the context of evolving Cuba-U.S. relations, it is important to point out that one of the persons interviewed (Cuba 03) predicted an increase in cooperation in health services, but a decline in terms of study exchanges for CARICOM students in Cuba, as well as cultural exchanges, since more provision would be made in these latter areas in North America.

Concluding Reflections

The cooperation arrangements between CARICOM and Cuba have extended to diverse areas, chief among them being the fields of health, education, disaster risk reduction, and cultural exchanges. Cuban doctors have saved Caribbean lives and the cooperation programs have impacted Caribbean societies in a positive and concrete manner. The island's scholarship program has changed life of young people all over the region.

Even as Cuba is committed to profound social and economic changes as part of its 2011 guidelines plan, the island "has continued its wide-ranging cooperation program, inspired by Fidel but tempered with Raúl's pragmatism" (Kirk 2016b). While Cuba's export of its trained professionals, especially its medical personnel, is a powerful tool of soft diplomacy, its Caribbean neighbors have also benefited from Cuban expertise in various fields and have trained their own human resources at Cuban universities.

Cuban cooperation in the Caribbean shows remarkable progress. Key reasons for its success are the absence of ideological-political conditions inhibiting such cooperation and the focus on promoting social goals. Cuba and CARICOM share similar development challenges. Both parties have found, through cooperation initiatives, a way to deepen cooperation and advance developmental goals. In the context of the normalization of relations between Cuba and the United States, there is room to enlarge these cooperation initiatives with the participation of the United States. Cuba and the United States share positive experiences of joint work in regional security, health, and cultural exchanges. The United States could be a valuable third party in triangular cooperation with Cuba-CARICOM and provide technology, financial, and professional resources. However, a key element for such partnership to work is that all parties restrain to advance their own political and ideological agendas that remain fundamentally divergent.

References

Bagri, Neha Thirani. 2017. An Adult Literacy Program Developed in Cuba Is Now Being Used in More Than 30 Countries. *Quartz*, March 30, 2017. Accessed February 9, 2019. https://qz.com/946299/an-adult-literacy-program-developed-in-cuba-called-yo-si-puedo-is-now-being-used-in-more-than-30-countries-including-brazil/.

Cabrera Domínguez, Alina. 2016. Ampliarán Cuba y Jamaica esfera de cooperación. *Radio Rebelde*, January 5, 2016. Accessed December 30, 2018. http://www.radiorebelde.cu/noticia/ampliaran-cuba-jamaica-esfera-cooperacion-20160105/.

Caribbean Community (CARICOM). 2005. Cultural Cooperation Agreement Between the Caribbean Community (CARICOM) and the Republic of Cuba. Press Release. December 8, 2005. Accessed December 30, 2018. http://caricom.org/communications/view/cultural-cooperation-agreement-between-the-caribbean-community-caricom-and-the-republic-of-cuba.

———. 2007. Travelling Caribbean Film Showcase to Be Launched in St. Kitts and Nevis. Press release 50/2007. February 21, 2007. Accessed February 7, 2019. https://caricom.org/media-center/communications/press-releases/travelling-caribbean-film-showcase-to-be-launched-in-st-kitts-and-nevis.

———. 2016. Regional Training Centre Being Established for Young People with Disabilities. December 8, 2016. Accessed February 9, 2019. https://caricom.org/media-center/communications/press-releases/regional-training-centre-being-established-for-young-people-with-disabilities.

Caribbean Community Climate Change Centre (CCCCC). 2012. *Delivering Transformational Change 2011–21*. Belmopan, Belize. Caribbean Community Climate Change Centre.

CARICOM Secretariat. 2006. *CARIFESTA IX Promoted at Caribbean Festival in Cuba*. Press Release 150/2006. July 12, 2006. Accessed February 7, 2019. https://caricom.org/media-center/communications/press-releases/carifesta-ix-promoted-at-caribbean-festival-in-cuba.

Charles, Dee Lundy. 2015. HOT Couture Celebrates 'Fashion for Freedom'. *The Saint Lucia Star*, April 18, 2015. Accessed February 7, 2019. https://stluciastar.com/hot-couture-celebrates-fashion-for-freedom/.

Communist Party of Cuba (PCC). 2011. *Sixth Congress of the Communist Party of Cuba Resolution on the Guidelines of the Economic and Social Policy of the Party and the Revolution*. Accessed June 9, 2017. http://www.cuba.cu/gobierno/documentos/2011/ing/l160711i.html.

Concepción Pérez, Elson. 2018. El Caribe que nos une y fortalece. *Cubadebate*, December 6, 2018. Accessed February 7, 2019. http://www.cubadebate.cu/opinion/2018/12/06/el-caribe-que-nos-une-y-fortalece/#.XGmkxaJKjIU.

Feinsilver, Julie M. 2010. Fifty Years of Cuba's Medical Diplomacy: From Idealism to Pragmatism. *Cuban Studies* 41: 85–104.

Gómez, Sergio Alejandro. 2017. The Caribbean: A Look at the Neighborhood. *Granma*, March 14, 2017. Accessed February 9, 2019. http://en.granma.cu/cuba/2017-03-14/the-caribbean-a-look-at-the-neighborhood.

González Núñez, Gerardo. 2002. Cuba's Relations with the Caribbean: Trends and Future Prospects: Executive Summary. *FOCAL*, September. Accessed February 9, 2019. http://www.focal.ca/pdf/cuba_Gonzalez_Cuban%20relations%20Caribbean%20trends%20prospects_September%202002_RFC-02-2.pdf.

Hamilton, Deandrea. 2017. Cuba Providing Technical Support for Regional School of Arts. *Magnetic Media*, January 26, 2017. Accessed December 30, 2018. http://magneticmediatv.com/2017/01/cuba-providing-technical-support-for-regional-school-of-arts-2/.

Hewlett, L.K. 2016. Latin Festival 7 – Cuban Edition – Launched! *West Indies News Network (WINN FM 98.9)*, September 30, 2016. Accessed February 7, 2019. https://www.winnfm.com/news/local/18813-latin-festival-7-cuban-edition-launched.

Hurley, Gail. 2017. Punching Above Its Weight: Cuba's Medical Internationalism. *Speri*, January 4, 2017. Accessed February 9, 2019. http://speri.dept.shef.ac.uk/2017/01/04/punching-above-its-weight-cubas-medical-internationalism/.

Jamaica Information Service. 2009. *26 Students Receive Scholarships to Study in Cuba*. June 15, 2009. Accessed February 9, 2019. http://jis.gov.jm/26-students-receive-scholarships-to-study-in-cuba/.

Juventud Rebelde. 2007. Firmarán convenio de cooperación ambiental Cuba, Haití y Dominicana. July 9, 2007. Accessed February 9, 2019. www.juventudrebelde.cu/cuba/2007-07-09/firmaran-convenio-de-cooperacion-ambiental-cuba-haiti-y-dominicana/.

———. 2014. La participación cubana en el enfrentamiento al ébola en África Occidental no es un hecho aislado. September 12, 2014. Accessed February 9, 2019. http://www.juventudrebelde.cu/cuba/2014-09-12/la-participacion-cubana-en-el-enfrentamiento-al-ebola-en-africa-occidental-no-es-un-hecho-aislado.

Kirk, J.M. 2016a. Cuban Medical Internationalism: Fidel Castro's Humanitarian Legacy. *IRIN News*, December 1, 2016. Accessed February 9, 2019. https://www.irinnews.org/opinion/2016/12/01/cuban-medical-internationalism-fidel-castro%E2%80%99s-humanitarian-legacy.

———. 2016b. *Salud pública sin fronteras: para entender la cooperación médica internacional cubana*. Santiago de Cuba: Editorial Oriente.

Kirk, John, and Michael H. Erisman. 2009. *Cuban Medical Internationalism: Origins, Evolution, and Goals*. Basingstoke and New York: Palgrave Macmillan.

Laguardia Martinez, Jacqueline. 2017. Cambio climático: efectos y acciones de cooperación en las pequeñas islas del Caribe. *Revista estudios del desarrollo social: Cuba y América Latina* 5, no. 3 (September–December). Accessed February 12, 2019. http://www.revflacso.uh.cu/index.php/EDS/article/view/204.

Márquez, Roberto. 2019. Caribbean Heroes Park Inaugurated in Havana. *Radio Reloj*, April 26. Accessed May 30, 2019. http://www.radioreloj.cu/en/news/caribbean-heroes-park-inaugurated-in-havana/.

Martin, Karina. 2017. Castro Regime Sends Scarce Items to Dominica While Cubans Struggle to Recover from Hurricane. *Panama Post*, October 23, 2017. Accessed February 7, 2019. https://panampost.com/karina-martin/2017/10/23/castro-regime-sends-scarce-items-to-dominica/.

Martínez Reinosa, Milagros. 2015. Las relaciones de Cuba con la Comunidad del Caribe (CARICOM): contando la historia y pensando el futuro. In *El ALBA-TCP: origen y fruto del nuevo regionalismo latinoamericano y caribeño*, compiled by Maribel Aponte García and Gloria Amézquita Puntieland edited by Pablo Gentili, 193–237. Buenos Aires: El Consejo Latinoamericano de Ciencias Sociales (CLACSO).

Martínez Reinosa, Milagros, and Tania García Lorenzo. 2013. La cooperación de Cuba y el Caribe: la práctica de la teoría. In *El gran Caribe en el siglo XXI: crisis y respuestas*, compiled by Luis Suarez Salazar and Gloria Amézquita, 327–358. Buenos Aires: CLACSO.

Ministry of Foreign Affairs of Cuba (MINREX). 2007. Presentation by the Minister of Foreign Affairs of the Republic of Cuba at the Cuba-CARICOM Second Ministerial Meeting, May 29, 2007.

———. 2017. How Does Cuba Cooperate with the Caribbean? Accessed February 7, 2019. http://misiones.minrex.gob.cu/en/articulo/how-does-cuba-cooperate-caribbean.

Ministry of Foreign Trade and Investment of Cuba (MINCEX). 2017. Press Conference, on the Occasion of the Senior Officials Segment Meeting of the Association of Caribbean States, at Hotel Tryp Habana Libre in Havana, Cuba, March 9, 2017.

Opciones. 2015. Cooperación Sur-Sur, una baza contra el cambio climático. August 6, 2015. Accessed February 3, 2019. www.opciones.cu/cuba/2015-08-06/cooperacion-sur-sur-una-baza-contra-el-cambio-climatico/.

Prensa Latina. 2016. Cuba: destacada experiencia en gestión de riesgo de desastres. *Bohemia*, October 29, 2016. Accessed February 7, 2019. bohemia.cu/ciencia/2016/10/cuba-destacada-experiencia-en-gestion-de-riesgo-de-desastres/.

———. 2018. Firman acuerdo Ministerio de Cultura de Cuba y organización caribeña. Cubasí, September 19, 2018. Accessed January 24, 2019. http://cubasi.cu/cubasi-noticias-cuba-mundo-ultima-hora/item/82642-firman-acuerdo-ministerio-de-cultura-de-cuba-y-organizacion-caribena.

Programa de Naciones Unidas para el Desarrollo (PNUD). 2015. Compartiendo experiencias: cooperación Sur-Sur para la reducción de riesgos de desastres en el Caribe. June 25, 2015. Accessed February 9, 2019. https://www.undp.org/content/undp/es/home/news-centre/news/2015/06/23/sharing-what-works-south-south-cooperation-for-disaster-risk-reduction-in-the-caribbean.html.

Programa de Naciones Unidas para el Medio Ambiente (PNUMA). 2016. Corredor biológico en el Caribe: ecosistemas conectados más allá de las fronteras. Regional Office for Latin America and the Caribbean, PNUMA. Accessed February 9, 2019. www.pnuma.org/informacion/articulos/2016/a20160708/index.php.

Programa Iberoamericano para el Fortalecimiento de la Cooperación Sur-Sur. 2016. México y Chile contribuyen con Cuba a mejorar la utilización de la información geográfica en los países del Caribe. *Cooperación Sur-Sur.* Accessed January 23, 2019. https://www.cooperacionsursur.org/es/noticias-de-cooperacion-sur-sur/1393-mexico-y-chile-contribuyen-con-cuba-a-mejorar-la-utilizacion-de-la-informacion-geografica-en-los-paises-del-caribe.html.

Redacción Internacional. 2017. Cooperation, Key to Caribbean Development. *Granma*, March 8, 2017. Accessed February 3, 2019. http://en.granma.cu/cuba/2017-03-08/cooperation-key-to-caribbean-development.

Rooplall, Rabindra. 2017. 790 Guyanese Doctors Trained in Cuba. *Guyana Chronicle*, September 4, 2017. Accessed February 7, 2019. http://guyanachronicle.com/2017/09/04/790-guyanese-doctors-trained-cuba.

Telesur. 2018. The Caribbean Celebrates the Fire Festival in Santiago de Cuba. July 8, 2018. Accessed February 7, 2019. https://www.telesurenglish.net/news/The-Caribbean-Celebrates-the-Fire-Festival-in-Santiago-de-Cuba-20180708-0013.html.

United Nations Educational, Cultural, and Scientific Organization (UNESCO) Havana. 2012. The Slave Route and the Travelling Caribbean Film Showcase, Two Projects Sponsored by UNESCO, in the 21st International Book Fair Cuba 2012. February 15, 2012. Accessed February 7, 2019. http://www.unesco.org/new/en/havana/about-this-office/single-view-havana/news/the_slave_route_and_the_travelling_caribbean_film_showcase/.

United Nations Information Portal on Multilateral Environmental Agreements (InforMEA). n.d. *Agreement Between the Government of the Jamaica and the Government of the Republic of Cuba on the Delimitation of the Maritime Boundary Between the Two States*. Accessed January 5, 2019. https://www.informea.org/en/treaties/agreement-between-government-jamaica-and-government-republic-cuba-delimitation-maritime.

CHAPTER 10

Cuba-CARICOM Trade and Economic Relations

In the Caribbean region, the favorable economic climate experienced at the beginning of the twenty-first century differs from the current scenario. Structural gaps hinder the development of Caribbean states: poorly diversified productive sectors and export base; insufficient participation in global and regional value chains; weak levels of innovation. Various social problems such as high maternal mortality, the spread of HIV, unemployment—especially among youth and women—and the persistence of poverty and inequality exacerbate development challenges. Caribbean small island developing states (SIDS) remain highly vulnerable to exogenous financial and economic instability as well as to extreme climatologic events and environmental disasters (UN ECLAC 2016).

In light of the above, this chapter examines the strategies that are employed by Cuba and the countries of the Caribbean Community (CARICOM) as they strive for economic growth and development. For Cuba, trade and economic relations with the CARICOM group is a strategic objective. CARICOM is recalibrating its foreign economic and trade relations and forging links with partners in Latin American and Caribbean.

The global economy is currently immersed in uncertainty. The decline in raw material prices contradicted ominous forecasts that predicted moderate growth and modest economic recovery. The commercial confrontation between the United States and China may have a negative impact globally and in the Caribbean region. The Caribbean has not escaped the effects of the global slowdown. This has been reflected in the sluggish demand for exports and the increased volatility of foreign direct investment (FDI) and remittance inflows. If all these major challenges are not tackled effectively, the developmental gains of the region can be eroded (Hendrickson 2017).

For the Caribbean, it will be difficult to boost economic growth and to make advancements on the 2030 Agenda for Sustainable Development without restructuring the region's economic strategy and external economic relations. In the attempt to reduce dependence on a few export markets and products, the Caribbean is forced to diversify its trading partners, increase competitiveness, and attract FDI. The classification of Caribbean Community (CARICOM) member countries—with the exception of Haiti—as high- and middle-Income countries has led to a decline in official development assistance (ODA) and the tightening of lending conditions (CARICOM Today 2018). The current scenario forces CARICOM member states to redefine strategies for economic growth and regional development, in order to adapt to a less dynamic trade environment and lower prices for its export products, in a context in which access to international financial markets and concessional financing has become more difficult.

Cuba faces similar challenges as the rest of the region. Since 2011, the Cuban government has been focused on the implementation of a new economic policy that pursues economic recovery while preserving the social achievements of the socialist model. The main guidelines for the reform were approved at the Sixth Congress of the Communist Party of Cuba (PCC), in a document titled "Lineamientos de la política económica y social del partido y la revolución" (Republic of Cuba 2011). In 2017, the Cuban parliament approved new guidelines for the period 2016–2021, together with a document for the conceptualization of the Cuban socialist economic and social model.

The hybrid economy that has grown due to the reforms initiated almost a decade ago has brought changes within the Cuban socio-economic ecosystem. The efforts to modernize Cuba's centrally planned economy have borne mixed results, with some initiatives moving forward, others delayed, and still others yet to begin. Small- and medium-sized private businesses exist, together with around 5500 agricultural cooperatives in operation (Jorgensen 2018). Over 40 new projects for the Mariel Special Development Zone (ZED Mariel) and 175 joint ventures have been approved since the enactment of a new foreign investment law in 2014 (Torres 2018). Even if ZED Mariel, highlighted in Box 10.1, constitutes an interesting investment possibility for foreign partners—including Caribbean companies—bureaucratic obstacles hinder its functioning.

> **Box 10.1 Key Facts About the Mariel Special Development Zone**
> - Officially established on January 27, 2014.
> - Located 45 km from Havana city.
> - Created to drive in foreign direct investment (FDI) in economic development.
> - No restrictions on foreign ownership.
> - Fiscal advantages for FDI in the zone versus other Cuban areas.
> - Owned by Almacenes Universales S.A., the largest transportation and logistics group in Cuba.
>   Managed by PSA International.
>
> Source: ZED Mariel (2017)

In 2014, only one business proposal was approved. In 2015, as in 2016, there were ten projects approved. Twelve business proposals were accepted in 2017, and ten in 2018. At the Cuban International Trade Fair, in October 2018, an updated portfolio of opportunities for foreign investment was released. The current version offers 525 projects for an estimated investment of USD 11,609 million (Cubatrade 2018).

The opening up of major economic sectors to foreign investment and allowing of the establishment of national private enterprises must be understood in the context of steadily declining productivity and a lack of sufficient public funds. The reform process is aimed at boosting the productive integration of Cuba into the world economy, especially in light of the Cuban government's awareness of the dissatisfaction in most parts of Cuban society about declining living standards and reduced social benefits, while bureaucratization and corruption are on the rise (Grabendorff 2017).

There are major economic challenges yet to be confronted. Critical monetary and political reforms have been postponed; wholesale markets are non-existent; FDI has not arrived in the amounts expected (estimates indicate that between USD 2 billion and USD 2.5 billion per year of FDI are required to boost Cuba's economy) (Terrero 2017); foreign trade and agriculture production have stagnated; and economic growth is weak. Lower real wages in the public sector, import restrictions, and daily challenges related to moving about Havana city and to finding everyday products easily[1] have accelerated Cuba's brain drain and stimulated black markets.

So far, the economic reform process seems to be based on a trial-and-error method that avoids major risks. Dramatic changes have been postponed until the gradual retirement of the Revolution generation, fast-paced in 2018 with the election of Miguel Díaz-Canel as President of the Council of State and the Council of Ministers. The transformations currently under way have produced notable results; however, the main goals have yet to be achieved in a context in which Cuba's foreign debt payment reaches between 30 and 35 percent of its current export income—quite a high percentage, according to international standards (Torres 2017).

Another significant factor to be considered for the future of social, political, and economic reform—which certainly has an impact on Cuba's international relations and foreign policy—is related to the transformation of Cuban society into a well-functioning transnational society. The changes that are occurring in this regard will be determined principally by intermestic factors, with the influence of different sectors of Cuban society within and outside the country playing out together with that of their foreign counterparts (Grabendorff 2017).

The importance of the Caribbean region for Cuba's trade and economic relations is recognized in the 2011 guidelines, which established that Cuba aims to:

> [k]eep an active participation in the economic integration process with Latin America and the Caribbean as a strategic objective, and maintain Cuba's involvement in the regional trade economic arrangements to which Cuba has adhered, including but not limited to the Latin American Integration Association (LAIA), the Caribbean Community (CARICOM), the Association of Caribbean States (ACS) and PETROCARIBE, and continue to strengthen the unity among the members of these arrangements. (Republic of Cuba 2011, 20)

The strategic vision for regional economic integration that includes the Caribbean space and—explicitly—CARICOM is maintained in the newest version of the guidelines (Republic of Cuba 2017).

As stated in Chap. 8, Cuba is not a CARICOM member state. Nevertheless, the relationship between it and the regional integration

---

[1] In December 2018, there was a "bread" crisis due to delays in flour imports and broken equipment in flour mills.

scheme has advanced in the past decades. Triennial summits, together with sustained cooperation in health, education, environment, and cultural issues, for instance, are testimony of the constructive relationship Cuba and its Caribbean neighbors have managed to build. The first Cuba-CARICOM summit was held in 2002 to commemorate the 30th anniversary of the establishment of diplomatic relations between Cuba and Barbados, Guyana, Jamaica, and Trinidad and Tobago. The sixth and most recent summit took place in December 2017 in Antigua and Barbuda.

Trade and Investment

In 1998, Caribbean Export sponsored a study on trade facilitation between Forum of the Caribbean Group of ACP States (CARIFORUM) member States and third countries. The report revealed that even with the establishment, in 1993, of the Joint Cuba-CARICOM Technical Commission and the political discussions that are continually held, the anticipated exchange of goods, services, and information and the standardization of rules of trade had not materialized for the business community (Trade Wins 2006).

Furthermore, the Caribbean Export Development Agency (commonly called Caribbean Export) opened a Trade and Investment Facilitation Office in Havana in 1999, with the objective of facilitating trade and economic relations between CARIFORUM and Cuba.[2] Aimed at assisting companies in penetrating the Cuban and Caribbean markets, the office offers

> market research/intelligence services; needs analyses; marketing advisory services (e.g. formulation of market-entry strategies); co-ordination of in-market promotion activities (e.g. trade fairs, trade missions, market visits and appointments); follow-up activities for companies (including payment collection); trademark and health registration; identification of export and investment opportunities (including joint venture partnerships). (Trade Wins 2000)

---

[2] CARIFORUM refers to the group of Caribbean States which are signatories of the Georgetown Agreement of 1975 by virtue of which the African, Caribbean, and Pacific Group of States (ACP) was created. All CARIFORUM States, with the exception of Cuba, are signatories to the Cotonou Agreement and the economic partnership agreement (EPA).

The CARICOM-Cuba Trade and Economic Cooperation Agreement (TECA) was signed on July 5, 2000, during the Cuba-CARICOM Joint Commission meeting in Santiago de Cuba. Two years later, in December 2002, during the First Cuba-CARICOM Summit, the TECA was ratified and a protocol for provisional application was signed (Martínez Reinosa 2015). The TECA is a partial scope agreement, mainly focused on the trade in goods. It creates a framework for the progressive liberalization of trade, while seeking "to lay the foundation for increased economic integration through new levels of partnership and the gradual reduction of tariffs and other obstacles to trade" (Trade Wins 2006). The TECA makes provisions for extensive duty-free treatment of specific products, which include, among many others, clothing, condiments, fruit juices, seasonings, and various sauces. It also makes duty-free treatment available for certain agricultural products at planned periods throughout the year. Several products have been allocated for the reduction and elimination of tariffs, a process that will be completed in phases (Trade Wins 2006).

The main products covered by TECA (Trade Wins 2006) fall within four categories:

1. CARICOM products allowed duty-free entry into Cuba, which include: animal feed; bags and cases; bulbs; cereals; chemicals and oxides; compounds and resins; cosmetics; eggs; fermented beverages; fish and seafood; footwear; fruits; furniture; glass products; hats; ice-cream; insecticides and fungicides; household electrical machinery and equipment; jewelry; juices; lamps; mattresses; meat; medicines; metal waste and scrap; metals and related products; milk and milk-based products; ores; poultry; vegetables; peas; petroleum products; sauces and condiments; spices; sugar confectionery and cocoa products; textiles and clothing; tiles; toys; transportation equipment; vegetable oils and extracts; water; and wood and paper products.
2. CARICOM products subject to phased duty reduction over four years by Cuba, which include: bags of paper; boxes; bread; cakes and biscuits; cartons; cases; cut flowers; fruits and nuts; packaging products; pasta; pastry; plastic builders' wares; plastic tableware and kitchenware; sausages and other prepared meat; and some sauces and condiments, among others.
3. Cuban products allowed duty-free entry into CARICOM member states classified as more developing countries (MDCs), which

include: alcoholic beverages; aluminum products; bags and cases; blocks; boilers; bricks; chemicals and oxides; cooking apparatus; cosmetic products; eggs; essential oils and extracts; fish and seafood; footwear; fruits and vegetables; furniture; glands and organs; glass products; hats and headgear; hides and skins; hormones; household and industrial electrical machinery, equipment, and parts; ice-cream; insecticides and the like; juices; knives; leather; live animals; meat; medicaments; metals and related products; motor vehicle parts and accessories; ores and other minerals; plastic products; potatoes; prefabricated buildings; pumps; safes; scientific instruments; soups and broths; stone products; sugar confectionery and cocoa products; textiles and clothing; tiles; tobacco products; toys; trunks; turbines; water; and wood and paper products.
4. Cuban products subject to phased duty reduction over four years by CARICOM MDCs, which include: boxes; cartons; cases and bags; cloth, coffee; grilled products; jams; jellies and marmalades; netting and fencing (iron or steel wire) pasta; plastic tableware and kitchenware; sausages; and soups and broths.

The TECA removes "regulatory and administrative barriers to bilateral trade and addresses issues related to investment, taxation, trade promotion and facilitation, tourism, and intellectual property rights" (McLean and Khadan 2015, 7). The agreement establishes lists of goods that would undergo phased reductions in duty and provides for special trading arrangements for a set list of agricultural products once imported into the CARICOM MDCs (Trade Wins 2006). Under TECA, the role of trade financing in the development of trade is also recognized (ExportTT n.d.).

CARICOM and Cuba aim to ensure that all participating countries are able to take advantage of the agreement, in spite of the differences that exist in terms of their capacity and level of economic development. To help accomplish this, the less developed countries (LDCs) of CARICOM are not obligated to grant duty-free access to goods, nor do they have to institute the phased reduction in duty (Trade Wins 2006).

CARICOM and Cuba agreed to trade under the agreement without applying any quota restrictions. Consideration is to be given, however, to their rights as stipulated by the World Trade Organization (WTO) and to the commitments of CARICOM member states under the Revised Treaty of Chaguaramas. Both parties also aim to ensure that technical regulations do not create any barriers to trade and to standardize their technical, and sanitary and phytosanitary measures (Trade Wins 2006).

Under the TECA, products manufactured in free trade zones and export-processing zones are subject to most favored nation (MFN) treatment. In practical terms, this translates into the fact that while duty-free access will not be given, these products will be subject to duties and tariffs that are no less favorable than the ones set for other countries not part of the agreement (ibid.). The TECA seeks to promote, protect, and facilitate investments between the trading partners through the development and adoption of an agreement based on "reciprocal promotion and protection of investments" (Trade Wins 2006).

According to the Export Trinidad and Tobago (simply called ExportTT) office, for the CARICOM member states, some of the benefits of exporting to Cuba are as follows:

1. Competitive market pricing for exported products covered by the TECA
2. Access to a large market considered a regional "virgin" market due to the limited presence of traditional competitors and dominant brands
3. Opportunities for investment, mostly on investments to develop productive capabilities, with emphasis in tourism and agriculture
4. Ability to capitalize on Cuba's strong areas as medicine, education, and services
5. Lesser need for resources to be expended on advertising and promotional activity

In spite of the TECA and the identified benefits of bilateral trade, commercial links between Cuba and CARICOM are not significant as both parties prefer to trade with traditional partners outside the Caribbean region. Nevertheless, trade between them has expanded since 2000, and CARICOM generates trade surpluses with Cuba (McLean and Khadan 2015). CARICOM exports to Cuba climbed from USD 13.7 million in 2000 to USD 46 million in 2008. The negative effects of the global economic crisis hit this trade, which declined in 2009 before a partial recovery in 2010, when exports reached USD 25 million (ONEI 2012).

Within the CARICOM space, Trinidad and Tobago, Jamaica, Guyana, and Suriname comprise the majority of Cuba's trade. Trinidad and Tobago, and Guyana are the major exporters to Cuba, and the member countries

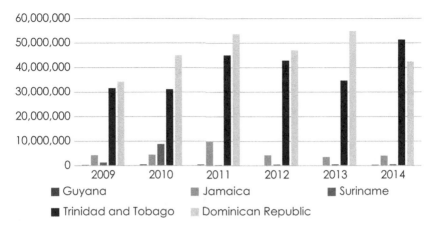

Fig. 10.1 Cuban imports of goods from main CARICOM trade partners and the Dominican Republic, 2009–2014 (in USD). Source: Based on figures in ONEI (2015)

of the Organization of Eastern Caribbean States (OECS) maintain minor exports to the island. However, CARICOM has some untapped prospects in the Cuban market. The Caribbean has comparative advantage in pesticides and disinfectants, organic chemicals, wood products, and non-alcoholic beverages (McLean and Khadan 2015). Figure 10.1 offers information in this regard.

CARICOM's imports from Cuba reached a top value of USD 107 million in 2007, followed by a decrease and a restricted recovery in 2009. From 2010 onward, the decline has sharpened, and with the exception of Guyana, previous import levels have not been equaled (ONEI 2012). Figure 10.2 illustrates the trends here.

Between 2014 and 2017, Antigua and Barbuda, Belize, and Barbados showed a certain dynamism in their trade with Cuba. In 2016, Barbados registered a surplus of USD 3.8 million in its trade with Cuba, mostly in beverages, spirits, and vinegar (International Trade Centre Trade Map 2015).

In January 2017, CARICOM and Cuba agreed on the expansion of preferential access to each other's markets. The agreement was reached during the 10th Meeting of the CARICOM-Cuba Joint Commission held in Guyana, and "[a] significant number of items from the Community, including beer, fish and other agricultural products, and manufactured

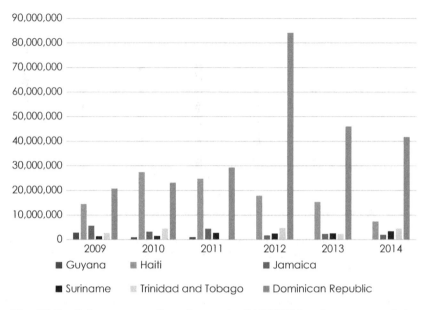

Fig. 10.2 Cuban exports of goods to main CARICOM trade partners and the Dominican Republic, 2009–2014 (in USD). Source: Based on figures in ONEI (2015)

goods, [was] approved for entry into the Cuban market free of duty once both sides formalize the agreement" (*Jamaica Observer* 2017). CARICOM member states also approved to allow duty-free access to Cuban goods, including pharmaceuticals. CARICOM MDCs will determine the level of preference to permit to Cuba on other items (ibid.).

Even as the current context seems favorable for CARICOM to expand its exports to Cuba, there are obstacles that hamper trade and investment flows between Cuba and CARICOM. Besides the global economic downturn, there are also the high cost of air and sea transportation, legal and institutional differences, scarce financial and credit mechanisms to support trade and investment, and the U.S. embargo against Cuba. Also, according to Lowe, a well-defined and articulated CARICOM trade policy toward Cuba cannot be identified (Lowe 2011).

In addition, the lack of export financing in several CARICOM countries—such financing is essential for penetrating the Cuban market—has been underscored by sub-regional economic operators. Moreover, the process for registering as a potential supplier in Cuba is deemed to be a very lengthy and complex one (McLean and Khadan 2015).

Even though the TECA considers the promotion of investments as part of its mandate and the Caribbean has proven that it can attract significant FDI, especially when compared to Latin America, only a few CARICOM countries have signed individual bilateral investment treaties with Cuba. They include Barbados (1996); Belize (1998); Jamaica (1997); Suriname (1999); and Trinidad and Tobago (1999) (UNCTAD 2013).

The promotion of FDI is very important for the Caribbean since domestic investment capability is insufficient. The majority of CARICOM governments could do more to exploit existing FDI in such a manner as to encourage economic growth, while some economies would have to first attract these bilateral investments before any noticeable positive impacts are experienced (UN ECLAC 2015).

According to data from the United Nations Economic Commission for Latin America and the Caribbean (UN ECLAC 2018), FDI is now back at 1997 levels after a gradual economic recovery following several years of recession. Greater interest in mining and oil was registered in 2017 and investments have increased in tourism, a key sector that was negatively hit following the economic recession started in 2008 when tourist arrivals and investments in the sector fell considerably. FDI in the Caribbean grew by 22 percent in 2017, reaching USD 6.074 billion. More than 50 percent of the total were directed to the Dominican Republic, followed by the Bahamas (15 percent) and Jamaica (14 percent) (Fig. 10.3).

Investors in Dominican Republic are attracted by the tourism sector, manufacturing, export services, the electricity sector and mining. On the other hand, inward FDI to Trinidad and Tobago was negative in 2016 due to lower oil prices and the maturity of the two-island state's oil fields (UN ECLAC 2018). Haiti usually receives scarce levels of FDI, but in 2017, inflows reached USD 375 million. The increase is attributable to the acquisition of DINASA by a French company. The clothing sector continues to grow due to investments made by Asian companies (ibid.).

As previously mentioned, in 2014, Cuba opened ZED Mariel, which was largely funded by Brazil. The port's closeness to the Panama Canal and to the United States could create opportunities, as long as Washington lifts economic sanctions against Cuba and pursues the normalization of relations (UN ECLAC 2015).

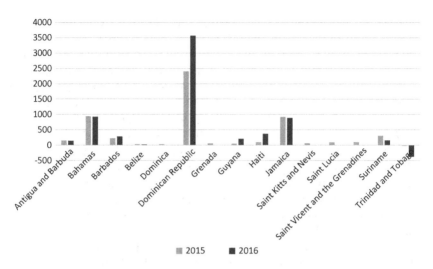

Fig. 10.3 The Caribbean (selected economies): inward FDI, 2015–2016 (millions of USD). Source: UN ECLAC (2018)

The Cuban Foreign Investment Act, introduced in 2014, updated the legislation in effect since 1995. The revised act aims at diversifying the production system, gaining access to advanced technology, substituting imports—particularly food imports—and encouraging integration into regional and global value chains. Another objective is to transform the energy environment by means of investments in renewable energy. Through this act, all sectors—apart from the education, health, and defense sectors—may receive FDI. Additionally, it determines the legal protections for investors, authorizes foreign investors to hold a greater share in an investment, and introduces tax incentives (UN ECLAC 2015).

As of 2015, Spain is the leading investor in Cuba, followed by other European countries, Canada, and the BRIC countries (Brazil, Russia, India, and China) (UN ECLAC 2015).

Tourism

In 2014, the year when Cuba and the United States resumed relations, the Caribbean received a record 26.3 million tourists, a 5.3 percent more compared to the previous year. These visitors spent USD 29.2 billion, a 3.9 percent increase on the USD 28 billion spent in 2013. The United

States established itself as the principal market, with almost 13 million U.S. arrivals in the region—representing just under 50 percent of total arrivals. An increase was also seen in visitors from Canada, with an increase of 5.7 percent in 2013; and for the first time since 2008, European visitors surpassed five million, recording a 4.6 percent increase in 2013. The overall 5.3 percent increase experienced by the region as a whole was higher than the global growth rate of 4.7 percent, as indicated by the United Nations World Tourism Organization (UNWTO 2015), and also nearly twice the predicted growth of 2–3 percent (CTO 2017b).

Two years later, the momentum continued for the region, with Cuba registering a significant increase in tourist arrivals as a direct consequence of its changing relations with the United States (see Chap. 5). In 2016, tourism in the Caribbean reached a milestone with a record of over 29 million arrivals, exhibiting growth in this area at a rate faster than the global average. In 2016, tourist arrivals in the region increased by 4.2 percent, a positive figure when compared to the overall increase of 3.9 percent in tourist arrivals at the international level. There were also record levels of visitor expenditure, which grew at an estimated 3.5 percent, reaching USD 35.5 billion (CTO 2017b).

In 2015, the United States remained the Caribbean's primary market with an increase of 3.5 percent in stay-over arrivals—equating to a total estimate of 14.6 million U.S. visitors. It is worth noting, however, that among the major source markets, it was European visitors that reported the highest rate of growth as a result of a strong increase from Germany (8.2 percent) and the UK (4.1 percent). Travel within the Caribbean reflected a 3.6 percent increase—marking the second consecutive year of growth—in spite of higher costs and air service fragmentation (CTO 2017b). Figures 10.4 and 10.5 highlight some of the details concerning visitor arrivals within the Caribbean.

Almost all CARIFORUM countries registered increases in 2016 arrivals, with a significant rise for Cuba and continental CARICOM members—Belize, Guyana, and Suriname. Decreases were registered in Haiti, Bahamas, St. Kitts and Nevis, and Trinidad and Tobago. In the case of Trinidad and Tobago—an oil and gas exporting country that has not relied heavily on tourism, unlike most of its Caribbean neighbors—the reduction topped 7 percent in the 2015–2016 period; a situation linked not only to the minor development of the tourism sector in Trinidad in particular, but also due to the economic recession and the upsurge in crime and insecurity that has affected the twin islands.

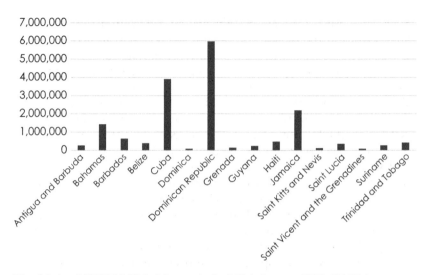

Fig. 10.4 CARIFORUM visitor arrivals, 2016. Source: CTO (2017a)

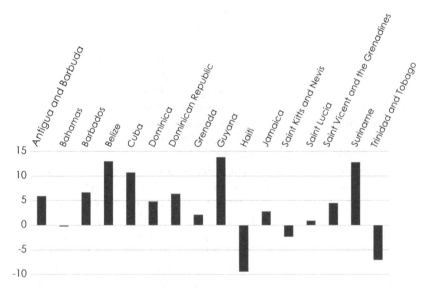

Fig. 10.5 CARIFORUM visitor arrival increases, from 2015 to 2016. Source: CTO (2017a)

Cuba and the CARICOM member states recognize the importance of the tourism sector for their economies, and have discussed the necessity of joining efforts to diversify their tourism offering and become a more competitive regional destination worldwide. Cuba and CARICOM have agreed to promote the development of tourism and to encourage multi-destination travel. As members of the ACS, they signed the Convention establishing the Sustainable Tourism Zone of the Greater Caribbean (STZC) in 2001 (ACS 2015).

The TECA undertakes to ensure cooperation in all areas of tourism development, including marketing. It comprises joint preparation and promotion of tourism products designed to develop multi-destination tourism as well as the diversification of the tourism offering. The agreement

> also provides for mutual technical assistance in the areas of human resource development, foreign language training, hospitality training, tourism planning and development, and hotel management training ... [and] encourages the participation of the business sector in special programmes dealing with the supply of goods and services for the tourism, travel-related and entertainment sectors. (ExportTT n.d., 9)

At the 38th regular meeting of the Conference of Heads of Government (CHG) of CARICOM in Grenada, in July 2017, Caribbean leaders recognized the necessity of addressing both current and continuing initiatives intended to inspire sustainable growth in tourism. They also agreed to extend engagement with CARICOM countries, companies, and intergovernmental organizations, in order to lend support to a regional tourism marketing and development enterprise, as well as to implement measures that would facilitate travel and consequently stimulate growth (CTO 2017a).

Concluding Reflections

Cuba and CARICOM SIDS share characteristics and circumstances that pose challenges to economic growth and social development. The economic slowdown that started in 2008 exacerbated long-standing economic problems, and Caribbean countries are forced to reorient their external relations, with a special emphasis on promoting trade and economic links with their neighbors in the region and in Latin America and elsewhere. In the case of Cuba, the deepening of regional economic links is a key element of the country's ongoing reforms.

There are important instruments already in place to boost trade, investments and joint initiatives in the tourist sector. The most relevant one is the TECA signed in 2000. Nevertheless, the use of the agreement has been limited and trade and economic relations between Cuba and the rest of the Caribbean has not developed as could be expected considering the state of political relations and cooperation initiatives.

Due to many factors that include different colonial histories, diverse paths followed to achieve political independence and current divergent political and economic models, it is difficult for Cuba and CARICOM states to advance easily on further economic links. However, common development challenges may be the trigger to pursue economic links in the future. Unfortunately, the growing animosity against Cuba manifested by the Trump administration may discourage Caribbean businesspersons and governments to advance economic relations with Cuba. The persistence of the U.S. embargo, in spite of the Obama administration's efforts to end it, also acts as a major obstacle to foster economic relations between Cuba and the rest of the Caribbean.

References

Association of Caribbean States (ACS). 2015. Sustainable Tourism Zone of the Greater Caribbean. Accessed July 18, 2017. http://stzc-acs.org/wp-content/uploads/2015/07/BookletfinalENGLISH.WEB_.pdf.

Caribbean Tourism Organization (CTO). 2017a. *Annual Statistical Report.* Accessed July 18, 2017. http://www.onecaribbean.org/wp-content/uploads/Sample-AR-2016-site.pdf.

———. 2017b. Caribbean Tourism Arrivals Hit All-Time High. *CTO News*, February 9, 2017. Accessed July 18, 2017. http://www.onecaribbean.org/caribbean-tourism-arrivals-hit-time-high/.

CARICOM Today. 2018. CARICOM Needs Very Concessional Financing for Climate Resilience – Secretary-General LaRocque. February 27, 2018. Accessed March 15, 2018. https://today.caricom.org/2018/02/27/caricom-needs-very-concessional-financing-for-climate-resilience-secretary-general-larocque/#more-26399.

Cubatrade. 2018. *Cuba Releases 2018–2019 Portfolio of Opportunities for Foreign Investment.* November 2, 2018. Accessed December 30, 2018. https://www.cubatrade.org/blog/2018/11/2/cuba-releases-2018-2019-portfolio-of-opportunities-for-foreign-investment.

ExportTT. n.d. *An Exporter's Guide to Cuba: CARICOM/Cuba Trade & Economic Agreement.* Accessed July 18, 2017. http://www.exportt.co.tt/sites/default/files/CARICOM%20CUBA%20booklet%20draft.pdf.

Grabendorff, Wolf. 2017. Cuba: The Challenges of Change. *Cuba y el proceso de actualización en la era de Trump in Pensamiento Propio* 45: 33–56.
Hendrickson, Michael. 2017. *A Framework for Caribbean Medium-Term Development.* ECLAC Studies and Perspectives Series, 52 (January). Accessed July 19, 2017. http://repositorio.cepal.org/bitstream/handle/11362/41043/1/S1601079_en.pdf.
International Trade Centre Trade Map. 2015. Accessed August 2017. http://www.trademap.org/Index.aspx.
Jamaica Observer. 2017. CARICOM, Cuba Sign New Trade Agreement. February 8, 2017. Accessed July 18, 2017. http://www.jamaicaobserver.com/news/CARICOM%2D%2DCuba-sign-new-trade-agreement.
Jorgensen, Gabrielle. 2018. The Dangers of U.S. Withdrawal from a Post-Castro Cuba. *Engage Cuba*, April 16, 2018. Accessed December 27, 2018. https://static1.squarespace.com/static/55806c54e4b0651373f7968a/t/5adbf66803ce64e6836f0c25/1524364904467/The+Dangers+of+US+Withdrawal+from+a+Post-Castro+Cuba.pdf.
Lowe, Michele A.M. 2011. *La integración CARICOM-Cuba: las iniciativas de comercio y cooperación económica en el marco de un CARICOM más amplio.* Paper presented at the Fifth International Conference of the Norman Girvan Chair of Caribbean Studies at the University of Havana, Cuba, December 8–10, 2011.
Martínez Reinosa, Milagros. 2015. Las relaciones de Cuba con la Comunidad del Caribe (CARICOM): contando la historia y pensando el futuro. In *El ALBA-TCP: origen y fruto del nuevo regionalismo latinoamericano y caribeño*, compiled by Maribel Aponte García and Gloria Amézquita Puntiel and edited by Pablo Gentili, 193–237. Buenos Aires: El Consejo Latinoamericano de Ciencias Sociales (CLACSO).
McLean, Sheldon, and Jeetendra Khadan. 2015. *An Assessment of the Performance of CARICOM Extraregional Trade Agreements: An Initial Scoping Exercise.* Santiago: United Nations Economic Commission for Latin America and the Caribbean (UN ECLAC). Accessed July 19, 2017. http://repositorio.cepal.org/bitstream/handle/11362/37612/lcarl455_rev1.pdf?sequence=5.
Oficina Nacional de Estadísticas e Información (ONEI). 2012. Anuario Estadístico de Cuba 2011. Accessed July 18, 2017. http://www.one.cu/aec2011.htm.
———. 2015. *Anuario Estadístico de Cuba 2014, Edición 2015.* Accessed July 18, 2017. http://www.one.cu/aec2014/08%20Sector%20Externo.pdf.
Republic of Cuba. 2011. *Lineamientos de la política económica y social del partido y la revolución.* Accessed July 18, 2017. http://www.cubadebate.cu/wp-content/uploads/2011/05/folleto-lineamientos-vi-cong.pdf.
———. 2017. *Lineamientos de la política económica y social del partido y la revolución para el periodo 2016–2021.* Accessed July 18, 2017. http://media.cubadebate.cu/wp-content/uploads/2017/07/PDF-321.pdf.

Terrero, Ariel. 2017. Inversión extranjera en Cuba: amenazas de la lentitud. *Cubadebate*, November 6, 2017. Accessed March 5, 2019. http://www.cubadebate.cu/opinion/2017/11/06/inversion-extranjera-en-cuba-amenazas-de-la-lentitud/#.XH80sMBKjIU.

Torres, Ricardo. 2017. El proceso de actualización del modelo económico y social de Cuba. *Cuba y el proceso de actualización en la era de Trump in Pensamiento Propio* 45: 57–80.

———. 2018.FIHAV y la nueva apuesta económica. *Progreso Semanal*, November 21, 2018. Accessed December 27, 2018. https://progresosemanal.us/20181108/fihav-y-la-nueva-apuesta-economica/.

Trade Wins. 2000. Trade and Economic Cooperation Between CARIFORUM and Cuba. *Critical Issues for Business*. Accessed February 9, 2019. http://carib-export.com/login/wpcontent/uploads/2010/01/Trade%20and%20Economic%20Cooperation%20between%20Cariforum%20and%20Cuba.pdf.

———. 2006. The CARICOM/Cuba Trade and Economic Co-operation Agreement Explained. *Critical Issues for Business* 2 (1) (November). Accessed July 18, 2017. http://www.carib-export.com/login/wp-content/uploads/2010/01/Final%20TradeWins%20revised.pdf.

United Nations Economic Commission for Latin America and the Caribbean (UN ECLAC). 2013. *Cuba: Bilateral Investment Treaties*. Accessed February 9, 2019. http:/investmentpolicyhub.unctad.org/IIA/CountryBits/52.

———. 2015. Foreign Direct Investment in Latin America and the Caribbean. Accessed July 19, 2017. http://repositorio.cepal.org/bitstream/handle/11362/38215/S1500534_en.pdf?sequence=4.

———. 2016. *Horizontes 2030: la igualdad en el centro del desarrollo sostenible*. Document LC/G.2660/Rev.1. Accessed July 18, 2017. https://repositorio.cepal.org/bitstream/handle/11362/40159/4/S1600653_es.pdf.

———. 2018. Foreign Direct Investment in Latin America and the Caribbean, 2018. Santiago. Accessed March 2, 2019. https://www.cepal.org/en/publications/43690-foreign-direct-investment-latin-america-and-caribbean-2018.

World Tourism Organization (UNWTO). 2015. *UNWTO Annual Report 2014*. Madrid: UNWTO.

ZED Mariel. 2017. Zona Especial de Desarrollo Mariel. *Una puerta abierta al mundo*. Accessed March 9, 2019. http://www.zedmariel.com.

CHAPTER 11

Conclusion

The book has examined the changing relationship between Cuba and the United States, with a view to understanding its potential implications for the Caribbean Community (CARICOM) and its relations with Cuba. This concluding chapter is organized as follows: first, we provide the rationale, outline, and key points of each chapter; second, we reflect on whether recent developments in Cuba-U.S. relations represent fundamental shifts in the relationship and in the global political economy; third, we outline the implications of these unfolding developments for CARICOM and Cuba-CARICOM relations; and finally, we end with some policy recommendations.

In Chap. 1, we started by providing a brief introduction of the developments in Cuba-U.S. relations from December 17, 2014 (17D), to the present—steps toward normalization under Barack Obama's administration and a partial reversal of this policy under the Donald Trump's presidency. This provided the foundation of the rationale for undertaking this book project and the point of departure of this work. By going beyond the implications of these developments for Cuba and the United States and by reflecting on how these developments might impact CARICOM and Cuba-CARICOM relations, we sought to fill an important gap in the scholarly literature. Not only is the substantive focus of the book novel, but it has been written by Caribbean academics, thus providing a unique Caribbean perspective on the subject matter.

The next task we undertook was to provide a broad overview of regional integration globally and in the Caribbean in particular; for the latter, we focused on CARICOM, whose member states are at the center of our analysis. In that vein, Chap. 2 provided an overview of global trends in regional integration and cooperation to present the context for understanding how these may affect the direction of CARICOM integration and what this in turn could mean for CARICOM cooperation and integration with Cuba. We saw how there have been both continuity and change in integration and regional cooperation globally: a movement away from predominantly traditional geographic configurations of regional cooperation; expanding South-South but continued North-South cooperation; the emergence of anti-hegemonic, neoliberal initiatives (particularly in Latin America); and an emerging trend toward the prevalence of inward-looking policies that could endanger regional cooperation in the United States, the West, and other parts of the world.

Chapter 3 aimed to give the reader an overview of the regional grouping, CARICOM, which is at the center of this book; specifically, its purpose and mandate, its institutions and governance structure, as well as its challenges and future direction. The chapter showed that the regional integration project, from the time of the West Indies Federation, has been driven to some degree by external forces; that economic rationale rather than identity considerations formed the basis of the Caribbean Free Trade Association (CARIFTA)—the predecessor of CARICOM—and regional integration was seen as a tool to attain (economic) sovereignty; that socio-economic development, foreign policy coordination, functional cooperation, and the promotion of security are at the heart of CARICOM's regional integration project; that CARICOM is a quasi-political body whose governance is based on a model of intergovernmentalism rather than supranationalism; that the regional agenda has sometimes been subordinated to independence and self-determination; that CARICOM faces several challenges emanating from internal and external factors; that CARICOM is increasingly complementing traditional North-South cooperation with non-traditional cooperation with the developed North as well as the global South as a means of meeting its developmental needs; and that CARICOM has been expanding its membership, by providing associate status to new members.

Chapter 4 offered an extensive examination of the political and economic history of Cuba and the United States. The chapter provided the background information important for understanding the significance of

17D. Conflict between Cuba and the United States originated from U.S. economic and geostrategic interests. These emanated in turn from the U.S. expansionist philosophy which saw Cuba as an extension of the United States. After the Cuban Revolution in 1959, tensions arose from ideological factors, but this was wrapped in existing U.S. economic and geostrategic interests linked to the Cold War. The research re-established that current U.S. attempts at improving relations with Cuba are not entirely new and that similar attempts were made—both during and after the Cold War—by previous U.S. administrations. Attempts made during the Cold War were unsuccessful, largely because of the strong ties between Cuba and the USSR during that period. Policy shifts under the Obama administration signaled a break from the past. President Obama was more successful than previous U.S. presidents, not only because his efforts were undertaken after the Cold War period, but also because he was serious about normalizing relations with Cuba, unlike President Bill Clinton (also a post-Cold War president) whose objective was primarily to improve rather than to normalize bilateral relations.

Chapter 5 provided the foundation upon which this book is based—the substantive and procedural changes that have been taking place in Cuba-U.S. relations since 17D. The chapter also highlighted some key areas of cooperation between the two countries since 17D. The resulting changes included the re-establishment of diplomatic relations and the easing of restrictions on the following: travel for non-tourist-related activities to both Cuba and the United States; remittances; telecommunications; and economic relations. Cuba was removed from the U.S. State Sponsors of Terrorism List, which in principle gives Cuba access to U.S. funding and to funding from international financial institutions and President Obama ended the wet-foot, dry-foot policy. The United States also ended the Medical Professional Parole Program, which had facilitated the defection of Cuban medical professionals working in third countries to the United States. The key areas of cooperation had been communications and transportation; security; scientific and cultural exchange; agriculture and the environment.

Chapter 6 sought to examine the obstacles, both past and present, that hinder the further advancement of Cuba-U.S. relations. The chapter outlined President Trump's policy toward Cuba and examined the challenges faced in the immediate post-17D period and under the Trump administration. The key changes during the Trump presidency have been the limiting of U.S. financial transactions with companies with ties to the Cuban military, intelligence, security services, and personnel and a ban on people-to-people travel together with the activation, for the first time ever, of Title III of the Helms-Burton Act of 1996. Some of the obstacles to normalization are the persistent U.S. policy of regime change in Cuba and the limits on trading with Cuba. Cuban exports to the United States are almost non-existent. The continuation of the U.S. embargo against Cuba and the Helms-Burton Act of 1996, which has not been revoked, serve to keep the ban on financial operations with Cuba in place, and U.S. investment in Cuba is not authorized under general licenses except in the case of telecommunications.

To expand the discussion, Chap. 7 examined the factors and actors that are variously driving and obstructing positive shifts in Cuba-U.S. relations. Apart from President Obama's charismatic personality and individual leadership style (see, e.g. Kumah-Abiwuon 2016; Hussain and Shakoor 2017, on the role of personality and leadership in foreign policy), 17D was fueled by strong economic and political impetus: the persistent and growing international and hemispheric consensus against the United States for its hostile policy toward Cuba; U.S. concern of diplomatic isolation in the hemisphere; President Obama's push for a more stable global system through a more inclusive multilateralist foreign policy; recognition by President Obama that the previous U.S. policy toward Cuba had failed; the Obama policy goal of formulating the perception that Cuba has been weakened by engaging with the United States; Washington's desire to undermine post-hegemonic regional integration; lobbying by a large number of powerful state and non-state actors favoring change in Cuba-U.S. relations; expanding economic opportunities in Cuba due to its economic reform process and U.S. fear of being left behind in a competitive economic environment; shared security concerns; and existing transcultural ties between populations on both sides. Actors pushing for positive Cuba-U.S. relations include: states, especially Canada and countries in Latin America and the Caribbean; a younger generation of Cuban politicians who were on the negotiating team; Pope Francis and the Catholic Church; progressive civil society, particularly from Latin America; increasing numbers of the U.S. public and Cuban Americans; various academics and think tanks; as well as segments of the U.S. business community and the U.S. political class.

Factors posing obstacles to the advancement of the relationship include: divergence of views on what normalization means—conceptually and concretely—between the United States and Cuba; economic and political asymmetries; persistent ideological differences between Cuba and the

United States on fundamental issues such as democracy and sovereignty; U.S. national interests; the continued presence of an official regime change policy at the core of the U.S. relationship with Cuba; Havana's mistrust of Washington; and unresolved issues in Cuba-U.S. relations surrounding sovereignty and territorial integrity. Within the same sectors supporting positive Cuba-U.S. relations are also actors who oppose the warming of relations. Actors openly opposing the changing relationship include pockets of the Cuban American community and the U.S. and Cuban political classes.

Chapter 8 presented the history of the Cuba-CARICOM relationship in light of Cuba-U.S. relations. The chapter also described the challenges experienced in the relationship and their causes. CARICOM has traditionally considered the Cuba-U.S. dynamic in its relationship with Cuba, but at the same time, has not been dictated by it. Historically, CARICOM countries have boldly pursed relations with, and supported, Cuba; in some cases, this has involved standing in direct opposition to, and in defiance of, the United States. The most significant and symbolic of these instances was the establishment of diplomatic relations by four Caribbean states with Cuba in 1972, at the height of the Cold War. Arguably, this may be viewed as the defining moment in Cuba-CARICOM relations and continues to be a reference point in the relationship between the two parties. At the same time, CARICOM's approach has also often been one of caution because of its own links with, and dependence on, the United States and fears of the spread of socialist ideology to its own member countries.

Although the end of the Cold War did not end tensions between the United States and Cuba, it created a more conducive environment for Cuba-CARICOM engagement. A shifting geopolitical climate, the declining geostrategic significance of the Caribbean to the United States, and the opening up of the global economy in the 1990s allowed for greater cooperation between Cuba and CARICOM. This period coincided with Cuba's new policy thrust toward greater South-South cooperation while seeking partnerships with developed countries (Byron 2000).

The enormous amount of development cooperation extended by Cuba toward CARICOM states is representative of the friendly bond that Cuba shares with CARICOM. Existing areas of Cuba-CARICOM cooperation cover a wide range of sectors including education, health, science, arts and culture, sports, physical infrastructure and industrial development, transport, agriculture, climate change, and disaster risk reduction, as well as energy. Progress made around development cooperation, though, has not been duplicated in the realm of trade and investment.

While CARICOM has "dragged its feet" in being more proactive in pursuing a mutually beneficial economic relationship with Cuba, the persistence of Cuba-U.S. hostility and, by extension, the embargo has been a hindrance to greater progress in this area. The embargo makes it extremely difficult and cumbersome for CARICOM to trade with Cuba, and there has always been apprehension on the part of CARICOM about breaching the embargo, being subjected to U.S. sanctions, and losing U.S. development assistance. The embargo has, therefore, been a key factor hindering the ability of the Cuba-CARICOM relationship to reach its full potential. The research identified other factors that have posed a challenge in Cuba-CARICOM relations, including: historical and cultural differences between the two sides; language barriers, particularly CARICOM member states' general lack of proficiency in Spanish; problems in CARICOM's regional integration project; lack of CARICOM proactivity in pursuing relations with Cuba; political and economic ideological differences between CARICOM and Cuba; mutual ignorance of the Cuban and CARICOM markets; CARICOM's dependence on, and its interdependence with, the United States; and fear and uncertainty about competition from Cuba because of the size of the Cuban economy vis-à-vis CARICOM states. These problems persist, and the uncertainty about competition has intensified, particularly as it relates to the diversion of development assistance, tourism, trade, and investments to Cuba. These concerns also relate to EU and Canadian relations with Cuba. CARICOM further fears that emerging powers, such as China and Brazil, could similarly favor relations with Cuba over CARICOM states.

Chapter 9 presented existing areas of cooperation to provide the background and foundation for discussing future Cuba-CARICOM engagement. The chapter outlined the key areas of cooperation between Cuba and CARICOM member states: health, education and training, climate change, disaster risk reduction, and cultural cooperation. These cooperation initiatives have been characterized by varying levels of success and challenges for both sides.

Because trade and economic relations have been the most problematic aspect of Cuba-CARICOM relations, we sought to emphasize their importance by dedicating a separate chapter to them. Chapter 10, therefore, considered the strategies employed by Cuba and CARICOM to foster economic growth and development. Cuba and CARICOM states face, to some extent, similar structural and other types of challenges. Amidst the persistence of unfavorable global economic developments, which have worsened existing challenges, both parties have to rethink their internal structuring as well as their external trade and economic relations. For Cuba, strengthening trade and economic relations with the Latin American and Caribbean region—and with CARICOM specifically—is a strategic objective. CARICOM, too, is recalibrating its foreign economic and trade relations and forging links with new extra-regional partners and neighbors in Latin America and the Caribbean. CARICOM trade and economic links continue to be predominately with traditional Northern partners. The CARICOM-Cuba Trade and Economic Cooperation Agreement (TECA) of 2000—a partial scope, goods agreement—is the framework that governs Cuba-CARICOM trade. While Cuba-CARICOM trade has only had modest results, it has expanded since 2000, and CARICOM has had a trade surplus with Cuba.

Having summarized the key points of the various chapters, we now reflect, in this concluding chapter, on the implications of changing Cuba--U.S. relations for international relations more broadly.

We argue that neither the policy position of President Obama nor that of President Trump points to a foundational shift in Cuba-U.S. relations; nor does either position fundamentally impact international political and economic relations. We make this claim on several grounds. First, although the changes initiated by 17D policies are significant, they have not shifted the underlying philosophy of U.S. engagement with Cuba. Despite the friendly and welcoming overtures made by President Obama toward Cuba, the relationship between the United States and Cuba did not change fundamentally: regime change remained at the center of U.S. policy toward Cuba under the Obama administration, albeit in an atmosphere of dialogue. The identical policy, although in a less conciliatory manner, also drives the partial reversal of the Obama package by the Trump administration. Second, although a soft power approach was the modus operandi under the Obama dispensation, 17D was not driven by altruism but, as in previous eras, by a realist philosophy. Among the main objectives of the new developments was the advancement of U.S. economic and political interests. These include counter-balancing EU and Chinese influence and market share in Cuba and seeking to access opportunities for U.S. business and investment. Third, and most important, the embargo was not terminated under the Obama administration, and it remains in place under the Trump administration. The embargo lies at the core of the hostility in Cuba-U.S. relations, and it adversely impacts all other aspects of the relationship: genuine and full normalization is not possible with the embargo in place.

What 17D and subsequent developments illustrate, therefore, are policy modifications rather than a paradigm shift in Cuba-U.S. relations. This can be likened to Hall's typology of policy change. According to Hall (1993), policy change occurs at three levels: at the first and second levels, there are modifications to certain elements of a policy. Third-order change is, however, a radical shift in the policy framework (Hall 1993). Third-order change mirrors Kuhn's concept of a "paradigm shift", which signifies a fundamental change from "universally recognized scientific achievements that for a time provide model problems and solutions to a community of practitioners" (Kuhn 1970, viii). In sum, the key pieces of evidence that argue against viewing 17D and President Trump's reversal of it as third-order change or a paradigm shift are the continuation and tightening of the U.S. embargo against Cuba; the persistence of realist motivations on the part of the United States; and the persistence of regime change on the U.S. agenda on Cuba.

Considering the above, we argue that current Cuba-U.S. relations represent epiphenomenal rather than fundamental shifts in international politics. In this, we follow a similar line of reasoning to Kennedy-Pipe and Rengger (2006) about the events of September 11, 2001. Kennedy-Pipe and Rengger (2006, 540) argue that some events that seem to symbolize radical shifts are "merely symptomatic of certain key aspects of world politics that should be familiar to all serious students of the field". Borrowing from this, we argue that 17D, as well as Trump's partial reversal of it, represents more continuity than change. Based on the evidence presented by recent developments in Cuba-U.S. relations, we conclude that these have not signaled change in international relations, nor do they challenge traditional international relations theories explaining state-to-state relations. We see more continuities than change in the foreign relations of the United States as a global actor as well as in its behavior toward other states, particularly toward those in less powerful positions. President Obama's policy changes toward Cuba did not alter the economic and political distribution of power in the world, nor in the Western Hemisphere for that matter. The United States remains, arguably, the most powerful political and economic actor in the Western Hemisphere and in the world. By virtue of the embargo, the United States is able to heavily determine the pace and direction of economic relations between Cuba and the rest of the world. Current relations between the United States and Cuba have not addressed global issues of political and economic asymmetries; the normalization process has not fundamentally challenged structural inequalities. The spread of global capitalism and neoliberal globalization as a development model continues unaffected. In fact, the opening up of Cuba to the United States has meant a step toward further liberalization of the Cuban economy and further opening up to the rest of the world for capitalist business ventures. In all these supposedly revolutionary shifts, states remain at the center of international negotiations and dialogue; and although we saw non-state actors playing an important role in the realization of 17D, states predominate, and non-state actors have not overtaken states as the main actors in global relations.

Arguably more important, a key lesson to be derived from changing Cuba-U.S. relations is that of the relevance of agency of small states. Although there is much literature on the weakness of small states by virtue of their smallness (see, e.g. Rustomjee 2016; UNCTAD 2007), there is an equal amount of writing on the notion that small states "punch above their weight" (see, for e.g. Edis 1991; Cassells 2016; Thorhallsson 2017). There is also literature indicating that smallness is not as important as the nature of the small state's relative position vis-à-vis other states; that is, the degree to which the relationship is equal or asymmetrical (Long 2017). This is how the real measure of states' agency could be ascertained. In this regard, Cuba-U.S. relations illustrate the case of a small state *really* punching above its weight in international relations. Although the entire world has been swept up by Westernization and Americanization since the early 1990s, Cuba—a small country, in very close proximity to the United States—has been able to withstand and successfully resist both U.S. and global forces for over six decades and has pursued an autonomous and an independent socio-economic development and political model. So far, as illustrated in this book, Cuba has demonstrated that it is opening up at its own pace, on its own terms, in a controlled fashion, and is not being swept up by the winds of change and the dictates of the United States and other actors.

What Does the Current Cuba-U.S. Dynamic Mean for CARICOM and Its Relationship with Cuba?

Our analysis is based on the view that President Trump is not likely to fundamentally reverse Obama-era policies in the short term. This projection is made on the grounds that the Trump administration is facing a myriad of other more pressing domestic challenges, which are of far greater priority than a further hardening of the U.S. position on Cuba. Changing Cuba-U.S. relations, notwithstanding the Trump administration's partial reversal of President Obama's normalization policies, present many challenges as well as opportunities for CARICOM (Bernal in Whitefield 2015), which we discuss in turn below.

First, there are concerns on the part of CARICOM countries that Cuba's opening up to the United States will eventually result in the former's adoption of an economic capitalist model and its economic attractiveness will surpass the rest of Caribbean. These fears stem from the view that as Cuba undertakes economic transformation, by virtue of its large size vis-à-vis CARICOM countries, it could have the competitive edge for U.S. investments, other business opportunities, and aid. CARICOM countries are also concerned that Cuba has the capacity to replace them in the export of goods to the United States, as well as to be a more attractive tourist destination (González Núñez and Verba 1997; IIR and University of Havana 2015; Sanders 2014).

Tourism is an area that has caused great anxiety for CARICOM in terms of potential competition from Cuba because of the opening up to the United States. Cuba is expected to attract more tourists because of the possibilities presented by the easing of travel restrictions, the potential use of credit and debit cards, and the ability to conduct direct transactions between U.S. and Cuban institutions (IIR and University of Havana 2015) (see Chap. 5).

The view is that Cuba presents a more attractive tourist destination because of the short physical distance between the United States and Cuba, which makes travel cheaper. Cuba is also a more interesting choice for potential visitors because of its unique history; their unfamiliarity with the country; the more diverse tourism product it offers; and the fact that Cuban society is diverse and its population multilingual. According to one source, "Cuba is not only rich in history and architecture, it is renowned for the excitement and excellence of its arts, including music, dance, poetry, and craft. Cuba also offers beaches as stunning as any of the other islands" (Sanders 2014). This is compounded by the fact that new infrastructure is being put in place to facilitate and boost sea and air travel. The development of new tourist locations across Cuba could potentially divert tourists from CARICOM countries to Cuba (Sanders 2014). With tourism being a major economic driver of Caribbean economies, this development could have adverse impacts on their growth potential (González Núñez and Verba 1997; IIR and University of Havana 2015; Sanders 2014).

Additional concerns about competition stem from the construction of the Mariel Special Development Zone (ZED Mariel) and the conversion of the Port of Havana into a tourism zone, both of which compete directly with development projects in CARICOM countries, notably the transshipment port project in Jamaica (IIR and University of Havana 2015).

While the fear of economic competition from Cuba was exacerbated by 17D-related developments in Cuba-U.S. relations, this concern did not emerge with the events of 17D, but rather has been an ongoing issue. It was a consideration in 1992, when Cuba's application to join the Caribbean Tourism Organization (CTO) was approved. CARICOM feared competition from Cuba for Canadian and European tourists. Considering the (partial) normalization of relations between Cuba and the United States, this anxiety has been heightened. However, the Trump renewal of restrictions on individual travel places the worries of CARICOM and the possibilities for collaboration in this sector on hold.

Second, U.S. overtures toward Cuba will have the effect of attracting further prospective partners and potentially intensifying existing partnerships. Cuba, too, now has greater confidence to be proactive in maneuvering in its new environment. If this is met with more willing and aggressive partners than CARICOM countries, economic imperatives will take preeminence over the feelings of solidarity that Cuba has long had for CARICOM. CARICOM's importance may be lowered on Cuba's list of economic relationships over time as more opportunities become available.

CARICOM may remain important, because with the embargo still in place, Cuba is not able to fully conduct business with the United States and other partners. However, this erosion of the economic importance of CARICOM to Cuba may happen if the embargo is lifted. The United States is Cuba's natural trading partner due to their geographical proximity and economic complementarity; therefore, short physical distance from each other and lower transportation costs will encourage expanded economic links between Cuba and the United States. Cuba could follow the path of Mexico, and the United States could become the former's main source of capital, trade, and investments, in which case CARICOM will diminish further in importance to Cuba (CARICOM 06).

Interviewee feedback affirmed that the new Cuba-U.S. dynamic could have both adverse and positive economic impacts on Cuba-CARICOM relations. Interviewees (CARICOM 05, Cuba 07) considered that an open Cuban economy could imply a diversion of foreign direct investment (FDI) away from CARICOM and toward Cuba. However, the current developments in Cuba-U.S. relations could have a positive impact and offer opportunities for CARICOM and Cuba-CARICOM relations. Moreover, some of the very challenges could be converted into opportunities.

We argue that the economic relationship between CARICOM and Cuba cannot be fully exploited with the embargo in place. U.S. business interests in Cuba could pressure the U.S. political elite to reverse the embargo. Signs of such pressure have been seen in the criticism expressed by business actors of President Trump's move to partially reverse Obama-era policies (see Chaps. 7 and 8).

With this in mind, what are the potential positive impacts on, and implications and opportunities for, CARICOM and Cuba-CARICOM relations?

First, although continuities in Cuba-U.S. relations hinder regional integration, 17D—and the fact that President Trump did not reverse the Obama package completely—provides some measure of hope for pushing on dismantling the embargo and for Cuba-CARICOM economic cooperation and integration. Cuba's location within the Caribbean Sea and the Greater Antilles and its close geographic proximity to other Caribbean islands provides additional incentives for greater economic cooperation and integration (SELA 2015). Up to 2013, Cuba was not on the agenda in relation to CARICOM's discussion of associate membership (Joseph 2013). Considering the strong bonds between CARICOM and Cuba, it is likely that Cuba's indifference to joining CARICOM is also related to the U.S. embargo.

Cuba's membership in CARICOM could increase CARICOM's weight and leverage in its external relations. In an interview with Mimi Whitefield, Richard Bernal, a longtime Caribbean diplomat, stated that "If Cuba were to join CARICOM ... it would double the population of the potential market and could change how agreements between the United States and the Caribbean region are negotiated"; and noted that "Cuba currently isn't part of any major free trade agreements" (Bernal in Whitefield 2015). Furthermore, and more generally, the Caribbean's voice would be strengthened, and the region could carry greater weight in international negotiations, global governance, and in its relations with external parties. CARICOM could also attract more foreign investment and on better terms.

Second, the mere fact that Cuba has been removed from the U.S. State Sponsors of Terrorism List provides a more comfortable environment for the Caribbean to engage with Cuba. Removal from this list means that, in principle, Cuba has opportunities to access international funding, albeit still with many challenges remaining. Apart from the indirect positive impact this could have on expanding economic ties with the Caribbean, it also removes any residual fear of political and diplomatic reprisals that the Caribbean may have had in engaging with a country labeled by the United States as a state sponsor of terrorism. This could, therefore, embolden the Caribbean to engage more confidently with Cuba.

Third, the termination of the wet-foot, dry-foot policy has removed an additional avenue of mobility for Cuban political and economic migrants. In recent times, the Caribbean has seen a greater flow of Cuban migrants than was seen before (CARICOM 06). This is illustrated by the increasing number of Cuban migrants and refugees, as well as the prominence of negative stories in the media about them (see, e.g. Dowlat 2018; La Vende 2018). This may have the unintended consequence of changing the Caribbean's nonchalance about Cuban domestic affairs and create additional areas for cooperation.

Fourth, notwithstanding the practical impediments that still exist to taking advantage of some of the policy changes of 17D, and in spite of the existence of the U.S. embargo and President Trump's partial reversal of the normalization policies, the current space for economic opportunities is greater than it was before 17D. Besides, 17D has made the possibility of full normalization of Cuba-U.S. relations seem not as distant or far-fetched as before.

An interviewee (CARICOM 01) pointed out that business relations between Cuba and CARICOM have been strong in recent years (especially since the signing of the TECA in 2000), and held the view that this has intensified since 17D. Another interviewee (Cuba 02) did not think that there would be significant change in terms of the nature or number of investments between Cuba and CARICOM, especially considering that Dominican Republic, Trinidad and Tobago, and Jamaica already have investments in Cuba. This interviewee (Cuba 02) mentioned, though, that these relations could extend to other CARICOM countries once the blockade (embargo) is removed. Similarly, yet another interviewee (CARICOM 02) offered the perspective that if Cuba can export more in the future, it is expected to do so to the CARICOM market. Additionally, once the embargo is removed, there will be greater legal and political security to invest in Cuba. Consequently, there will be an increase in Cuban business with CARICOM and in opportunities for joint multilateral investments between Cuba and CARICOM as well as extra-regional partners.

Fifth, if Cuba's relations with the United States and other Northern partners are fruitful, this could have positive impacts on CARICOM. If CARICOM positions itself strategically, it could benefit from the spin-off effects of Cuba's economic prosperity. CARICOM could benefit through the greater opportunities that will be created in Cuba due to developments such as improvements in infrastructure, and the expansion and strengthening of the private and cooperative sector. A strengthened Cuban economy means that the country could import more from CARICOM and increase intra-regional trade. Cuba will also have greater capacity to engage in regional projects and development cooperation, including through technical assistance in specialized areas such as medicine, pharmaceuticals, and innovation. Overall, Cuba could contribute even more significantly to regional development from which the Caribbean can benefit (CARICOM 06).

Sixth, despite the regression under the Trump administration, 17D has created an atmosphere for dialogue to take place and for enhanced awareness among CARICOM states and the private sector of the potential benefits that can be derived from a more strategic and deliberate economic engagement with Cuba. The opening up of Cuba and the development of the necessary infrastructure for facilitating business had been in progress and had been accelerating in previous years, but 17D has further fueled or highlighted these processes. Another unintended consequence of the (partial) normalization of Cuba-U.S. relations could be that the potential for private sector engagement in specific areas could boost the confidence of the regional private sector to venture into Cuba in an attempt to replicate existing successes.

Seventh, normalization or its reversal has implications for the tourism sector in the Caribbean. Although tourism continued to be excluded under the Obama normalization package, with the easing of travel restrictions and starting of flights, additional avenues were created for travelers to find ways to engage in leisure activities. This more attractive option led to a pull of visitors toward Cuba. At the same time, this could provide opportunities for the Caribbean to draw these visitors already in one Caribbean destination (see Chap. 5). According to the Latin American and Caribbean Economic System (SELA), tourism projects involving "multiple destinations", port infrastructure and connectivity, and conservation of shared natural resources give renewed vigor to the possibilities for expanding and deepening Cuba-CARICOM relations (SELA 2015). The continuation of restrictions on travel for tourism and the reversal of people-to-people travel by the Trump administration could mean more tourists for CARICOM countries.

Eighth, regarding President Trump's America First policy, this could signal further reduction in funding for overseas development initiatives that are not amenable to U.S. national interests. This provides additional reason to strengthen and promote Caribbean regional integration and CARICOM's ties with Cuba, with a view to advancing the development of its member states.

Ninth, the loosening of travel restrictions to Cuba could boost development cooperation, particularly among non-state actors who are critical elements in the overall development process. The developments around 17D offer opportunities for expanded and deepened state-to-state engagement and for public-private partnerships as an additional mode for Cuba-CARICOM engagement. President Trump's announcement of the re-tightening of travel restrictions could, however, hinder the possibilities discussed above.

What then are the practical considerations for the way forward for CARICOM and its relations with Cuba? We provide some policy recommendations for the tourism sector and other areas below:

1. By virtue of the relative diversity of CARICOM states and Cuba, there could be collaboration to provide multi-destination tourism packages to CARICOM states and Cuba. The possibility, therefore, exists for joint-venture activity in the tourism sector for this purpose (SELA 2015). Interviewees (CARICOM 02, 05; Cuba 02, 04) were of the view that this means that CARICOM countries would have to work at making their respective tourist industries more efficient and attractive to keep up with regional changes in the tourism sector. We maintain that this also applies to Cuba.
2. CARICOM could adjust its national and regional external policies to rethink the international dimension of its development strategies. There is a need to perhaps identify collectively what the new possibilities for South-South cooperation are, in order to enable more effective engagement by CARICOM countries with Cuba and to maximize the potential of the Cuba-CARICOM relationship.
3. CARICOM could consider restructuring and advancing its own integration process, in order to make this more sustainable and relevant in a rapidly changing regional and international context

and to take advantage of the new dynamic with Cuba and the United States.
4. Both CARICOM and Cuba could perhaps seriously consider Cuba's membership in CARICOM. Cuba could be a valuable addition to the CARICOM membership. Cuba has made an outstanding contribution to regional development, especially in areas such as health care, education, environmental protection and culture. Cuba possesses economic potential and diplomatic capital with the capacity to increase CARICOM's negotiating leverage in multilateral fora. Cuba is recognized for its activism on behalf of developing countries and the global South and for its support for Latin American and Caribbean integration (González Núñez 2002).
5. Cuba's membership in CARICOM could be used as a tool to provide a stronger and more united position on, and strengthen the call to end the embargo against Cuba—a cause CARICOM has long actively supported. This could be done in additional international fora as well as in regional spaces such as the Community of Latin American and Caribbean States (CELAC). CELAC is a valuable mechanism for coordinating the positions of Latin American and Caribbean states on a wide range of issues, and could provide an effective platform for addressing the embargo.
6. 17D has stimulated more discussion, analysis, and research about Cuba-CARICOM relations than ever before. This abundance of emerging information can uncover new insights and assist in developing policy positions aimed at refining the contours and direction of CARICOM's relationship with Cuba. The University of the West Indies (UWI) can provide leadership in developing research projects with the aim of enhancing the Cuba-CARICOM relationship. One of the most pertinent areas could be how to enhance complementarity between the Cuban and CARICOM markets to reduce the fear and reality of competition.
7. Initiatives toward fostering greater understanding of the Cuban market to take advantage of opportunities in Cuba and the rest of Latin America when they arise could be helpful (see Montoute et al. 2017). CARICOM-Cuba cooperation in Spanish language learning could help bridge this gap.
8. CARICOM could consider being more proactive and repositioning itself, since there is great potential for the expansion of trade and investment between Cuba and CARICOM. ZED Mariel can

provide the space for CARICOM investment. There is also potential for increased investment in the expansion of trade in the services sector, from which CARICOM can benefit. Cuba and CARICOM can also benefit considerably from cooperation in the much-needed areas of air and sea transportation, and communication through joint partnerships (see, e.g. SELA 2015).
9. CARICOM countries wishing to export to Cuba would benefit more from exporting to Cuba collectively rather than as individual countries (CARICOM 01). The challenges associated with entering the Cuban market in general would be exacerbated by the limited resources of the small islands of the Caribbean.
10. Improved infrastructure for business and investment as well as other areas of engagement (see Chap. 10) could be exploited by CARICOM to boost various aspects of its relationship with Cuba as well as for triangular cooperation. Improvements in telecommunications and related technologies have upgraded the infrastructure for business and investments.

REFERENCES

Byron, Jessica. 2000. Square Dance Diplomacy: Cuba and CARIFORUM, the European Union and the United States. *European Review of Latin American and Caribbean Studies* 68: 23–45.

Cassells, Elsada Diana. 2016. Cuba: Still Punching Above Its Weight. In *Diplomatic Strategies of Nations in the Global South: The Search for Leadership*, ed. Jacqueline Braveboy-Wagner, 319–344. New York: Palgrave Macmillan.

Dowlat, Rhondor. 2018. Cuban Refugee Protest Grows Outside UN House. *Trinidad and Tobago Guardian*, November 12, 2018. Accessed March 7, 2019. http://www.guardian.co.tt/news/cuban-refugee-protest-grows-outside-un-house-6.2.713480.779528519f.

Edis, Richard. 1991. Punching Above Their Weight: How Small Developing States Operate in the Contemporary Diplomatic World. *Cambridge Review of International Affairs* 5 (2): 45–53.

González Núñez, Gerardo. 2002. Cuba's Relations with the Caribbean: Trends and Future Prospects: Executive Summary. *FOCAL*, September. Accessed February 7, 2019. http://www.focal.ca/pdf/cuba_Gonzalez_Cuban%20relations%20Caribbean%20trends%20prospects_September%202002_RFC-02-2.pdf.

González Núñez, Gerardo, and Ericka Kim Verba. 1997. International Relations Between Cuba and the Caribbean in the 1990s: Challenges and Perspectives. *Latin American Perspectives* 24 (5): 81–95.

Hall, Peter. 1993. Policy Paradigms, Social Learning, and the State: The Case of Economic Policymaking in Britain. *Comparative Politics* 25 (3): 275–296.

Hussain, Nazir, and Fatima Shakoor. 2017. The Role of Leadership in Foreign Policy: A Case Study of Russia Under Vladimir Putin. *IPRI Journal* 17 (1): 1–25.

Institute of International Relations (IIR) and University of Havana. 2015. Seminar on the *Cuba and CARICOM: Challenges to Regional Development and Cooperation*. Institute of International Relations, the University of the West Indies, St Augustine, Trinidad and Tobago, November 3–6, 2015.

Joseph, A. Lawrence. 2013. How Soon Will Cuba Be Given the Option to Join CARICOM. *Now Grenada*, September 4, 2013. Accessed February 7, 2019. http://www.nowgrenada.com/2013/09/how-soon-will-cuba-be-given-the-option-to-join-caricom/.

Kennedy-Pipe, Caroline, and Nicholas Rengger. 2006. Apocalypse Now? Continuities or Disjunctions in World Politics After 9/11. *International Affairs* 82 (3): 539–552.

Kuhn, Thomas. 1970. *The Structure of Scientific Revolutions*. Chicago: University of Chicago Press.

Kumah-Abiwuon, Felix. 2016. Leadership Traits and Ghana's Foreign Policy: The Case of Jerry Rawlings' Foreign Economic Policy of the 1980s. *The Round Table: The Commonwealth Journal of International Affairs* 105 (3): 297–310.

La Vende, Jensen. 2018. Cuban in Custody for Stabbing Wife. Trinidad and Tobago Newsday, December 2, 2018. Accessed March 7, 2019. https://newsday.co.tt/2018/12/02/cuban-in-custody-for-stabbing-wife/.

Latin American and Caribbean Economic System (SELA). 2015. *Assessment of the Economic and Cooperation Relations Between Central America, the Caribbean and Mexico*. SELA. Document SP/Di No. 9–15. September.

Long, Tom. 2017. It's Not the Size, It's the Relationship: From 'Small States' to Asymmetry. *International Politics* 54 (2): 144–160.

Montoute, Annita, Andy Knight, Jacqueline Laguardia Martinez, Debbie Mohammed, and Dave Seerattan. 2017. *The Caribbean in the European Union-Community of Latin American and Caribbean States Partnership*. Hamburg: EU–Latin America and Caribbean (EU-LAC) Foundation.

Rustomjee, Cyrus. 2016. *Vulnerability and Debt in Small States*. CIGI Policy Brief 83 (July). Centre for International Governance Innovation. Accessed February 7, 2019. https://www.cigionline.org/sites/default/files/pb_no._83web.pdf.

Sanders, Ronald. 2014. *Cuba's New Relationship with the US: Challenges and Chances for the Caribbean*. December 25, 2014. Accessed February 7, 2019. http://www.sirronaldsanders.com/viewarticle.aspx?ID=479.

Thorhallsson, Baldur. 2017. Small States in the UNSC and the EU: Structural Weaknesses and Ability to Influence. In *Small States in a Legal World: The World of Small States*, ed. Petra Butler and Caroline Morris, vol. 1, 35–64. Cham, Switzerland: Springer.

United Nations Conference on Trade and Development (UNCTAD). 2007. *'Structurally Weak, Vulnerable and Small Economies': Who Are They? What Can UNCTAD Do for Them?* Trade and Development Board, Fifty-Fourth Session, Geneva, Switzerland, October 1–11, 2007. Accessed February 7, 2019. https://unctad.org/en/Docs/tdb54crp4_en.pdf.

Whitefield, Mimi. 2015. Emerging Cuba Worries Caribbean. *Miami Herald*, November 30, 2015. Accessed April 24, 2017. http://www.miamiherald.com/news/nationworld/world/americas/cuba/article47182355.html.

Appendix A: Interviewee Profiles

Interview reference number	Country/Region	Sex	Professional area
CARICOM 01	CARICOM	Male	Public officer
CARICOM 02	Dominican Republic	Male	Diplomat
CARICOM 03	CARICOM	Female	Public officer
CARICOM 04	CARICOM	Male	Diplomat
CARICOM 05	CARICOM	Male	Academic
CARICOM 06	CARICOM	Male	Academic
Cuba 01	Cuba	Female	Public officer
Cuba 02	Cuba	Male	Academic
Cuba 03	Cuba	Male	Academic
Cuba 04	Cuba	Male	Public officer
Cuba 05	Cuba	Male	Academic
Cuba 06	Cuba	Male	Academic
Cuba 07	Cuba	Male	Public officer
Cuba 08	Cuba	Male	Academic
US 01	USA	Female	Academic
US 02	USA	Female	Academic
US 03	USA	Male	Academic

Appendix B: Interviewees by Region of Operation

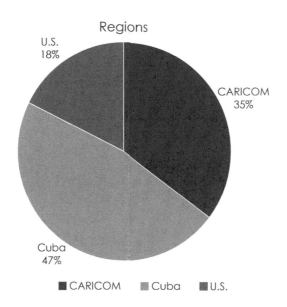

Appendix C: Interviewees by Areas of Work

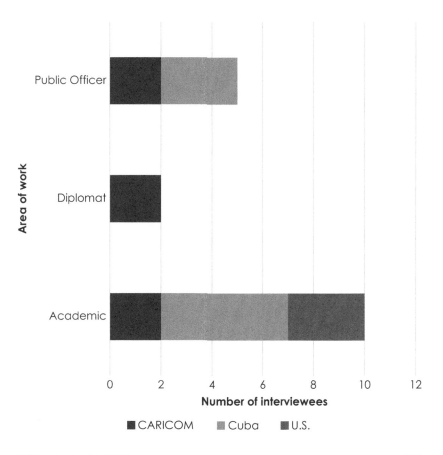

Index[1]

A
ACP, *see* African, Caribbean, and Pacific
African, Caribbean, and Pacific (ACP), xiii, 12, 23, 146, 158, 181, 181n2
Agriculture, 40, 68, 71, 72, 79, 96, 101, 114, 115, 130, 179, 184, 199
ALBA-TCP, xiii, 113, 158
Antigua and Barbuda, 19n1, 31n9, 159, 162, 165, 167, 170, 171, 181, 185
Argentina, 14, 16, 21n2, 73, 80, 95, 128

B
Bahamas, 97, 146, 159, 165, 189
Barbados, 19n1, 29, 31n9, 47, 143, 159, 162, 165, 169, 181, 185, 187
Batista, 41

Belize, 29, 31n9, 159, 162, 165, 168, 185, 187, 189
Bilateral, 1–3, 42, 46, 50–54, 63, 65, 67, 70, 83, 93–96, 100, 101, 103, 113, 114, 116, 120, 121, 125, 126, 132, 149, 151, 157, 158, 169, 170, 183, 184, 187, 197
BIS, xiii
Blockade, 46, 49, 68, 115, 118, 123, 124, 129, 132, 154, 207
Brazil, xiii, 12, 14, 16, 21n2, 94, 96, 128, 187, 188, 200
Brexit, 14–16, 32, 33
BRICS, xiii, 12
Bush, George H. W., 50, 53, 54
Business, 23, 50, 53, 62, 65, 66, 74, 81–83, 95–98, 105, 121, 123, 124, 126, 129, 131, 146, 147, 150, 152, 179, 181, 191, 198, 201, 203–208, 211

---

[1] Note: Page numbers followed by 'n' refer to notes.

C

CACR, xiii, 48n5, 54, 61, 99, 122
Caribbean, i, v, vii, xi–xvi, 1–4, 6, 9, 12–14, 13n4, 16, 19–33, 38, 45, 47, 54, 55, 68–72, 75, 79, 100, 105, 112–114, 118, 123, 127, 143–154, 143n1, 157–172, 177, 178, 180, 181, 181n2, 184, 185, 187–189, 191, 195, 198, 199, 201, 204–208, 210, 211
Caribbean Community (CARICOM), v, xiii, xiv, 2–4, 6, 16, 19–23, 26–33, 31n9, 115, 118, 121, 125, 126, 143–154, 157–172, 177–192, 195, 196, 199–201, 203–211, 215
Caribbean Free Trade Association (CARIFTA), xiii, 20, 23, 196
CARICOM, *see* Caribbean Community
CARICOM Single Market and Economy (CSME), xiv, 21, 23, 30, 31
CARIFORUM, 146, 158, 181, 189, 190
Carter, Jimmy, 50–53, 126, 127n2, 127n3
Castro, Fidel, 1, 41–43, 45–47, 49, 52, 61, 98, 120, 122, 126, 127, 129, 132, 153, 154, 170
CDA, xiv, 48, 48n4, 49, 52, 122, 130, 145
CELAC, *see* Community of Latin American and Caribbean States
Chile, 14, 16, 114, 128, 160, 161
China, 12, 13, 16, 42, 44, 73, 96, 103, 105, 113, 161, 200
Clinton, Bill, 49, 50, 52–54, 127n2, 197
Cold War, i, 4, 7–11, 15, 20, 21, 29, 51–55, 129, 149, 150, 154, 197, 199
Communication, 1, 64, 66–67, 121, 168, 211

Community of Latin American and Caribbean States (CELAC), xiv, 14, 28, 113, 128, 158, 210
Congress, 39, 47, 48, 50, 52, 54, 66, 101–105, 120, 122, 123, 130, 131, 159, 178
Cooperation, 1–3, 5, 6, 9, 10, 12–14, 19–22, 24, 25, 28, 29, 32, 54, 65, 67–72, 77, 79, 80, 100, 101, 112, 113, 118, 119, 144, 145, 147, 151, 153, 154, 157–162, 164–172, 181, 191, 196, 197, 199, 200, 206–209, 211
Cuba, i, v, xi, xiv–xvi, 1–4, 6, 16, 32, 33, 37–56, 48n4, 48n5, 61–84, 93–105, 111–133, 133n4, 143–154, 157–172, 177–192, 181n2, 195–211, 215
Cuba-CARICOM, 143, 148, 151, 154, 159, 163, 182, 195, 199, 200, 205, 206, 210
Cuban Adjustment Act, 47
Cuban-American, 38, 50, 53, 54, 66, 105, 123, 130, 131
Cuban Revolution, 43, 45, 46, 52, 55, 105, 113, 126, 150, 160, 197
Cuba-U.S., v, 1, 3, 4, 16, 32, 37–56, 63, 65, 67, 71, 76, 83, 100, 101, 103, 111–133, 144, 148, 149, 168, 171, 195, 197–211
Cultural, 49, 50, 52, 55, 64, 77, 78, 81, 83, 101, 116, 169–171, 197, 200
Culture, 7, 20, 26, 77, 145, 169, 170, 199, 210

D

Declaration of Havana, 44
The Department of Homeland Security, 63
Development, 3, 8, 11–13, 20, 22, 24–26, 28–30, 32, 41, 42, 97, 105, 113, 115, 122, 145, 148,

151, 154, 157, 158, 162, 168, 171, 172, 177–179, 183, 189, 191, 199, 200, 203–205, 208–210
Díaz-Canel, 103, 105, 121, 153, 180
Diplomacy, xi, 11, 41, 53, 111, 127, 160, 172
Diplomatic, 1, 2, 33, 39, 42–45, 47, 50, 51, 55, 63, 65, 67, 70, 93, 113, 116, 128, 129, 143–145, 151, 154, 181, 197–199, 207
Direct investment, xiv, 41, 55, 114, 178, 179, 205
Disaster management, 181
Disaster risk reduction, 3, 200
Dominica, 19n1, 29, 31n9, 159, 162, 163, 165, 167, 170, 171

E
EAR, xiv, 61, 99
Economic Development, 26
Economic integration, 20, 23, 25, 27, 28, 30, 127, 180, 182
Education, 3, 20, 41, 78, 151, 157, 158, 160, 162, 164–166, 170, 171, 181, 184, 188, 199, 200
Eisenhower, Dwight D., 42, 43, 45, 47
Embargo, 4, 46–50, 48n4, 48n5, 53, 64, 68, 84, 95, 97–99, 103–105, 112, 118, 121, 122, 124, 126–130, 133, 144, 145, 150, 186, 198, 200–202, 205–207, 210
Environment, 79, 167
Environmental cooperation, 160
European Economic Community (EEC), xiv, 8, 9, 20
European Single Market, 11
European Union (EU), xiv, 10, 33, 114, 168
Exports, 31, 38, 42, 62, 80, 81, 93–95, 101, 102, 104, 114, 122, 146, 161, 178, 184–186, 198

F
Foreign Direct Investment, 80–81

G
Good Neighbor policy, 41
Grenada, 19n1, 31n9, 144, 145, 149, 159, 163, 165–167, 191
Guantánamo, 52, 64, 69, 105, 118, 125
Guyana, 29, 30, 31n9, 143, 148, 149, 158, 159, 163, 165, 167, 168, 170, 171, 181, 184, 185, 189

H
Haiti, 21, 40, 69, 71, 74, 146, 151, 158, 159, 162–171, 178, 189
Health, 3, 20, 41, 63, 68, 71, 77, 83, 113, 129, 151, 157, 158, 160–164, 168, 171, 181, 188, 199, 200, 210
Helms-Burton Act, 48, 53, 62, 68, 96, 122, 130, 148, 198
House of Representatives, 130
Humanitarian, 44, 44n3, 49, 50, 52, 54, 62–64, 71, 73n2, 95, 120, 165

I
Imports, 41, 42, 94–96, 121, 180n1, 185, 188
Investments, 97–98

J
Jamaica, 19n1, 20, 31, 31n9, 40, 143, 149, 153, 158, 159, 161–165, 167–171, 181, 184, 186, 187, 205, 207

K
Kennedy, John F., 45, 46, 48, 50, 202

L

Latin America, xi, xii, xvi, 1, 7, 11, 13, 14, 16, 28, 39, 40, 43, 44, 50, 54, 55, 104, 112–114, 116, 118, 123, 127, 128, 159, 163, 180, 187, 191, 196, 198, 210
Limits, 3, 28, 49, 62, 72, 93, 104

M

Manifest Destiny, 37
Mariel, xvi, 51, 71, 97, 99, 129, 178, 179, 187, 205, 210
McKinley, William, 39
Migration, i, 6, 15, 40, 47, 50, 52, 54, 68–70, 74, 101
Military, 8, 15, 39, 44–46, 55, 68, 69, 99, 103, 116, 121, 124, 125, 149
Monroe Doctrine, 4, 39, 39n1, 44
Montserrat, 19n1, 31n9, 165

N

Nationalism, 14–16
Normalization, 2, 50, 51, 55, 63, 65, 67, 76, 80, 84, 96, 100, 104, 111, 115–119, 121, 125, 126, 129–133, 148, 195, 198, 202–205, 207, 208

O

OAS, xv, 8, 43, 44, 114
Obama, Barack, 1–3, 49–56, 61–67, 70, 72, 74, 76, 80, 81, 84, 96–100, 102, 105, 112, 119–124, 126, 128, 129, 132, 195, 197, 198, 201–203, 206, 208
OECS, xv, 149, 170, 185

P

PCC, xv, 117, 153, 159, 178
Platt Amendment, 39–41

R

Rapprochement, 112, 144
Reagan, Ronald, 50, 130
Regional cooperation, 10, 20, 196
Regional integration, 5–16, 19–33, 113, 154, 180, 196, 198, 200, 209
Regionalism, 3, 5–7, 5n1, 9–14, 13n4, 133
Regionalization, 5
Remittances, 52, 54, 61, 64, 76, 83, 102, 115, 123, 197
Restrictions, 52, 62, 81, 96, 101, 104, 121, 123, 179, 183, 204, 208
Reversals, 55, 62, 63, 76, 99–101, 103, 126, 132, 207, 208
Roosevelt, Franklin D., 41
Roosevelt, Theodore, 37
Russia, 10, 12, 16, 73, 96, 103–105, 113, 152

S

Sanctions, 47, 48, 48n4, 48n5, 52, 55, 62, 80, 84, 97, 101, 103, 104, 122, 123, 125, 150, 187, 200
Security, i, xi, 4, 7–11, 13, 23, 24, 26, 37, 38, 44–46, 51, 52, 55, 63, 64, 67–72, 83, 98–100, 103, 105, 113, 116, 124, 148, 171, 196–198, 207
Senate, 101
17D, v, xiii, 3, 53–54, 61, 63, 67, 73, 76–80, 83, 93, 97, 112, 114, 118, 121, 123, 129, 143–148, 152, 153, 195, 197, 198, 201, 202, 205–210
SIDS, 167, 177, 191

Soft power, 121, 126, 201
St. Kitts and Nevis, 31n9, 159, 165, 168, 169, 171, 189
St. Lucia, 19n1, 31n9, 159, 165, 167, 169–171
Strategies, 2, 3, 28, 99, 158, 167, 177, 178, 181, 200, 209
St. Vincent and the Grenadines, 29, 31n9, 159, 165, 167, 168, 170, 171
Summit of the Americas, 53, 65, 114, 127, 128
Suriname, 29, 31n9, 159, 162, 165, 167, 171, 184, 187, 189

T
TECA, xv, 146–148, 182–184, 187, 191, 201, 207
Tourism, 68, 71–74, 98, 100, 101, 115, 121, 122, 124, 130, 133, 145, 147, 152, 183, 184, 189, 191, 200, 204, 205, 208, 209
Trade, xii, 3, 6, 7, 9–12, 14, 20, 22, 23, 26, 31, 31n9, 32, 38, 41, 42, 44, 44n3, 48–50, 48n4, 52, 55, 61, 64, 65, 67, 70–72, 80, 81n3, 83, 84, 93, 95, 96, 101, 104, 114, 115, 122, 128, 145–148, 150, 152, 158, 164, 178–188, 191, 200, 201, 205, 206, 208, 210
Transport, 74–75
Travel, 1, 50, 52, 54, 61, 62, 65, 70, 72, 75, 81, 82, 99–102, 104, 115, 122, 124, 128, 191, 197, 204, 205, 208, 209

Treaty of Chaguaramas, 21, 23, 30, 143n1, 183
Trinidad and Tobago, i, xii, 19n1, 20, 29, 31, 31n9, 53, 143, 150, 159, 165, 167, 168, 171, 181, 184, 187, 189, 207
Trump, Donald, 1–4, 14, 16, 55, 62–64, 76, 78, 79, 93, 98–105, 119, 121, 123, 124, 126, 132, 195, 201–203, 205–209
TSRA, xvi, 50, 72, 94, 122
TWEA, xvi, 47, 123

U
United Kingdom (UK), xvi, 14–16, 32, 33, 189
United Nations, xi, xvi, 8, 47, 65, 84, 95, 103, 116, 127, 144, 166, 168, 187, 189
United States (U.S.), i, v, xiii–xvi, 1–4, 6, 8–16, 32, 33, 37–56, 39n1, 48n4, 48n5, 61–84, 93–105, 100n2, 111–133, 133n4, 143–146, 148–150, 152–154, 160, 168, 186–189, 195–210
U.S. Department of Commerce, xiii, xiv, 93
U.S. Department of State, 46, 47, 52, 69–71, 74, 95, 99, 100, 119
U.S. Department of the Treasury, xiii, xv, 52, 54, 61, 62, 78, 80, 82, 114

W
"Wet foot, dry foot" policy, 47